Praise for
"Ace the SAT Writing Even If You Hate to Write"
By Tamra B. Orr

"Today's teens are faced with the daunting task of taking the 'new and improved [illegible] pressure is on. Take a deep breath and relax. *Ace the SAT Writing Even If You Hate to Write* is to the rescue. Its lively and engaging style will painlessly take you through the essay-writing process specifically geared for the writing section of the SAT. The book explains what determines a 'good' writer, the ins and outs of the scoring process and the ever important skills to become an awesome writer. Sample essays and discussion of the multiple choice section round out this extremely valuable resource."

–Christine Florie, Editor, Marshall Cavendish Benchmark

"Finally! A book about writing that actually helps students who don't like to write! It is more than a quick guide to how to do it–it actually helps students become better writers. And for students who don't like to write, you will find out more than advice to get through the essay section of the SAT–with no mind-numbing exercises. If you don't like to write, or if you aren't very good at it, this is the book for SAT writing prep."

–Samuel Barnett, Ph.D., Certified Educational Planner

"Learn how to get your words down on paper and polish them to make them the best they can be."

–Pam Rosenberg, Editor, Editorial Directions

"Writing can be fun and this book proves that even writing for the SAT can be less painful than you ever imagined. What should you do first when you open the writing section of the new SAT? By following the advice in this book, you will avoid that pounding panic that can overtake anyone. You will learn the best ways to approach and master the writing situation. The information is not only helpful and to the point, but it also explains what test scorers are looking for in top rate exams. The book examines the skills of good writers and shows you how to use those skills yourself. Included are 30 essays, both good and bad, to study as examples. It also includes information and help to overcome the dreaded multiple choice portion of the SAT. Study this book carefully, and you can confidently master the writing section of the SAT."

–Sandra Roy, Educational Test Writer

"A rare combination of verve and precision. In this time of high-stakes accountability, *Ace the SAT Writing Even If You Hate to Write* provides an accessible way for students to get through the SATs. The author has an insider's perspective on assessment having participated in all aspects of test development. She knows what the test writers are looking for because she is one of them. Her knowledge of assessment combined with her writing talents make this book a 'must' for students who want to help themselves and improve their test scores."

–Brenda Thomas, Educational Editor

Ace the SAT Writing Even If You Hate to Write

- Second Edition -

By Tamra B. Orr

Author of "America's Best Colleges for B Students"

Ace the SAT* Writing Even If You Hate to Write (2nd Edition)
By Tamra B. Orr

Published by SuperCollege, LLC
3286 Oak Court
Belmont, CA 94002
www.supercollege.com

Cover design by TLC Graphics, www.TLCGraphics.com. Design: Monica Thomas.

ISBN: 9781932662306

Manufactured in the United States of America

10 9 8 7 6 5 4 3 2 1

Cataloging-in-Publication Data
Tamra B. Orr
Ace the SAT Writing Even if You Hate to Write 2nd Ed.
p. cm.
Includes appendices.
ISBN 9781932662306
1. Test Preparation I. Title
2. Reference 3. Education

Contents at a Glance

Table of Contents

To my kids who brighten my life, my husband who enriches my life and my parents who gave me life.

When Writing Equals a Root Canal... (without an Anesthetic!)

When Writing Equals a Root Canal... (without an Anesthetic!)

If you ask your parents whether anything in life is inevitable, they will probably tell you yes: "death" and "taxes." Chances are you are way too young to worry about either one of these yet, but don't think you are off the hook that easily. The one inevitable event in the life of a student is taking the SAT. And you'll just have to accept it. It's one of those parts of life we have to tolerate, whether we want to or not. It's like cleaning out underneath your bed, getting a camp physical, having the stomach flu or running out of chocolate: you have to get through it and do the best that you can in the process.

And just to add a little sadistic twist to the knife–the new SAT now includes a pretty extensive writing portion. Lucky test takers such as you get to answer 60 multiple choice questions about various aspects of the English language. And the new bonus is that you also get to write a timed essay. (I don't hear you cheering yet!)

Have you wondered why the powers that be (PTB) decided to add an essay portion to the new SAT? You aren't the first. Contrary to what may first come to mind, it was not to (a) torture you, (b) humiliate you, (c) annoy you, (d) depress you or (e) all of the above. Simply put, according to the experts at the College Board, they believe the "addition of writing encourages and supports the teaching of writing at every grade level...The College Board, and its many member advisers, strongly believes that making the writing section required and not optional sends a strong message about the importance of writing for success in college and the workplace."*

In other words, the College Board thinks that the ability to write a strong, clear essay is one of the most essential skills you will need to get through college, as well as succeed in a wide variety of careers. To see if you can pen such an essay, they are giving you a limited time to put one together. For the students in your English class who *always* get A's on their papers, know what every single vocabulary words means and think research papers are lots of fun (gag!), this new requirement is a piece of cake. (Go ahead; stick your tongue out at them right now!) For the rest of us, however, it can be as terrifying as a root canal without an anesthetic (hence the title of this chapter!)

There's nothing to writing. All you do is sit down at a typewriter and open a vein.

~ Walter Wellesley "Red" Smith, famed sports writer

If the idea of writing an essay for the new SAT makes you turn pale, hyperventilate and break out into a cold sweat, you have come to the right place. Even if you can hold your own on a term paper, the thought of writing a timed essay for an important standardized test is enough to send a chill down many a student's spine. This book will show you simple steps to improve your writing, gain confidence in your abilities and (most importantly) raise your score–even if writing is next to scrubbing the toilet on your list of exciting things to do.

The dirty little secret about the SAT is that you don't have to be a Fitzgerald or a Hemingway (heck, you don't even have to know who they are!) to do well on the test. Through the techniques you learn in this book you will learn how to put words on paper in a coherent and effective fashion. Not only will these skills boost your test score on the SAT but they will also help you in other areas of your life such as finding jobs, getting jobs and keeping jobs. Hey, it might even help you write an effective plea to your parents for more money when you are in college. In other words, good writing skills are not just useful for the SAT but they are useful for life.

*From the College Board website at: www.collegeboard.com/about/news_info/sat/faqs.html

Writing is easy: All you have to do is sit staring at a blank sheet of paper until drops of blood form on your forehead.

~ Gene Fowler, screenwriter and director

Here is an overview of what *Ace the SAT Writing Even if You Hate to Write* will show you:

- In the **first section**, we will dissect a professional writer to see what she does that non-writers may not know about. (We promise it won't hurt her though.)

- In the **second section**, we will chat with some of those lovely people (no, they cannot be bribed) that read and score your essay. We want to know what they look for, what matters most and what we can just quit worrying about.

- In the **third section**, we give you so much information that you had better have at least two highlighters ready. This info will make that SAT essay easier, but it will also help you to write well in almost any present or future situation. Get ready to learn all about everything from prewriting techniques, outlines, thesis statements and transitions to examples and anecdotes, good old grammar, big words, legible handwriting and writing FAST.

- In the **fourth section**, we will show you example after example of essays written by students just like you. You will get to see the "before" and "after" shots of some of them, like those weight loss ads you see on television. The "before" version shows how the essay was handed in and the score it would get. And if it rates a 3 or less, it will be followed by an "after"–what could have been done to make it better so that it received a higher score. By the time you have read through all of them, you should be an expert yourself.

- In the **fifth section**, we will spend time talking about the three kinds of multiple choice questions you will deal with on the SAT: error identification, improving sentences and improving paragraphs. (Where *is* that cheering?)

Other perks to this book are the handy-dandy charts of info, as well as a number of practice questions designed to make sure you understand what you just read and can apply the information. Ideally, you are reading this book several months before you need to take the SAT. Hopefully, it's not 48 hours before the SAT starts and you plan to read, gulp coffee, munch chocolate and read until the test. (If you are, however, pass some of that chocolate over, please.) However much time you have, this book can help you; so sit back, grab a pencil (no, it doesn't have to be a #2) and let's take a look at what writing is all about.

POP QUIZ:

To make sure you got the highlights of the intro, and to give you some great practice for the SAT exam, here are a couple of multiple choice questions to get the brain cells in gear:

(1) The reason the College Board added an essay portion to the SAT is because they:

(a) will make more money from this longer, updated version
(b) want to make sure students can actually write an essay
(c) are lonely, bored, retired teachers and need something to read
(d) have personal vendettas against high school seniors
(e) love reading student essays more than anything else in life

(2) Fitzgerald and Hemingway are:

(a) journalists
(b) animal trainers
(c) authors
(d) circus acrobats
(e) janitors

(3) The best part of reading this book is that it will teach you how to:

(a) write a solid essay
(b) win a Pulitzer Prize
(c) score a perfect 2400
(d) get a girl/boyfriend
(e) win the local lottery

Answer key: (1) b; (2) c; (3) a

Hint: The multiple choice questions on the SAT are a tad bit more difficult than the ones you will encounter in this book, but these will help you feel proud of yourself and still get the point across.

SECTION 1

The (Relatively Painless) Anatomy of a Writer

Highlights: What you will (hopefully) learn in this chapter...

- Understanding the intuitive part of writing
- Utilizing the power of thinking positively and paying attention
- Calling on all of your resources
- Focusing on the words, not the count
- Reading your work to get a sense of "rightness"
- Putting together a puzzle of words
- Learning the huge importance of practice

The (Relatively Painless) Anatomy of a Writer

And by the way, everything in life is writable about if you have the outgoing guts to do it and the imagination to improvise. The worst enemy to creativity is self-doubt.

~ Sylvia Plath, Pulitzer Prize winning poet

Do you remember the part in the "Matrix" movies when Trinity and Neo could learn how to do just about anything by having it directly downloaded into their brains? Need to know how to fly a fancy helicopter? There it is. Want to know powerful martial arts (not to mention levitate at the same time) in a few seconds? Voila. You got it. Sadly, the closest we have to the Matrix technology so far is tight, black leather outfits, but that ability to learn something instantaneously would be pretty darn handy. Before you walked in to take the SAT, for instance, you could just download how to be a natural writer straight into your brain. In lieu of that, let's take a look inside the brain of a writer–the old fashion way–to see how he or she thinks and works.

If you ask writers–either straight A English students or authors of dozens of books–how they do what they do, it is unlikely that they will be able to tell you. It is largely intuitive. It is simply an inherent part of who they are. That is true of almost anyone who is successful in some genre. For example, think of something at which you personally excel. Perhaps you can fly around the high school track in record time; maybe you can do trig problems blindfolded and with both hands tied behind your back; possibly you can play the clarinet way better than Kenny G. Do you know HOW you do it? It is usually a combination of intuition, natural skill, tons of practice and education. The same is true for writing. While you may not be a natural born writer, there is no reason you cannot learn the skills, practice and become a truly competent writer.

As a full time writer, I have written more than 50 books and 1,000 magazine articles. I can write several thousand words almost in my sleep (you should see me right before deadline!). When I try to dissect exactly how I do what I do, it is very difficult. I struggle to break it down into steps because it is all such an integral part of who I am and how I think. (Example: I'm terrible with a face-to-face confrontation, but I can write a *mean* letter to the editor!) Most of my writing is done at the unconscious level. After thinking and analyzing, however, here is a list of writing hints that I find helpful in my writing:

1. *Thinking positively and paying attention.* When I approach any writing assignment (read "SAT test" for you), I do it with confidence that I will do a good job. I psyche myself up to concentrate on the topic at hand and I don't let myself get distracted. If my attention wanders to the summer day outside, the comfy hammock in the back yard or the good book waiting on my night table, I am lost. The same principle applies when you go in to take the SAT. If you are busy thinking about how you did or will do in another section of the test, or whether or not your socks match or if the cute guy/girl sitting behind you is free later, your writing will suffer for it.

   How much influence do your attitude and attention have on what you write? Bunches–but don't just take my word for it! Sit down and try to write something coherent and interesting if you are either thinking about something else and/or telling yourself negative thoughts. See how it turns out.

   In the book, *Blink: The Power of Thinking without Thinking,* Malcolm Gladwell explained how attitude can substantially affect your ability on an exam. Gladwell described an organization that came up with a unique test. A group of people were told that they were going to answer 42 relatively difficult questions from the board game "Trivial Pursuit." Before they answered these questions, however, they were told to imagine what it would be like to be a college professor. They were instructed to take five minutes and write down what a job like that might involve. Another group was also ready to play the game, but for their five minutes, they were told to think about kids having fun kicking a soccer ball around. When the two groups began to answer the "Trivial Pursuit" questions, the group that imagined being a professor did substantially better (55.6 percent right) than the soccer group (42.6 percent). Was one group smarter than the other? Not at all. "They weren't smarter or more focused or more serious," writes Gladwell. "They were simply in a 'smart' frame of mind, and clearly, associating themselves with the idea of something smart, like a professor, made it a lot easier–in that stressful instant after a trivia question was asked–to blurt out the right answer. The difference between 55.6 and 42.6 percent, it should be pointed out is enormous," he continues. "That can be the difference between passing and failing."

What all this means to you is that when you write the SAT essay (or any other writing assignment), you need to go into the room with confidence and in the right frame of mind. If you are filling your head with statements like, "I am going to bomb this thing," "I don't know how to write" or "This is going to be just horrible," then don't be surprised if each statement comes true. After all, you just told your brain that you were going to fail, so why would it try to do anything else? Instead, you need to program your mind with the same kind of thoughts professional writers (like me!) do. I often say, "This chapter will turn out just the way I want it to," or "This book is coming together perfectly." Try positive thoughts such as "I am going to do my best on this essay," "I am ready to do a great job" or "This is going to go very well." It isn't a guarantee (be prepared: there are no guarantees) but it is one important step you can make to become a better writer.

2. *Using all of your resources.* When I write a book or an article, I often have several types of sources that I need to seamlessly blend together. I have my research, a few quotes, occasionally some interview notes and my own personal experiences. All of these have to work together to support the central idea I am writing about. If I leave any one of them out, there will be a gap in my writing. Without an integration of ideas, people will be confused when they read what I have written (or, more likely, an editor will be yelling at me over the phone). It is the same thing when you write your essay. You need to reach down inside and draw upon your life experience and knowledge to support your point of view or main topic. Don't be afraid to use personal experiences and bits of knowledge that you've collected in your SAT essay.

3. *Focus on the words, not the word count.* Just like you have a certain number of lines to fill on the SAT essay; I have a specific word count to meet, regardless of what I am writing. If I focus solely on meeting the word count instead of just covering the subject thoroughly, however, I start making mistakes. I say ten words when I only need four; I repeat myself; I concentrate on the wrong thing. That magic number has suddenly become more important than my actual message. If you focus on filling up the lines of the exam instead of on writing well, you are almost sure to make those same errors.

Writing comes more easily if you have something to say.

~ Sholem Asch, novelist and playwright

4. *Reading it over to get a "sense."* When I have finished writing something, I don't hit the send or the print button until I have done one more thing–I make my husband read it out loud to me while I listen with my eyes closed. I am a very auditory person and so while he reads, I listen for errors. If he stumbles or pauses over how I phrased something, I know a reader may stumble over it too. If I hear a repeated word, an awkward phrase or something that just doesn't flow, I have him mark the spot and I go back and fix it. When you write your SAT essay, read it (silently) to yourself and "listen" for mistakes. Everyone perceives errors differently. I *hear* them, but you might *see* or feel them, depending on your own personal style.

5. *Putting together a puzzle.* If you have ever assembled a puzzle (and who hasn't?), you know that you have to take many different pieces and slowly fit them together so that they make a clear and understandable picture. When I write something, I am doing the same thing, but each one of the pieces is an idea. I can't throw them together in any order, just like you can't put a puzzle piece anywhere that you want. The result in both cases would be a jumbled mess. I have to make sure that each sentence connects to the one next to it in a logical way. The ideas have to flow together; they have to fit. When you write your SAT essay, the sentences must flow together in a clear and logical order. One must smoothly lead to the next one. If you–or I–jump around and write without continuity, confusion ensues. I get in trouble with the boss; you get a lower test score.

6. *Practice, practice, practice.* Because I am a full time writer, I get lots of practice putting words together. On a typical day, I write no less than 30 or 40 emails, as well as several thousand words on one project or another. At least six hours (and up to 16!) a day are devoted to playing around with words in one way or another. I can write much faster than I could five years ago. I am quicker and better today because of the daily practice I get. I've trained my brain to think and write faster. You may write things for school, but chances are you only spend a few hours each year writing essays. In order to be good at it, you need to spend several hours each week writing essays. Think of it this way. If you were on the football team, how well would you play if you skipped practices and just showed up for the games? You would have missed learning new skills, finding out new plays and getting to know your teammates. *Anything* that you want to do well takes practice. Not a little, not some, but A LOT.

If you are not a person who writes very often, even practicing writing an essay may seem intimidating. Here is something to try instead. Have a friend or parent read a writing prompt to you. Then respond to it verbally. Say what you would normally have to write. If you practice responding to this kind of question orally, at least your brain will get used to the format. If you do it enough, it will become more familiar and easier to translate into words on paper later.

One of the best pieces of advice this writer can give to you, the so-called non-writer, is simply this: "To become, act as if." In other words, to become a good writer, act as if you already are one. By copying the traits and habits of a professional writer, you will be much closer to actually becoming one yourself.

POP QUIZ:

(1) What is one of the main things a professional writer uses when putting words together?

(a) thesaurus
(b) chocolate
(c) intuition
(d) whiskey
(e) printer

(2) How does thinking positively affect your overall performance?

(a) It makes you go at least 44.2 percent faster.
(b) It uses less gas overall than a typical SUV.
(c) It guarantees perfection in any arena.
(d) It gives you all the right answers.
(e) It puts you in the right frame of mind to do well.

(3) When you are writing your essay, you should concentrate mainly on:

(a) the clock
(b) your message
(c) how many lines you have left
(d) what color to dye your hair next
(e) what your girlfriend/boyfriend is wearing

(4) Which of the following is a good resource to use while writing your essay?

(a) quotes
(b) personal experiences
(c) examples from history
(d) examples from literature
(e) all of the above

(5) If there is a number one key to writing well on a regular basis, it is:

(a) cheating
(b) copying
(c) spelling
(d) practicing
(e) avoiding

Answer Key: (1) c; (2) e; (3) b; (4) e; (5) d

An Inside Look at Scoring

Highlights: What you will (hopefully) learn in this chapter...

- Exactly how your essay will be graded
- Exactly what elements you need to receive a score of 1 to 6
- Exactly who SAT essay graders are
- Tips from those who work with your essays on a regular basis

An Inside Look at Scoring

Let's take a moment to think about the people who hold your SAT essays in their hands (or on their computer screens) and give you that magical score. Just who are they? The vast majority of them are high school and college teachers who have been specifically trained to read and score SAT essays. The primary qualification is a minimum of three years teaching at the high school or college level during the last five years. To be selected, they must go through an online training program and complete a qualifying scoring test. SAT graders are taught to do the following things:

- Read through the essay quickly (the average scorer does not look at your essay for more than two minutes and often less)
- Read the essay from beginning to end before determining a score
- Follow a specific scoring guide (see below)
- Reward things done well, not punish those done badly
- Judge by quality, not length (read more about this in the chapter on appearance)

For sitting and reading essays and giving them a score, these readers are paid between $17 and $22 an hour.

The QUICK Guide to Scoring

6 Outstanding
5 Solid
4 Adequate
3 Limited
2 Flawed
1 Deficient
0 Off topic

Essays are graded "holistically." At first blush, the term "holistic" might make you think that the graders are all New Age advocates who rake their Zen gardens and meditate in between reading essays! That would be interesting, but it's just not the case. Holistic scoring simply means that the essay is evaluated as a whole, not in individual pieces. In other words, SAT essay graders read an entire essay and then give it a score.

SAT essays are usually evaluated by at least two graders. First, one grader reads the essay and gives it a score of 0 to 6. Then the essay goes to another professional scorer. He or she reads it and gives it a score of 0 to 6 as well.

No student's score rests solely with the opinion of one grader because the two scores are averaged together. But what happens when scorer A gives you a 5 and scorer B gives you a 4? Does this mean you will get a 4.5? No, there are no half scores. Instead, the essay is sent to a third scorer. Any essay that has one point or more difference between the two scores is always sent to a third grader, whose score will determine what you get. This is rare, however. The College Board states that less than eight percent ever go to a third scorer.

A Breakdown of What the Scores Mean

Since you're probably wondering what the different scores are supposed to represent, here is a summary from the official score guide. (Reprinted by permission of the College Board, the copyright owner. Disclaimer: Permission to reprint SAT materials does not constitute review or endorsement by Educational Testing Service or the College Board of this publication as a whole or of any other questions or testing information it may contain.)

SCORE OF 6

An essay in this category is outstanding, demonstrating clear and consistent mastery, although it may have a few minor errors. A typical essay:

- effectively and insightfully develops a point of view on the issue and demonstrates outstanding critical thinking skills, using clearly appropriate examples, reasons, and other evidence to support the writer's position
- is well organized and clearly focused, demonstrating clear coherence and smooth progression of ideas
- exhibits skillful use of language, using a varied, accurate, and apt vocabulary
- demonstrates meaningful variety in sentence structure
- is free of most errors in grammar, usage, and mechanics

SCORE OF 5

An essay in this category is effective, demonstrating reasonably consistent mastery, although it will have occasional errors or lapses in quality. A typical essay:

- effectively develops a point of view on the issue and demonstrates strong critical thinking skills, generally using appropriate examples, reasons, and other evidence to support the writer's position
- is well organized and focused, demonstrating coherence and progression of ideas
- exhibits facility in the use of language, using appropriate vocabulary
- demonstrates variety in sentence structure
- is generally free of most errors in grammar, usage, and mechanics

SCORE OF 4

An essay in this category is competent, demonstrating adequate mastery, although it will have lapses in quality. A typical essay:

- develops a point of view on the issue and demonstrates competent critical thinking skills, using adequate examples, reasons, and other evidence to support the writer's position
- is generally organized and focused, demonstrating some coherence and progression of ideas
- exhibits adequate but inconsistent facility in the use of language, using generally appropriate vocabulary
- demonstrates some variety in sentence structure
- has some errors in grammar, usage, and mechanics

SCORE OF 3

An essay in this category is inadequate, but demonstrates developing mastery, and is marked by ONE OR MORE of the following weaknesses:

- develops a point of view on the issue, demonstrating some critical thinking skills, but may do so inconsistently or use inadequate examples, reasons, or other evidence to support the writer's position
- is limited in its organization or focus, or may demonstrate some lapses in coherence or progression of ideas
- displays developing facility in the use of language, but sometimes uses weak vocabulary or inappropriate word choices
- lacks variety or demonstrates problems in sentence structure
- contains an accumulation of errors in grammar, usage, and mechanics

SCORE OF 2

An essay in this category is seriously limited, demonstrating little mastery, and is flawed by ONE OR MORE of the following weaknesses:

- develops a point of view on the issue that is vague or seriously limited, demonstrating weak critical thinking skills, providing inappropriate or insufficient examples, reasons, or other evidence to support the writer's position
- is poorly organized and/or focused, or demonstrates serious problems with coherence or progression of ideas
- displays very little facility in the use of language, using very limited vocabulary or incorrect word choices
- demonstrates frequent problems in sentence structure
- contains errors in grammar, usage, and mechanics so serious that meaning is somewhat obscured

SCORE OF 1

An essay in this category is fundamentally lacking, demonstrating very little or no mastery, and is severely flawed by ONE OR MORE of the following weaknesses:

- develops no viable point of view on the issue, or provides little or no evidence to support the writer's position
- is disorganized or unfocused, resulting in a disjointed or incoherent essay
- displays fundamental errors in vocabulary
- demonstrates severe flaws in sentence structure
- contains pervasive errors in grammar, usage, or mechanics that persistently interfere with meaning

SCORE OF 0

Essays not written on the essay assignment (topic) will receive a score of zero. (Ouch!)

Chatting with the Experts

To get more of an insider's look at how SAT essays are scored, I talked to several experts in the field. Ned Johnson, for example, has been tutoring students for the SATs and other exams for more than 13 years. He is based in Washington, D.C. and runs a company called PrepMatters. Johnson has spoken personally with SAT scorers and shares his opinion of them. Johnson says, "They are often disgruntled, underpaid and on their 14th cup of coffee. You want to make it easy for them to score your essay."

Johnson believes in employing a basic strategy when writing the SAT essay–write about what you know. "When test-takers can use strong examples, they can quickly and confidently write well and a lot," he says. "Confident writing with specific and detailed examples allows writers to avoid the written equivalent of stammering." He has the perfect story to illustrate this point too.

The most essential gift for a good writer is a built-in, shockproof #&$ detector. This is the writer's radar and all great writers have had it.*

~ Ernest Hemingway

Johnson remembers helping to prep a young man for a writing test much like the new SAT. "Sean was profoundly non-verbal," explains Johnson. "His first stab at an essay could not have been worse–painful even–likely a score of four or five out of 12. He felt compelled to use a literary example, a poor choice that utterly doomed his essay." A series of questions led Johnson to the conclusion that Sean rarely even read. He paid attention in class, used Cliffs Notes, but did not really read. "Quite possibly the last book he'd read cover to cover was *Clifford, the Big Red Dog,"* continued Johnson. So he asked him what he knew about–what he was an expert in. "Sports!" was his emphatic reply. "Anything else?" he asked. Loooooonnnnnngggggg pause. "Um, basketball." Sports it was.

"He wrote practice essay after practice essay," says Johnson. "Topics about success, overcoming adversity, teamwork, etc. all elicited tales about Michael Jordan and the Chicago Bulls. Failure, conflict and the like brought accounts of the (then) lowly Washington Bullets," he adds. "The essays were good."

The day of the actual test brought "Describe an event that changed history" as a topic. Sean's answer? "When Michael Jordan entered the NBA draft in 1984, it was an event that changed history. Not only did he set new standards for what it meant to be a professional basketball player, but he redefined the role of professional athletes as spokesmen and icons in society." Then, Sean simply rewrote the main body paragraphs he had written so many times in practice. His score? Ten out of 12. "A miracle in my mind," says Johnson.

You will find the strategy of writing practice essays repeated throughout this entire book. Ned Johnson is a huge advocate of the idea, believing in practicing long before the test. "Find a topic and do a little research so you have some details and practice," he recommends. "The key is being organized and detailed!"

Johnson's last piece of advice: Get enough sleep several days before the test. "Emotional control and verbal recall are two of the first things that are negatively affected by sleep deprivation," he reminds students.

Dr. Samuel Barnett, a Certified Educational Planner, agrees with that recommendation. "Being awake and functioning at top efficiency between 8 and 9 a.m. is incredibly important," he says. Barnett has been working with students preparing for the SAT since the early 1990s. He believes that "the best way to learn to write is to write. It just takes practice and the willingness to grasp the basics of writing mechanics," he says. "Based on the scoring guide, students should practice developing a position and showing two or three pieces of evidence which support that position. They also need to learn mechanics so the reader doesn't lose the overall impression that they can express themselves."

According to Barnett, the bottom line to success with the new SAT is "being able to understand how to respond to a prompt which is asking you to form an opinion quickly and then define it without repeating yourself, using examples, illustrations or arguments beyond your immediate social experience, along with writing competent sentences and paragraphs."

One grader I interviewed, who wishes to remain anonymous, has been involved with scoring tests for more than a decade. She has a no-nonsense attitude towards the SAT essay. "Length counts," she says, "but B.S. does not. And please do not think that scorers are too dumb to figure out that you are repeating the same thing over and over." According to her, a score of 6 is rare; 5 is decent; 4 is an attainable goal for students and is the level required to be able to handle college work; 3 is a sure miss; and 2 and 1 "we just don't want to talk about." She advises students to "pick the side of an issue that you have the most examples for, not necessarily the one you agree with, then use examples, examples, examples. I cannot say that enough. USE EXAMPLES."

This grader also stresses that scorers look for a beginning, middle and end to an essay, as well as sentence variety. "State what you are going to do and then do it," she says. Her final words of advice? "Stay far away from writing second person (you). It is the sign of a poor writer. Try to keep with third person instead." She reminds students that if even they write, "When John F. Kennedy was President in World War II" for part of an example, they will not be negatively scored just because they have their history mixed up. "Include names, people, places and dates," she adds. "Scorers are not reading for accuracy."

The people quoted here are the ones who know both the proverbial and literal score. They know what your essay needs and what numbers you will get if you do or do not follow through with those requirements. Listen up!

POP QUIZ:

(1) Who are the main scorers for the SAT essay?

(a) underpaid college students
(b) unemployed circus workers
(c) current and retired teachers
(d) College Board employees
(e) national test writers

(2) What does the term "holistic" mean when applied to scoring your essay?

(a) scored and drinking herbal tea
(b) scored while practicing yoga
(c) scored by individual paragraphs
(d) scored in its entirety
(e) scored on a computer screen

(3) What was Johnson's main piece of advice?

(a) write about sports
(b) write about what you know
(c) write after studying all night
(d) write as fast as possible
(e) write about Michael Jordan

(4) What did Barnett say was extremely important?

(a) getting enough sleep beforehand
(b) eating a nutritious breakfast
(c) studying spelling and punctuation
(d) learning sentence variety
(e) using first person experiences

(5) What is one thing our anonymous grader said *not* to use in your essay?

(a) sentence variety
(b) slang terms
(c) quotes
(d) examples
(e) second person

ANSWER KEY: (1) c; (2) d; (3) b; (4) a; (5) e

SECTION 3

I'm Gonna Make a Writer Outta You!

This part of the book is like a crash course in Writing 101 (no helmets required). It is divided into a dozen different sections and each one is pretty darn important. When you put them all together, you not only have everything you need to know to write a great SAT essay, but anything else you will be called on to write now or in the future. Hang on to this book; its shelf life may be amazingly long. (Better yet! Buy multiple copies and give them out for birthday gifts!)

In this version of SAT Boot Camp, you don't have to wear a nasty looking uniform; you won't be awakened at 5 a.m. by "Taps;" you don't have to do 100 push-ups if you don't understand something and you don't have to eat unidentifiable food dumped onto a plastic tray. You do, however, have to learn a great deal of material fast and be able to turn around and use it. (And I wouldn't mind if you saluted me now and then too.) Ready? Take a deep breath and let's go.

Part 1:

Boot Camp

Getting Familiar with the SAT's Format

The more you get to know about something, the less intimidating it can be. For example, I have spent most of my life deathly afraid of bats. At my children's insistence, I learned about the nocturnal creatures. When I found out that (a) bats eat mosquitoes and (b) they are really nurturing mothers, I was much less afraid of them. It can be the same with the test. By learning what the new SAT looks like, you will know what to expect and it will be less frightening. It may even become, dare I say it, *comfortable*? Okay, I'll stick with *familiar*.

The writing portion of the SAT is divided into two sections: the essay portion and 60 multiple choice questions. In the last section of this book, we will take a long and detailed look at the multiple choice portion of the test. We will talk about what it involves and how to approach the questions. Right now, it's enough to know that you have 40 minutes to complete it and the questions will cover three skills: identifying sentence errors, improving sentences and improving paragraphs. Now, does that sound like fun, or what?

The Essay, Up Close and Personal

Your essay will be written in an official test booklet. There are 46 lines, not 45 and not 47. FORTY-SIX. You don't get any extra paper to write on either. Within a time period of 20 minutes, the average student can fit between 300 and 500 words on those lines. Although length supposedly does not count for or against you, according to the PTB at the SAT (fun rhyme there), it really does. (See comments from graders in last chapter). So filling up most of the lines is *good*. But beware; filling up the lines by doing *any* of the following is *BAD:*

writing very, very big

indenting each paragraph more than necessary

skipping every other line

There will be more about this in the section on overall essay appearance, but for now, it's important that you know that those tricks just do not work. They will only count against you as graders see students who are trying to fool them into thinking they wrote more than they actually did.

First, let's consider the typical directions that go with the essay. Read them CAREFULLY. They are helpful. They remind you of important points. Although the wording may vary a little from test to test, they generally look like this:

> This essay gives you the chance to show how effectively you can develop and express ideas. You should, therefore, take extra care to develop your point of view, present your ideas in a clear and logical order and use precise language.

These are reminders that you are expected to <u>choose</u> a side and then organize your thoughts.

> Your essay must be written on the lines provided on your answer sheet. You will not receive any other paper on which to write. You will have enough space if you write on every line, avoid wide margins and keep your handwriting to a reasonable size. Remember that people who are not familiar with your handwriting will read what you write. Try to write or print so that what you are writing is legible to those readers.

This is another reminder to not make those mistakes listed above.

> You have twenty-five minutes to write an essay on the topic assigned below. DO NOT WRITE ON ANOTHER TOPIC. AN OFF-TOPIC ESSAY WILL RECEIVE A SCORE OF ZERO.

Hopefully you will not miss this clue since it is IN CAPITALS. Staying on-topic is absolutely essential if you want an actual score.

Example Essay Prompts

Think carefully about the concept presented in the following excerpt and the assignment below. You will be given a quote or a discussion of a concept. Here is a sample writing prompt from the College Board, the makers of the SAT:

> Many persons believe that to move up the ladder of success and achievement, they must forget the past, repress it and relinquish it. But others have just the opposite view. They see old memories as a chance to reckon with the past and integrate past and present.

After the writing prompt, you will see the official assignment. Usually it will ask for your opinion or point of view on the quote or the concept at hand. You will be told to think about it carefully. Here is the one the SAT used in conjunction with the prompt above:

> **Assignment:** "Do memories hinder or help people in their effort to learn from the past and succeed in the present? Plan and write an essay in which you develop your point of view on the issue. Support your position with reasoning and examples taken from your reading, studies, experience or observations."

If you responded to this prompt by telling about one of your past memories or how Alzheimer patients often lose their memories, you would probably get a zero. Why? Because that is NOT what you were asked to address. You veered too far off track and went into "off-topic land" where the only score you can get is a lousy ZERO.

Here is another prompt from the College Board. Read it over. These examples will help you get comfortable (okay, *familiar*) with the format you will see on test day:

> Most of our schools are not facing up to their responsibilities. We must begin to ask ourselves whether educators should help students address the critical moral choices and social issues of our time. Schools have responsibilities beyond training people for jobs and getting students into college.
>
> **Assignment:** Should schools help students understand moral choices and social issues? Plan and write an essay in which you develop your point of view on this issue. Support your position with reasoning and examples taken from your reading, studies, experiences or observations.

Other writing prompts on the essay portion will center around one longer quote or two shorter quotes that are being compared. Here is a typical example of the comparison type:

> Author Abraham Joshua Herschel has been credited with saying, "Wonder, rather than doubt, is the root of knowledge." Author Antoine de Saint-Exupery wrote, "If you want to build a boat, do not drum up people to collect wood or assign them tasks or work, but rather teach them to long for the endless immensity of the sea."
>
> **Assignment:** Both of these quotes are talking about the concept of curiosity. Do you believe that knowledge leads to wonder or that wonder leads to knowledge? Plan and write an essay in which you develop your point of view on this issue. Support your position with reasoning and examples taken from your reading, studies, experiences or observations.

Hopefully, these three prompt examples will give you a better idea of what to expect when it is your turn to hold the #2 pencil and read the test question. It brings you one step closer to acing that SAT.

Part 2:

Tick, Tick, Tick

Managing Your Time as the Clock Keeps Ticking Away

Have you ever noticed that time seems to go by at vastly different paces depending on what you are doing? Usually if you are having fun–maybe instant messaging with your friends on the computer or watching your favorite television show–the minutes fly by. But if you are stuck babysitting your younger brother or watching your Aunt Ethel's video of her trip to Rome, time tends to crawl.

When it comes to writing the SAT essay, you will have a total of 25 minutes from the moment the prompt is read until the time you are told to put down the pencil. That is not a lot of time by any means and if you do not use it wisely and efficiently, it will be gone in the blink of an eye. This is a situation that calls for solid planning if you are going to get everything done in less time than it takes to watch an episode of "Friends" (in reruns, of course).

Let's break the essay down into a minute-by-minute plan. Are you going to be able to stick to it like Crazy Glue from start to finish? Not likely. You may take a few extra minutes for one step and a few less on another. It will vary from individual to individual.

Before the time starts, be sure to take several deep breaths. Relax your shoulders. Stretch your arms. You need your energy to write a solid essay. You aren't doing yourself any favors when you siphon energy into tense muscles. And it's not likely that being up-tight will help your score.

Each skill listed in this timed plan will be discussed thoroughly in the next sections. If you find yourself reading it now and saying, "What the heck is this person talking about?", don't give up on me. Hang in there because it will all be explained eventually. Here is the basic format (can you hear the ticking clock like they play on "Jeopardy"?):

Minute 1: Plan to spend just about one minute reading the prompt, making sure you understand exactly what it is asking and then determining your point of view on the statement. It is essential that you read the prompt carefully and read the ENTIRE assignment from beginning to end.

Minutes 2-3: Brainstorm your ideas and responses to the prompt. This is where you will choose the best examples to support your opinion.

Minutes 4-7: You have three to four minutes to put together an outline. Organize the introduction, body and conclusion now.

Minutes 8-23: This is your biggest slice of time. Obviously, it will be used for actually writing the essay itself. You have 15 minutes to put those thoughts from your outline down onto paper.

Minutes 24-25: Time to proof your essay. Scan it carefully, looking for errors in grammar, spelling, punctuation or flow.

Time is up: When "Time" is called, pencils are put down. You can breathe a sigh of relief. Those manic minutes are over–for now.

When you start practicing writing essays later on (and yes, you will be doing that or else you are wasting your time reading this book), it will be important to set a timer so that you start and stop in that 25 minute period. Get a stopwatch or at least a watch that measures the seconds. Analyze how long it takes you to do each phase of the essay. I can almost guarantee that it will take you longer than the time allotted to complete each one. It's easy to spend 20 minutes brainstorming. It's even easier to spend 20 minutes outlining. With class papers, this is fine; with the SAT, it's a catastrophe. That is why practice is absolutely mandatory. You have to learn to speed up.

I am guessing I do not even have to tell you this, but I am going to say it anyway –just to be on the safe side. **Do not practice your essays on the computer**. I know that actually writing something out by hand is almost as archaic as putting a letter in the mailbox; but nonetheless, your essay must be written in your own handwriting. Practicing on the computer will throw your times completely off as most people can type far faster than they can write. With a computer, you also have all of those handy-dandy features like spell check–which you won't have the day of the SAT exam–so computer essay writing is unrealistic practice since it gives you an unfair advantage. All of your practice essays must be written by hand only. Get it? Got it. Good!

Time yourself each time you practice and see which stage slows you down. Ask yourself questions like these: How long did you spend reading the prompt and figuring out what it was asking you to do? Did you spend too much time brainstorming or creating an outline? Did you write too slowly to get the essay done in 15 minutes? Did you have any time left over to proof your writing?

Find your weakness and through practice, improve on it. Wouldn't you rather discover what skills need sharpening ahead of time than realize it with horror during the test when it counts against you? Practice is the key. Remember that. You will probably get sick of my saying it but it certainly bears repeating. PRACTICE! You can even use the form I have created to do so. List the topic and how long it took you to do each stage of the process.

EXAMPLE PRACTICE FORM						
Topic	**Read**	**Think**	**Outline**	**Write**	**Proof**	**TOTAL**
Justice	3	5	7	24	4	43
Courage	2	4	6	20	3	35
Honesty	1	2	3	16	3	25

YOUR PRACTICE FORM						
Topic	**Read**	**Think**	**Outline**	**Write**	**Proof**	**TOTAL**

Watch for signs of improvement as you work. You want the numbers to go down. Ideally, you'd like to reach 25 minutes and stay around there. Do it often enough that it becomes both natural and quick.

Part 3:

Take Cover!

It's Time to Brainstorm

If you have ever taken part in any kind of competition, you know that you have to get your mind (and often, your body) prepared before you start. If you don't stretch before walking on stage to dance, a muscle cramp may be in your very near future. If you don't do some scales before singing a solo, your voice and throat may not cooperate. The same is true with taking a big test like the SAT. Before launching into writing those first words on the page, you need to go through other vital steps. Not too shockingly, the first one is called *prewriting techniques*. Catchy name, eh? Usually it is referred to as *brainstorming*, but it can also involve free writing, list making or clustering. All of these accomplish the same thing; it just depends on whichever works best for you and feels the most natural.

Prewriting is simply an exercise of the mind to get ready to actually (can you guess it?)…write! If you look back at the time schedule of your SAT, you've already spent one minute reading the quote and assignment. Now, you have one to two minutes to start putting together your initial response to what you just read.

Remember that you are primarily writing a persuasive essay. This is essential! Stop. Read that statement again. This is not a definition essay. It's not a narrative. It is mainly *persuasive.* You are taking a stand, stating an opinion, choosing a position on what you have read. It is your job to convince the reader that you are right, whatever your viewpoint may be. You have four possibilities to choose from. You can:

- agree completely with the statement
- agree with some reservations
- disagree completely with the statement
- disagree with some reservations

As you write down ideas during the prewriting stage, you are looking for reasons, examples, stories, quotes or any other resource you can think of to support your opinion. There are several ways to get the words flowing. Let's take a look at these to see which ones you find most helpful (and yes, they are very similar so you may find one method overlapping another one.)

Brainstorming: Based on the question about a quote or a concept, start writing down any ideas or thoughts that come to mind in association with it. They can be words, phrases or sentences. You might think of something you read on the same topic, your dad once told you, you have seen at work, your friend did or you saw in a movie. All of these examples can be relevant, so jot them down. At the end of a minute, try to pick out the three most important or strongest points. Cross out the ones that you know won't work. This prewriting technique is also called *free writing*. Both words represent basically the same concept.

Listing: Make a numbered list of the concepts that come to mind as you think about a quote or question.

Clustering: Draw a circle, put the main subject in it and start shooting lines out of the circle with words on the end of each one. Each word should relate directly to the topic.

Let's practice this a little bit. Using any of the three methods listed here, what ideas can you come up with in association with the following, general statements?

(1) Beauty is only skin deep.

____

____

____

____

(2) Never a borrower or a lender be.

____

____

____

____

(3) Go confidently in the direction of your dreams. Live the life you've imagined.

____

____

____

____

Can you see how doing this helps you to focus on the topic as you gather ideas? It is truly an insightful thing to do. For the sake of good old illustration, let's use the following prompt as an example:

> President Calvin Coolidge once said, "Nothing in the world can take the place of persistence. Talent will not; nothing is more common than unsuccessful men with talent. Genius will not; unrewarded genius is almost a proverb. Education will not; the world is full of educated derelicts. Persistence and determination alone are omnipotent. The slogan 'Press on' has solved and always will solve the problems of the human race."
>
> **Assignment:** While persistence is important, do you think it more important than talent, intelligence and education in solving problems? Plan and write an essay in which you develop your point of view on this issue. Support your position with reasoning and examples taken from your reading, studies, experiences or observations.

Fill your paper with the breathings of your heart.

~ William Wordsworth, British poet

What things come to mind when you read this? Let's think it through together. First, decide on whether you agree or disagree with the statement. Is persistence the most important element to solving the world's problems? Yes or no? Once you have your position (and keep in mind, the essay graders do NOT care what your opinion is, just that you have one and support it!), write down as many relevant thoughts as you can. For example, what people come to mind? You might think of someone you know who has been persistent. It could be a relative, friend or co-worker. It might even be someone in the news, in a book you read or a historical figure. Hey, it might even be you! Write down the name(s). What else can you think of? Jot down some world problems. How could persistence affect them? At this point, just put down whatever comes to mind. You will be weeding out the ones that don't apply in a few minutes.

By having these words written down in front of you (in your test booklet), you have a place to begin. No longer are you simply staring at a blank page. You have a few concepts to flesh out. This is your starting point for the next step–the outline. Ready? Let's keep moving.

[illegible]

[illegible]

[illegible]

[illegible]

[illegible]

Part 4:

Just Add Water

Making Instant Outlines

Today's top prize question: What are the three basic parts of the typical essay? (Go ahead and think about it. I will wait. *twiddling thumbs*)

Okay, time's up. Know the answer? If you guessed the (1) introduction, (2) body and (3) conclusion, pat yourself on the back. Good job. Fifty points for you in the SAT lottery.

You have already used up the first three minutes of the writing time. Now you have three to four minutes to put together an outline. I can see you now, shaking your head at me. "Nah, man, not me. I don't need no silly outline. I'll just wing it, man." (You have to say it with a Cheech Marin accent though. If you don't know who he is, ask your parents.)

Even the best writers use an outline. Ask me what I did before I started writing this book. Really–ask me. *Hey, Tami, what was the first thing you did before you started writing this excellent book?* Hey! Thanks for asking. Actually, I wrote an outline (just ask my editors). I had so much great stuff to tell you but I wanted to make sure I did it in the right order. This book would be less helpful if I just threw chapters in any order. What is the point of reading about prewriting techniques AFTER the chapter on proofing the essay? Since one of the most important things your essay will be graded on is organization, putting things in a logical order is essential. The key to that is...can you guess? Yep, it's the outline.

I know you've heard this analogy a hundred times, but let's go with it again because it is such an accurate one. Your outline is your MAP. If you put it together correctly, the hardest work is done. As you are writing, you won't get lost because all you have to do is consult your map. *Okay, I just finished that point...where am I supposed to go next? Glance at the outline. Aha! Got it.* If you stick with the map and follow its directions, you will reach your destination safe and sound. In the case of the SAT essay, the end of the trip is putting down your pencil and turning in the test.

So, how do you put together an outline in just a matter of minutes? Most likely, the other outlines you've done for term papers or other writing assignments have taken an hour or more. Right now, you have a maximum of 180 seconds. Here is how to use those precious moments best:

Start with the introduction. Here you will simply state your opinion on the issue. Let's look at the example we used in the last part:

> President Calvin Coolidge once said, "Nothing in the world can take the place of persistence. Talent will not; nothing is more common than unsuccessful men with talent. Genius will not; unrewarded genius is almost a proverb. Education will not; the world is full of educated derelicts. Persistence and determination alone are omnipotent. The slogan 'Press on' has solved and always will solve the problems of the human race."
>
> **Assignment:** While persistence is important, do you think it more important than talent, intelligence and education in solving problems? Plan and write an essay in which you develop your point of view on this issue. Support your position with reasoning and examples taken from your reading, studies, experiences or observations.

REMEMBER! You are writing a persuasive essay. You must convince your reader. Let's assume (uh-oh) that you agree with President Coolidge's statement; persistence truly is the most important element in solving a variety of problems. That opinion is your introduction. Fill it in on the form below. You can use words, phrases or sentences; just be quick and be able to remember what you were referring to when you start writing. (Shorthand is only helpful if you can decipher it later.)

Now, look back at all of the words you put down during the brainstorming process. Slash those that just won't work in the scope of this short essay. Some might be too complex; some could be too vague on the details to write about reliably. Look through the names you jotted down. Susan B. Anthony, Rosa Parks and the Wright Brothers. Hmmmm. You might be onto something here. Those are three very solid examples. They belong in the outline. Decide which one you think is the strongest and use it as the first example. Plug it into the outline, along with the other two supporting examples (more on how to choose the right examples in part 6).

Okay, 30 seconds left. You need a conclusion. Wrap it up. Show how the examples supported your original opinion. Voila! You're done!

Introduction:	Persistence is the most important element in solving problems.
Example 1:	Susan B. Anthony–push for women's right to vote
Example 2:	Rosa Parks–bus boycott
Example 3:	Wright Brothers–first flight
Conclusion:	Persistence is the key to finding solutions that other skills like education, intelligence and talent alone cannot accomplish.

Remember that you don't have to write it this way. You may be writing something that looks more like this, especially considering the limited time you have:

> Intro–agreed
>
> #1–Susan B. Anthony
>
> #2–Rosa Parks
>
> #3–Wright Brothers
>
> Con–all other skills can't accomplish

However you choose to write it is fine; just be sure you know what you mean when you start putting those first words onto paper.

Let's go back for a moment to the analogy of the outline as your map. Anyone who has ever taken a road trip, even if it's just to the next town, knows that detours can sometimes be fun. You might just discover something wonderful if you have to deviate from the map and take an alternate route. This is true with the outline as well. As you begin writing, you may suddenly have one of those "lightbulb-over-your-head" moments when you think of the perfect story or example to use. If you do, go ahead and plug it into the outline and use it. The problem is if you fill out the outline, start writing, get half way through and start to question yourself. You simply do not have time to start over. Keep on the same pathway and save that brilliant thought for another time.

Now, let's get some practice on creating an outline. Here is another sample prompt to try:

> One of the biggest growing controversies in education today is the concept of home schooling. Over two million children of all ages are taught at home in the United States and the number is growing by approximately 15 percent per year. Some families feel that this is the best way to give their children a strong education, while some educators believe that home schooling is detrimental to kids.
>
> **Assignment:** Do you think home schooling helps or hinders a child's education? Plan and write an essay in which you develop your point of view on this issue. Support your position with reasoning and examples taken from your reading, studies, experiences or observations.

You've read it through, so you understand what you are supposed to write about (home schooling: yea or nay?). You've brainstormed and have a half a page full of words, notes and phrases. It's time to create an outline. Fill in the form below. Notice that the examples I provide are written in ever so nice, complete sentences. This is just to make sure that they are clear for you. Chances are you will not do that in your outline. It takes too much time.

Introduction: ______________________________

____

____

(Examples: I think that home schooling is one of the best educational decisions parents can make for their child OR Teaching your child at home deprives them of some of the world's most important lessons.)

Example #1: ______________________________

____

____

____

(Examples: My best friend is home-schooled and I am constantly amazed at all that she does in a typical week OR I know several home-schooled kids and they just do not seem to communicate with others like public schooled kids do.)

Example #2: ______________________________

____

____

____

(Examples: I recently read an article on CNN about home schoolers and was amazed at how high they tend to score on standardized national tests OR According to a story in *Time* magazine, home schoolers rarely get the same athletic and scholastic opportunities as public schooled kids do.)

Example #3: ______________________________

____

____

____

(Examples: There have been times in my life when I have wanted to be home schooled also OR I would hate being home-schooled because I need a much more active social life.)

Conclusion: ______________________________

____

____

(Examples: The millions of families home schooling in this country do so for valid reasons that I both understand and support. Although it may not be a popular decision with everyone, it is a dedicated and wise one for many OR Although homeschooling parents may be trying to help their children, their decision is one that will result in multiple deficiencies and losses that they can never regain.)

Let's try another one.

> Ever since television was first invented, there has been controversy over its value. Some believe that it is one of the best inventions of the century, capable of educating viewers and connecting them to the rest of the world. Others think that it is an "idiot box," dumbing down viewers and alienating them from the rest of the people in their families.
>
> **Assignment:** Do you think television is an improvement to society or a detriment? How does it affect society as a whole? Plan and write an essay in which you develop your point of view on this issue. Support your position with reasoning and examples taken from your reading, studies, experiences or observations.

You've read it through, so you understand what you are supposed to write about (television: good or evil?). You've brainstormed and have a half a page full of words, notes and phrases. It's time to create your outline. Fill in the form below.

Introduction: ____________________

Example #1: ____________________

Example #2: ____________________

Example #3: ____________________

Conclusion: ____________________

What ideas did you come up with for this one? Did you create an outline that will lead you to writing a solid essay? Hopefully, by now, you can see how a thorough outline can make writing the essay much easier. It truly is a map to guide you right from the first word to your last.

Part 5:

Ready, Aim, Fire!

Finding Your Target

The prompt is read, the brainstorming is done, the outline is written and finally it is time to start putting words down on paper. The first thing you are going to write is a *thesis statement.* Don't let the terminology scare you. This is just a sentence that shows what idea you plan to convey within the essay. It is your point of view, your opinion.

Look at this way. Let's say you are thinking about going to the mall because you need a new pair of shoes. Your shopping thesis statement would be, "I'm going out to buy some sandals." It gives you direction. You won't wander around the mall, stopping in the bookstore, the drug store or the clothing store. You won't spend hours walking around and achieving little to nothing. Instead, you will go straight to the shoe store and get those sandals.

So, you hate to go shopping? Fine. Let's try another example. Imagine that you are in the mood to bake. You look through the cookbook and find just the recipe you want. Your thesis statement would be, "I'm going to bake oatmeal cookies this afternoon." By stating that, you don't have to get out the pound of bacon, the can of pureed tomatoes or the jar of curry (unless you make some very odd oatmeal cookies!) You can go straight for the brown sugar, flour, eggs and oatmeal. You won't get lost along the way because you have a direction.

All right. I can hear you from here. You don't like to shop or bake. Let's try one more. Imagine you are on the high school track team. You want to do well in the next meet's 100-meter sprint. You develop the thesis statement, "I want to cut a full second off my time in the 100-meter sprint." By doing this, you know that you don't need to waste time working on kicks, jumps, backstrokes or serves. Instead, you will work on endurance and speed.

Hopefully, these examples show you the point of having a thesis statement when you write the SAT essay: It provides your entire direction. It tells you where to go next, so that you will not get lost along the way. This is absolutely essential too; going off-topic in the essay is the only thing that will guarantee you a score of zero.

"Great," you say. The thesis statement is the best thing to come along since a compass, but how do I get one? It is pretty simple: read the prompt and choose an opinion about it. (As the parent of one former and two current teenagers, I know you have opinions!) Remember, your choices are to agree completely, agree with reservations, disagree completely or disagree with reservations. So, let's walk through the process:

1. Read the prompt. Make sure you understand it.

2. Did you have any kind of immediate reaction? If so, go with it.

3. If you did not have any particular reaction, read it over again (fast!).

4. Now decide if you agree or disagree with the prompt. Do you agree/disagree completely or is your head saying, "Well, yes, that is true BUT…" or "That's just nonsense EXCEPT for…"? If you honestly don't know one way or another, choose the perspective that seems more comfortable or the one that you have the most examples to support.

5. Take the wording of the prompt and use it as the basis for your thesis statement. Try your best not to copy it word for word, however. Rephrase the prompt but make your opinion clear. If you can, make it a powerful, strong statement. That makes a better impression.

6. Remember that this is YOUR opinion only, not your teacher's, the test scorer's or your parent's. This is only your opinion.

7. Also remember that there is no right or wrong answer to these essays. You do not have to be remotely PC (politically correct). You can write the wildest, most controversial thesis statement in the world as long as you adequately support it.

Let's practice writing a few thesis statements. What would you write in response to the quote, "Beauty is in the eye of the beholder"?

____

____

____

____

____

When you read the quote, did you find yourself going, "Right!" or "Wrong!"? Let's assume you agree with the statement. In that case, you might write, "What makes one person beautiful to another varies from individual to individual." This sentence sets you up for giving examples of how one thing is beautiful to one person but not to another. If you disagree with the statement, you might write, "Beauty is a universal concept and everyone agrees on what is beautiful and what is not." This would lead you to listing examples of how beauty is universal.

How about another one? What would you write in response to this statement? Many educational experts believe that all schools should be equipped with metal detectors and have periodic locker inspections.

____

____

If you agree with this statement, you might write, "By making metal detectors and locker inspections part of a school's security system, schools will be safer places." If you disagree, however, you could write, "Metal detectors and locker inspections will only frustrate and anger students rather than making them feel safer."

Okay, we will do one more. (I can tell how entertaining you find these.) Think of a thesis statement in response to this quote by Henry David Thoreau: "Do not worry if you have built your castles in the air. They are where they should be. Now put the foundations under them."

Did you agree or disagree with Thoreau's statement? If you agree, you could write something along the lines, "Building castles in the air is what imagination is for and putting the foundations underneath them is what intelligence is for." If, on the other hand, you disagree, you could write, "Building castles in the air is a waste of time and putting foundations under them is completely unnecessary."

The Mini-Me of Thesis Statements

Have you come across the term *topic sentence*? If so, you might be confused about what it means and how it relates to the thesis statement. Okay, most likely you've never given it any thought at all, but for the sake of learning about it, let's pretend that you did.

Just as a thesis statement sets the direction of your entire essay, the topic sentence is the one that sets what each individual paragraph is going to be about. Again, it lends you additional direction and organization. For example, look at this paragraph from an essay about what loyalty means.

> <u>Loyalty to your friends is not always easy</u>. A few years ago, one of my closest friends was involved in an illegal activity. I was emotionally torn between keeping it a secret for him or talking to his parents. Just last week, another friend asked me not to tell anyone that she has an eating disorder. These situations force you to ask the question, How far do loyalty and friendship go?

The topic sentence of this paragraph is underlined. Do you see how it sets up what will come next? It lets the reader know the paragraph is going to be about loyalty and friends; and, indeed, that is exactly what the examples are centered on.

Here are a couple of topic sentences for you. What do you think the paragraphs would be about? What kind of examples will they contain?

1) While some authors have multiple bestsellers, others write one single blockbuster and then never pick up the pen again.

This paragraph is going to be about...

(Suggested answer: examples of authors (such as Margaret Mitchell or Harper Lee) who wrote huge books, only to never write again)

2) Hurricane Katrina changed the lives of people in New Orleans, as well as the rest of the world.

This paragraph is going to include examples like...

(Suggested answer: how people in New Orleans lost their homes, belongings and even family, while the people of the country lost their confidence in the nation's ability to respond to major disaster)

Now let's look at this topic sentence thing from the opposite angle. Here are two paragraphs. What would be a good topic sentence for each one of them?

1) They began hitting old balls against a concrete wall at their home in Compton, California. Now the sisters are two of the top-ranked tennis players in the entire world. They have competed in some of the world's most challenging tournaments and always amaze the crowds with their power and speed.

The topic sentence for this paragraph would be something like...

(Suggested answer: Venus and Serena Williams have come a long way since they were small children.)

> 2) Research has shown that they help decrease a school's problems with teasing and they appear to bring a semblance of equality to the classrooms. With everyone wearing the exact same thing, however, there is no room for individuality.

The topic sentence for this paragraph would be something along the lines of...

____

____

(Suggested answer: School uniforms may have some good points, but in the end, I believe they are a mistake.)

Topic sentences are not absolutely essential in your essay, but if you use them, it will be easier to organize your points. They are like a big sign post telling you to go THIS WAY. In other words, it makes your job easier. And hey, who would mind that?

Once you have a thesis statement and topic sentences in place, it is time to move on to finding the best examples to support them. We will look at how to choose them in the next section. (Is that a spiffy segue between topics or what?)

Part 6:

I Need Some Support

Using the Best Examples and Illustrations

If you look back at the section where graders and other test experts gave some insight and advice, you will see that the general consensus is that the more solid examples in the essay, the higher it will score. Once you've formed an opinion and put it into a thesis statement, you need the info to back it up.

Think of it this way. You don't stand up and announce to your friends that you are the best guitar player to play in their band and then not be able to play a note. You don't walk into a job interview and say you're the best salesperson ever but you don't have a clue how to sell a single thing. You don't tell your friends you can ace the math test if you aren't even sure what chapters the test is covering. In other words, if you are going to claim something (your thesis statement), you had better be able to give the solid evidence (your examples) to prove it true.

There are a variety of kinds of examples you can use. All of them have merit, although some of them (history, literature, art and science) carry a little bit more authority than others (sports, personal experience, family stories). Here is a list of the primary types you can use in the essay:

- historical references (mentioning or quoting a historical figure, event, date, etc.)
- literature references (discussing or quoting a book or author)
- current event references (facts or quotes garnered from the radio, television, magazines or newspaper)
- science (studies done in the fields of biology, chemistry, physics, etc.)
- politics (activities and quotes from various parties, representatives, politicians or government officials)
- art (events happening in the movies, plays, music, theatre and television)
- sports (information about track, basket/base/football, soccer, Olympics, etc.)
- personal experience (yours, your family's, your friend's, your neighbor's, etc.)
- family stories (your family, their family, our family, anyone's family)

Pretend for a moment that you are a world famous detective. You can be Inspector Clouseau, Sherlock Holmes, Miss Marple, Hercule Poirot, Scully or Mulder or Adrian Monk. The point is that you are a great detective. You have gathered all of the murder suspects into one room and you boldly announce, "I know who the murderer is!" Everyone looks at you expectantly, each person holding his or her breath in great anticipation. You dramatically point to the guilty party and...what? What comes next? The evidence, of course! You have to present the proof or else your accusation will be nothing but a bunch of hot air (and people will be understandably annoyed with you).

It is the same thing with the essay. You have made this terrific statement agreeing or disagreeing with some universal concept (justice, hope, love, compassion, etc.) and now, in order to convince others that you believe what you have written, you need evidence. This is where those wonderful examples come in. You can use quotes, stories, facts and opinions. Just remember to *support* what you have said.

May I Quote You on That?

I would imagine about now, you are thinking to yourself, "Well, yeah, a quote would be great to put in my essay because I carry hundreds of them verbatim (good vocabulary word–don't know it? Look it up!) in my head at all times. Yes ma'am, I am a veritable (another one!) font (not the computer kind) of quotations."

To this, I would reply: "Pshaw! If pressured under threat of death, dismemberment or listening to Barry Manilow records nonstop, you might be able to pull up a couple of quotes. And most of us (including me) do not walk around with word-for-word quotes and their sources in our heads. We have much better stuff taking up that room, right? (Like the lyrics to four million songs and old locker combinations.)"

So, clearly this means you can just give up on using a quote, right? Nope. Here are ways to slip in that great thought without messing up. You preface (those vocab words just keep on rollin'!) that quote that you only semi-remember hearing or reading with any of the following:

- According to a physician/philosopher/author/writer/teacher/expert...
- I recall reading/hearing that...
- A recent study showed that...
- According to current reports...
- I remember once being told...
- A recent newspaper/magazine article stated that...
- Someone once told me...

Since it is rare that you will be able to recall an entire quote from beginning to end, you can always *paraphrase,* or summarize what you think the quote was primarily about. For example, perhaps you only know a portion of the quote, "The most beautiful thing we can experience is the mysterious. It is the source of all true art and science," by Albert Einstein. You could paraphrase it by writing, "Albert Einstein once said that there is nothing better to experience in life than the mysterious." Remember that no one is fact checking your essay. No one is going to make sure that your quote is totally correct. If you say that former president Harry Truman once said, "Obi-Wan Kenobi is a true representative of courage and the strength of conviction," the scorer may chuckle (or wince) but will not give a lower score for the inaccuracy.

While you do not carry exact word-for-word quotes in your head (well, I suppose there are a FEW of you who do), you probably have heard or partially remember a number of them. For instance, how many of the following can you complete:

(1) "Give me liberty or ____ ____ ____!" (3 words)

(2) "A thing of beauty is a joy ____." (1 word)

(3) "To err is human, to forgive ____ ____." (2 words)

(4) "God helps those who help ____." (1 word)

(5) "Never leave off till tomorrow what you can do ____." (1 word)

(6) "Early to bed and early to rise, makes a man ____, ____ and ____." (3 words)

(7) "You can fool some of the people all of the time, and all of the people some of the time, but you cannot fool ____ ____ ____ ____ ____ ____ ____." (7 words)

(8) "To be or not to be, ____ ____ ____ ____." (4 words)

(9) "One small step for man. One giant leap ____ ____." (2 words)

(10) "Frankly, my dear, I don't give a ____." (1 word)

Getting the Right Slant

Do you remember the story you read way back in the section about scorers? A young man was practicing writing essays and no matter what topic he got, he found a way to relate it to the one subject he knew well–sports, specifically his hero Michael Jordan. You can do this too. Start by asking yourself what areas you know a lot about. In what do you invest your passion? What topic could you speak on ad nauseum? It can be something academic, technical, social, professional, personal or any other category you can think of. Put these things on a list. For example, here is what I would say if I were making out a list:

Technical: writing educational material for grades K through 12

Social: organizing support groups, hosting potluck dinners

Professional: writing nonfiction books, succeeding as a freelancer, public speech

Personal: raising children, living in the Pacific Northwest, counted cross-stitch

You might list things like playing a musical instrument, singing, running, reviewing movies, playing sports, babysitting, volunteer work, part-time job, going to camp, traveling to another country or anything else that is part of your life that you know well enough to talk–or in this case–write about. Go ahead and fill out this form:

Academic: ____________________

Technical: ____________________

Social: ____________________

Professional: ____________________

Personal: ____________________

Okay, now you have an idea of some of the topics you know best. How does this help with the SAT essay? Reflect back on that story in the scoring section. The student found a way to relate his passion for sports to any question he was asked. While this may not always be possible, try spending some time thinking about familiar topics. Then practice writing answers that involve things, ideas or people in those fields. If you can relate your writing to those concepts, you will have a stronger essay.

Let's practice this concept for a moment: Imagine that the question on the essay is this: Shakespeare once wrote, "Never a borrower or a lender be." Do you agree or disagree with this statement? Is there harm in both borrowing and lending from someone? Plan and write an essay in which you develop your point of view on the issue. Support your position with reasoning and examples taken from your reading, studies, experience or observations.

There are a number of ways you could address this question, depending on what stories and ideas come to mind. Based on my own knowledge, personal experiences and opinions, here are several ways I could address it (these are my thesis statements, followed by examples):

Lending can be a compassionate and generous thing to do, as long as you are prepared for the fact that what you lent to someone may never be returned. Examples include: loaning books to friends and never getting them back and loaning money to family members and having it returned several times over.

If everyone took this statement to heart, the world would be a much sadder place. Examples include: countries that would be destitute if not for financial assistance from other countries, people who would never own homes if not for financial assistance from banks and libraries that would be out of business if not for their policy of lending books to the public.

Lending and borrowing teach vital life lessons for all ages. Examples include: watching my children learn the concepts of generosity, trust and the karmic philosophy of what goes around, comes around.

Author Doris Lessing once said, "Borrowing is not much better than begging; just as lending with interest is not much better than stealing," and there are times I have to agree with her. Examples include: credit card companies with extremely high interest rates and the problem with addiction gambling with its inherent philosophy of borrowing just long enough to win it back.

Ben Franklin, a man of much wisdom, once equated borrowing with regret and I can understand why. Examples include: borrowing money and the burden of paying it back, as well as loaning money to a friend which was never returned.

Note that in the fourth example of a thesis statement, I included an entire quote, while in the fifth, I paraphrased something Ben Franklin once said. (The actual quote is "He that goes a borrowing goes a sorrowing.") Other people could bring in historical examples of lending and borrowing, scientific knowledge that has been shared with others and much more. It simply depends on your area of expertise and experience. What ideas did you come up with when you read the quote?

Here are a few more quotes. After each one, jot down a couple of ideas that pop up that you could confidently write about.

"Education is not the filling of a pail, but the lighting of a fire."

(Hint: you can write about your educational experience, compare your experience to your parent's or grandparent's, delve into how your favorite subject has lit a fire of curiosity underneath you, etc.)

Idea #1: ____

Idea #2: ____

"I wanted to change the world. But I have found that the only thing one can be sure of changing is oneself."

(Hint: Did your favorite sports player change the world of sports? Did your favorite music group alter rock as we know it? Did your favorite author write a world-changing book [at least for you!]? Remember, you can slant your answer to whatever you know best as long as you keep [say it with me now] ON TOPIC.)

Idea #1: ____

Idea #2: ____

"How we learn is what we learn."

(Hint: good quote to use for some personal experiences–something you have learned, whether in or out of school, that has influenced you. You can write about learning styles, based on a book you read or how someone you know used his education in an interesting way.)

Idea #1: ______________________________

Idea #2: ______________________________

"Newspapers are unable, seemingly, to discriminate between a bicycle accident and the collapse of civilization."

(Hint: think about a newspaper article you have read at home or in class. What did you think of how the journalist handled it? You could write about the media in general–does it tend to dramatize everything? What are some good examples?)

Idea #1: ______________________________

Idea #2: ______________________________

Putting It All Together

Now you know that (1) you need evidence/proof/support for your essay; (2) the various kinds of supporting information that you can use and (3) how to slant this to your areas of expertise. The only other question is how to organize those pieces of support. There are several different methods. One is the *order of importance.* Some experts suggest that you write about your strongest example first, while others recommend you wait and list it last. If you had lots of time, I would suggest trying it both ways and seeing which works better for you. Obviously that will not work because you hardly have time to write it down at all. So, what is my profound and amazingly insightful advice? Do it either way–just do it and get it down on paper.

Another way to organize your support is in *chronological order.* If you are using three historical examples, it makes sense to list them in the order they occurred. If you are talking about three personal experiences, you might want to list them in time order as well.

Overall, the things to remember when it comes to using support examples are as follows:

- use solid examples from any of the sources listed above
- practice coming up with possible examples for different quotes
- know how to paraphrase a quote or use the information without knowing the exact wording

- organize your support in order of importance or chronological order–if you have the time to do so

As you hopefully remember from earlier reading, the strongest thing scorers look for in your essay is a solid thesis statement with a set of organized and relevant examples to back it up. Don't allow yourself to be the detective who is standing in the middle of the room looking foolish because you forgot to gather together the evidence. It definitely does not make for a happy ending for a movie or for your test score.

Part 7:

Gruesome Grammar and Painful Punctuation

Just the Facts, Please

I will let you in on a little known secret: even the majority of English teachers do not like grammar. They like it *in principle.* There is a reason for grammar (and it isn't just to torture you either!). It gives all written communication a pattern to follow so that people can understand it. Grammar is like all of the rules you had to learn before you could drive. You have to obey speed limits (really!), stay in the correct lane, use turn signals, stop at stop signs, etc. This makes it possible for the majority of people to drive down the street relatively safely. It gives a pattern to follow so that the drivers around you will understand what you are going to do. Just like driving rules, however, grammar rules are often boring, tedious and no fun to learn. But once you do, you can get in the car and drive–or pick up a pen and write.

Now, I will tell you an even bigger secret: professional writers rarely ever think about grammar rules. Fortunately, the basic lessons are so ingrained into their heads, they don't have to. It's like the basketball player who doesn't have to think about his footing when he does a lay-up or the pianist who gives no thought to where her hands are supposed to go on the keys. It is also like all of those things you first learned when you took driver's ed. Look in the side mirrors. Look in the rearview mirror. Check your speed. Look at cars ahead and behind you. Check the traffic light. At first it seems overwhelming. How will you ever remember all of these steps every time you slide into the driver's seat? It didn't take long though, before those steps were just a natural habit. It really can be the same with grammar as long as you get lots of (can you guess?) PRACTICE.

So, I am going to zip you right through this section about grammar and punctuation. If you haven't learned most of it already, you most likely won't get it all between reading this chapter and taking the test either. This is just to serve as a basic reminder because YOUR ESSAY WILL NOT BE GRADED ON GRAMMAR AND PUNCTUATION, right? As you will see in some of the essays in the next section, however, if there are enough grammar (spelling, confused words, etc.) and punctuation errors, it is really difficult to follow what the writer is trying to convey. You get lost and confused, because you *cannot follow the pattern.* It's like driving behind a car that goes 20 miles under the speed limit, veers into the wrong lane and has no brake lights. The pattern the driver is supposed to be following just isn't there and you aren't sure what to do.

Let's get through this together as fast as possible, because the last secret is: I despise grammar just as much as you do! Shhhhh!

The Top Five Grammar Mistakes

There are tons and tons of grammar mistakes that you can make in an essay but here are the five most common ones. If you are a glutton for punishment and want to know all the errors you can make, grab a good grammar book and read up. For now, here are the ones that stick out and catch your scorer's eye:

PRONOUN AGREEMENT: Do you remember what pronouns are? They are the little words that replace nouns. They come in flavors known as personal, objective personal, subjective personal, possessive personal, demonstrative, interrogative, relative, indefinite, reflexive–the list goes on and on. Do you need to know what all of those are? Well, to be honest, I don't. They include:

this	theirs	us	she
that	they	you	her
these	them	he	hers
those	I	him	we
their	me	his	it
mine	yours	ours	its

The important thing to remember about pronoun agreement is that the noun and pronoun must match. For example:

Ignorant people think it is the noise which fighting cats make that is so aggravating, but it ain't so; it is the sickening grammar that they use.

~ Mark Twain

Lisa was so happy that _____ did a little dance.

Only a limited number of pronouns will work here. "She" is the best answer because it matches "Lisa." "He" would be confusing. So would "you." Others might work but only if the sentences around it explain it. For instance, you could say, "Lisa was so happy that they did a little dance" as long as it was clear who else constitutes the "they." If you start to write a pronoun, think about who or what you are talking about. Then make sure you choose the right pronoun.

PRONOUNS: A pronoun should be used when you wish to rename the subject. Be careful to avoid writing sentences that don't show to whom or what the pronoun refers. Look at these examples:

Jenny went over to Laurel's house and she looked fantastic.

Who looked good? Jenny or Laurel? The "she" doesn't tell you.

The notices are posted on the two bulletin boards. They are light brown.

What is light brown? The notices or the bulletin boards?

Only in grammar can you be more than perfect.

~ William Safire

The cat is chasing the dog and now it wants in.

What wants in? The cat or the dog?

Whenever you use a pronoun, just check to make sure it is clear to what it is referring.

VERB TENSE: It is annoyingly easy to shift verb tenses when you are writing. You are writing in the present and suddenly you find yourself in the past (and it isn't a flashback either!) For instance:

I am taking the class and you should took it too.

You went from present progressive tense (taking) to past tense (took).

The airplane was full and so is the next one.

You went from past tense (was) to present tense (is).

DANGLING MODIFIERS: Sounds a little illicit, doesn't it? Well, in this case a dangling modifier just means that you have added some kind of detail to describe something (the modifier) but you put it in an inappropriate place in the sentence so it adds descriptive details to the wrong thing. Here is what I mean:

After finishing the book, the movie was started.

The movie finished the book? I don't think so. It should read: After finishing the book, I started watching the movie. The modifier of "after finishing the book" describes "I."

Whizzing past at 60 miles per hour, I looked at the cars.

This sounds like "I" is moving fast, rather than the cars. It should read, "I looked at the cars, whizzing past at 60 miles per hour."

One more, okay?

While singing a solo, the concert hall's lights went out.

Since concert halls traditionally cannot sing, it should read, "While I was singing a solo, the concert hall's lights went out."

CHANGING "PERSON": Sounds like a multiple personality disorder, doesn't it? You will see references to this in the section where we analyze different essays because it is a common writing error. Look at the shift in this example:

I think that bravery is a rare trait in today's world. One should respect it in others. They rarely exhibit in current culture. I almost never see it except on the news. You could develop it in yourself.

Is your head swimming yet? That's because it went from "I" to "one" to "they" back to "I" and then on to "you." First person (I, me, mine, we, us, ours) is fine to use in your essay, but if you start there, stay there. The same is true for third person (he, him, his, she, her, hers, they, them, theirs). If you use it, stick with it.

And What about Punctuation?

My spelling is Wobbly. It's good spelling but it Wobbles and the letters get in the wrong places.

~ A.A. Milne/Winnie the Pooh

For the punctuation section we are going to look at: colons, semi-colons, dashes and hyphens, ellipses and quotation marks. I am not dwelling on periods, commas, apostrophes, question marks and exclamation marks because I think you already know them fairly well. It boils down to this:

PERIODS–use them a lot; you need one at the end of every thought.

COMMAS–you will almost certainly forget one where you need it 'cuz we all do, so don't dwell on it.

APOSTROPHES–these are used for the missing letter in a contraction or to show possession.

QUESTION MARKS–this is a tough one: they are used when you ask a question. (Duh, huh?)

EXCLAMATION MARKS! These show excitement! If you overuse them, your reader will get weary quickly! So, please, use them sparingly! Please!

Okay–how was that for an overview? Now, let's look at the slightly more tricky ones.

COLONS: Colons are used when you are going to introduce a **list** such as:

Colin decided he wanted everything he possibly could fit in his sandwich: pickles, peppers, cucumbers, tomatoes, lettuce, ham, bacon, turkey, cheese and mustard.

A colon can also be used to introduce a lengthy **quote**, such as this one:

President Dwight D. Eisenhower once stated: "I can think of nothing more boring for the American people than to have to sit in their living rooms for a whole half hour looking at my face on their television screens."

Are there other uses for colons? Yup, such as in letters (Dear Sir:), times of day (8:30) and *Bible* quotes ("If God is for us, who can be against us?" Romans 8:31). Chances are you won't need these in your essay but there they are–today's bonus material.

SEMI-COLONS: *The Complete Idiot's Guide to Grammar and Style* calls the semi-colon "the love child of the comma and the period." Gives you an all new respect for punctuation, eh?

The main way you will use a semi-colon is between two independent clauses. HEY! Come back here. I saw that. You were running in the opposite direction just because I mentioned one of those grammatical technical terms, weren't you? Stop worrying. It's not that complicated! If you have two complete sentences that are closely related and you are not using a conjunction (but, and, for, or, not, yet) in between them, you need a semi-colon. Here is what I mean:

Kathryn slept late today; she was on the telephone until two in the morning.

Don't forget to take out the garbage; your life may depend on it.

Enjoy your new computer; it will be obsolete by the time you wake up in the morning.

See? Not so tough. Yeah, there are other ways to use the semi-colon but they get rather technical and I don't want you to go screaming out into the night. Chances are the only way you will need the semi-colon in your essay is in the instance described here.

DASHES/HYPHENS: Ah yes, these can be confusing little fellows. The dash is a bit longer than the hyphen and it is used to indicate a sudden change of thought. For example:

The guilty party–and you know who you are–will be caught within the hour.

Cathy, I need you to stay later–of course not tonight–all next week.

The hyphen, on the other hand, is the shorter of the two marks and is generally found in things like compound nouns (step-mom), fractions (one-third) and numbers (ninety-two). It is also commonly used to indicate a break in the word from one line to another. (Wasn't that clever?)

ELLIPSIS: These should not be confused with eclipses although they are both somewhat rare events. An ellipsis is not a period with a stutter either. Instead it is used to show that you have taken out some words or sentences from something that you are quoting. It can also show some kind of hesitation in what you are thinking. Here are a few examples:

Let's suppose that the original quote reads: "*It takes a good deal of physical courage to ride a horse. This, however, I have. I get it at about forty cents a flask and take it as required.*"

You could rewrite it as, "*It takes a good deal of physical courage to ride a horse…I get it at about forty cents a flask and take it as required.*" The ellipsis shows where you removed a few words.

Another use for the ellipsis is to indicate a pause in your thinking, such as in this example:

I have always found this concept to be true…except for that time in New Jersey.

The concert was fantastic…until they started playing their new songs.

QUOTATION MARKS: These punctuation marks let your reader know that those profound words were not yours. How is that a good thing again? If you try to claim it, it's called plagiarism although no, your grader won't lower your score for it. However, your quotes are part of your support so you want to make sure they are noticed. The key with quote marks is to put them before the first word of the quote and after the last word. Not so complicated, right? Let's try a couple:

Bernard Williams once said, "There is no psychiatrist in the world like a puppy licking your face."

"I've missed more than 9,000 shots in my career," says sports great Michael Jordan. "I've lost almost 300 games. Twenty-six times I've been trusted to take the game winning shot and missed. I've failed over and over and over again in my life. And that is why I succeed."

Note how in the second example you have to remember to add extra quotation marks since you are breaking the quote into two parts.

YEAAA! Another Pop Quiz!

You know it all now, right? You're a grammar and punctuation expert. Put your pencil marks where your mouth is and answer the following questions that test you on everything we just covered. (WERE YOU PAYING ATTENTION?) I'll give you a hint–there is a mistake in every sentence.

(1) Yesterday the teacher said we would see a film and then she says we would all be tested on it later.

(2) Roger and Matthew headed off to class at the same time but he was late.

(3) Heather hugged her youngest brother and it smiled at her.

(4) Raised on the coast, it is understandable to miss the smell of the ocean.

(5) I love spaghetti. They think it is wonderful.

(6) You are never given a wish without also being given the power to make it come true, according to well-known author Richard Bach. You may have to work for it, however.

(7) There are sixty–seven seats available-at least for tonight's show-in the theatre.

(8) The time is now the place is here.

(9) I am only taking the absolute essentials to camp clothes, shoes, sleeping bag, pillow, toiletries, portable CD player, CDs and headphones.

Answer key:

(1) Yesterday the teacher said we would see a film and then she said we would all be tested on it /verb tense.

(2) Roger and Matthew headed off to class at the same time but Roger was late / pronoun use.

(3) Heather hugged her youngest brother and he smiled at her / pronoun agreement.

(4) Since you were raised on the coast, it is understandable that you miss the smell of the ocean / dangling modifier.

(5) I love spaghetti. I (or we) think it is wonderful / pronoun agreement.

(6) "You are never given a wish without also being given the power to make it come true," according to well-known author Richard Bach. "You may have to work for it, however." / quotation marks.

(7) There are sixty-seven seats available–at least for tonight's show–in the theatre / dashes and hyphens.

(8) The time is now; the place is here / semi-colons.

(9) I am only taking the absolute essential to camp: clothes, shoes, sleeping bag, pillow, toiletries, portable CD player, CDs and headphones / colons.

Part 8:

When Words Matter

The Semi-Importance of Vocabulary

Although vocabulary is not going to count in your essay, per se, it is still quite important for you to think about and *practice.* (Sick of that word yet?) The use of an expanded vocabulary makes details more clear, arguments more persuasive and the overall essay stronger. There are some really neat ways to buff up your vocab choices. Go to your favorite bookstore or the public library and check out the line of books by Sagebrush and other publishers who put out great novels (mysteries, drama, humor, etc.) that slip in SAT vocab words as part of the story. You could also grab any number of vocabulary books that introduce you to new words and help you remember their meaning.

Two of the best ways to expand your vocabulary are to learn to recognize vague terms and replace them, plus get familiar with synonyms and antonyms (make friends with your neighborhood thesaurus!) The more words you have in your head to call on when writing, the better. Vague, abstract terms can dull your essay and muffle the details. For example, look at the difference between these sentences:

She grabbed her stuff and headed out the door really fast to catch the bus.

She grabbed all of her luggage and headed out the door, racing to catch the bus.

She grabbed her backpack and school books and headed out the door in a rush to catch the bus.

Do you see how each sentence changes as you expand on the word "stuff" and "really fast"? It alters the meaning of each one. The person in the second sentence probably has a different destination than the one in the third sentence.

Here are some extremely vague words that are commonly found in student essays. After each one, fill in some other possibilities that would work much better. If you get stuck, open up your thesaurus for some assistance. I'll give you an example to get started:

some	quantity	several	various	a number of
stuff	________	________	________	________
things	________	________	________	________
good	________	________	________	________

bad ________ ________ ________ ________

young ________ ________ ________ ________

old ________ ________ ________ ________

sometimes ________ ________ ________ ________

bunch ________ ________ ________ ________

A Different Kind of Colorful Language

A synonym is a word you use when you can't spell the other one.

~ Baltasar Gracian

Besides using more vivid and descriptive words, you can also liven up your writing by using metaphors and similes. If you are like me, you confuse the two of them and the truth is they are almost twins. They are both working for the same goal: they are comparing two unlike things. The only real difference is that one uses the words "like" or "as," while the other doesn't. Here are a few examples of both:

Instead of "*It thundered very loudly,*" you could write, "*It thundered like horse's hooves*" (simile).

Instead of "*The flowers were colorful,*" you could write, "*The flowers were rainbows*" (metaphor).

Instead of "*She had long, smooth hair,*" you could write, "*Her hair was silk*" (metaphor).

Instead of "*The house was cold inside,*" you could write, "*The house was as cold as a morgue*" (simile)

Why don't you try a few of your own? Just fill in the blanks below.

The ____________ were as hard as ____________.

Your __________ are like ____________.

The ______________ was/were ____________.

Her ___________ was/were ____________.

Too Much of a Good Thing

While words are a wonderful thing, there is such a thing as too much of them. When you have so many lines to fill up, it is tempting to start getting wordy. You use phrases that mean little to nothing and have no other purpose but to take up some of that room. If you find yourself using them, stop. They don't add anything to your essay at all. Here are some of the most common ones:

As a result of	Due to the fact that
In spite of the fact that	It is my opinion that
In the event that	The fact of the matter is that
A great number of	At that time
In this day and age	At this point in time
In this paper I will show that	I continue to conclude that

The word "good" has many meanings. For example, if a man were to shoot his grandmother at a range of five hundred yards, I should call him a good shot, but not necessarily a good man.

~ G.K. Chesteron

Having a strong vocabulary does more for you than simply raising your chance of a good score on the SAT. It helps you to communicate better, both on a written and spoken basis. This can have a positive effect on your personal relationships, your college career or your current and future jobs and perhaps even your whole life. And you thought vocabulary wasn't that important! Ha!

Part 9:

Lookin' Good

Appearance Counts

If you go out, you probably take some time to put on clean clothes, brush your hair and teeth and generally work to make sure that you look nice. You hope that when people glance at you, they get a favorable first impression. Such attention to appearance is even more important for your SAT essay.

For just a moment, I want you to put yourself in the shoes of an SAT grader. (Sorry if they pinch your toes. At least it is temporary.) You have been sitting in the same room, reading essay after essay after essay after essay for the past three hours. You have seen the same quotes repeatedly; you have skimmed hundreds of papers. Your eyes are dry and red from staring at the computer screen, you are tired of sitting in the same chair and your morale is starting to seriously deteriorate. You've had enough coffee to keep you walking back and forth to the bathroom for the rest of the night and at this point, you are even tired of chocolate.

With a sigh, you pick up the next essay. Your eyes scan the entire thing as a whole first. What do you see? If there are obvious attempts to make it look longer, if the handwriting is challenging and if there are a lot of scratch outs, arrows and insertions, how hard will it will be for you to give that essay a fair chance? You are trained to do it, but let's admit it, we are all human and an essay that is hard to read–even if it is brilliant–is at a real disadvantage. Fair or not, appearance counts, so let's make sure that your essay looks the best that it possibly can.

There are five things to consider with the appearance of your essay. As you practice writing them (which you will do…and doing them on the computer doesn't count), pay attention to each one of these elements. They are:

- length
- handwriting
- scratch outs
- insertions
- indentations

LENGTH: Statistics show that every single essay that has ever scored high has had at least five paragraphs and each paragraph has had at least three sentences. Filling out all of those lines is important. Skipping lines or double spacing, however, is not acceptable. It just looks like you are trying to fool the grader–and that usually doesn't make for the best impression or the highest score.

HANDWRITING: I know we have been over this before, but it bears repeating. You need to write *legibly.* If you are not sure how clear your handwriting is, have others look at it. Ask your parents to read something you've written; ask your friends or siblings. Do they struggle? Do they say, "Hey, what is this word…and this one…and this one?" If they do, that's a pretty good clue that your penmanship isn't what it should be. In this day and age of keyboards where virtually everything you have to write is done on the computer, it can be easy to overlook your handwriting. Take the time to analyze yours and if there are problems with it, start fixing them now. Experiment with writing cursive and printing to see which is clearer. Perhaps writing in all capitals works best for you. Fine. Just make sure the grader is able to spend time reading your words, not trying to decipher them.

The appearance of your essay also includes the size of your handwriting. Many students before you have attempted to make their essays look longer by writing quite largely. And there have been those who tried indenting an inch or more with each new paragraph. Both of these techniques are really quite silly and neither makes the positive impression on the grader that you are hoping for.

SCRATCH OUTS: When you reach the proofing stage of the essay, you may find that you want to replace one word with another or even that you want to eliminate an entire sentence. If this happens, the key is to simply draw one straight line through the word or sentence. Don't scribble; don't "x" things out. Keep it as neat as possible. Obviously, you want as few of these scratch outs as you can manage.

INSERTIONS: Occasionally as you read over the essay, you will notice that in your haste, you completely left out a word here or there. In that case, just make a caret (it looks like an upside down V) and write the word in. Don't draw arrows or write the word in the margin. Just make the appropriate mark and put the word where you want it to go.

INDENTATIONS: The optimal amount for your paragraph indention is about half an inch. Now, I don't expect you to have a ruler in your pocket, so this is a general rule. Just be reasonable; make it clear that there is an indentation there so the paragraphs do not run together, but don't indent so much that it looks ridiculous–and like a pathetic attempt to take up room.

It is important to remember that the average grader looks at the essay for two minutes or less. Yeah, I know…hundreds of pages, multiple lessons, all of this practice and countless sweat, worry and angst for two minutes, but that is how it is. They are trained to look fast, skim thoroughly and make quick judgments in less than 120 seconds. You can make their jobs easier. Turn in an essay that is lookin' good.

Part 10:

Beyond the Basics

Going beyond Boot Camp

You already have read about the basics of a good essay. Now, let's take it just a few steps further. The information in this chapter will deal with the "fine-tuning" of the essay. Here are some finer points that can help you bump up that score.

Writing an essay can really be a bummer. You just have to except it. I mean, it is no walk in the park, that's for sure. If you want it to amount to more than a hill of beans, you have to bust your butt. To make sure you don't blow it, there are a few things you need to avoid using like the plague. Dude, any guesses what they may be?

Did you notice anything odd about the last paragraph? I hope so! It was loaded with several things you do not want to use in the essay: idioms and slang. *Idioms* are terms that do not literally mean what the words themselves imply. The term *slang* refers to words that are known only in certain places or within certain groups. Both of these forms of language are very trendy; but remember that what is used in daily conversation this year may well be forgotten by next year. By using slang and idioms in the essay, you are making your thoughts less clear and too trendy. If you want to pepper your conversation with them, go ahead. Your friends will understand it and your parents will tolerate it (sprinkle a few "cools" in there–that is one they remember). Don't put them in the essay though. Those scorers are not going to be impressed one bit.

COMMON IDIOMS

He gets in my hair.

Go fly a kite.

He is on top of the world.

She blew her stack.

Hold your horses.

You're in the doghouse.

What a pain in the neck.

Have you lost your marbles?

Don't bite my head off!

Lend me a hand.

It's not worth a hill of beans.

I have too many irons in the fire.

Keep your shirt on.

For crying out loud!

COMMON IDIOMS (Continued)

You hit the nail on the head.	I had to blow off steam.
That rings a bell.	Somehow I held my tongue.
I'm in hot water.	That helped break the ice.
Does he have cold feet?	Time to make hay.
It's as easy as pie.	She is bent out of shape.
I'm all ears.	Let's call it a day.
He is down in the dumps.	Easy does it.
It got out of hand.	Let's grab a bite.
Keep an eye out.	It is state of the art.
I'm under the weather.	It broke my heart.

Slang is a language that rolls up its sleeves, spits on its hands and goes to work.

~ Carl Sandburg

SLANG

bummer	chill out	hip	for real?
get outta here	dude	rap	phat
bling-bling	homey	sweet	wacked
cool	dawg	tight	yo
wazzup	tight		

Here's a new bonus question for you. (Oh! Did I hear a couple of cheers there?) Reread the first paragraph of this section. I know that by now you should (hopefully) recognize the slang and idioms in it. Did you happen to notice any other error? If you spotted the mistake in the second sentence, you earn another 50 points in the SAT lottery. The sentence reads, "You just have to except it." The word "except" should be "accept." Did you confuse those two? Don't feel badly if you did; you aren't the only one. In fact, this is one of the most typical mistakes to show up on the "Commonly Confused Words" chart shown below. And there are several others. Make sure you know the difference between them so you don't mix them up in the essay. (If you read through all of the essays in the next section–and you had better!–you will find one essay where the writer continuously mixed up "wonder" and "wander" and in doing so, completely lost the reader.) Read over this list. If you are not sure of the difference between the words or when one should be used over another, get out the dictionary and find out!

COMMONLY CONFUSED WORDS

accept/except	all ready/already	allusion/illusion
assure/insure/ensure	complement/compliment	confident/ confidante
council/counsel	elicit/illicit	affect/effect
eminent/imminent	invoke/evoke	lay/lie
older/elder	persecute/prosecute	sit/set
wonder/wander		

One of the elements of a good essay which has been stressed again and again throughout this book is *organization.* You have learned that the essay should flow smoothly from introduction to example(s) to conclusion. One way to help make that happen is through the use of effective and appropriate transitions. Think of a good transition as a nice person who escorts you from one room to another in an unfamiliar place. You were in a room and it was time to move on, but you weren't entirely sure where to go. Then a kind and mannerly person took your arm and guided you to the next room. A transition can do something like that in an essay. These words or phrases connect your ideas and make it easy to understand how they go together.

Below is a list of some of the most common transitions. Scan them so you have a good understanding of what they are. "But how can I use them in my essay?" you ask. Think for a moment. Imagine you are writing a persuasive essay about how imagination can lead to success. Your example may be J.K. Rowling (author of the *Harry Potter* series) and how she went from a single mother on welfare to one of the most well-known and wealthy authors in the world. You might say that FIRST she wrote the book, NEXT she talked to agents, LATER she was accepted and FINALLY she was published. These transitions lead the reader from one point to another in chronological order. They give your organization strength.

Let's think of another example. Perhaps you have been asked to write on the concept of how friends can help you cope with the complications of life. Perhaps you decide to use three examples from your own life to illustrate the thesis statement. You can begin example one with the transition of FOR INSTANCE. The next one can start with TO ILLUSTRATE and the third can be FOR EXAMPLE. This helps the reader connect one idea to the next one.

Do not put statements in the negative form. And don't start sentences with a conjunction. If you reread your work, you will find on rereading that a great deal of repetition can be avoided by rereading and editing. Never use a long word when a diminutive one will do. Unqualified superlatives are the worst of all. De-accession euphemisms. If any word is improper at the end of a sentence, a linking verb is. Avoid trendy locutions that sound flaky. Last, but not least, avoid cliches like the plague.

~William Safire, "Great Rules of Writing"

TRANSITION WORDS

		Time		
after	as	at last	before	during
eventually	finally	first	last	later
meanwhile	next	now	second	since
soon	then	when	while	afterward
currently	earlier	immediately	recently	then
subsequently	simultaneously			
		Importance		
above all	best	especially	in fact	in particular
most	worst	most important		more important
		Example		
for example	for instance	for one thing	one reason	namely
specifically	to illustrate			
		And		
additionally	also	and	another	as well as
besides	furthermore	then	in addition	moreover
again	besides	further	equally important	
		But		
although	but	however	in contrast	nevertheless
instead	still	on the contrary		in spite of
notwithstanding		on the other hand		on the one hand
		So		
as a result	because	finally	so	therefore
		Conclusion		
finally	in a word	in brief	in the end	in conclusion
on the whole	thus	to conclude	to summarize	in sum
in summary	in the final analysis			

Will forgetting to use a transition, slipping and using a slang term or accidentally including an idiom in your essay reduce your score? It's not likely–but it's possible. If you pay close attention to details like this, however, you can write a more solid essay and improve your overall writing skills.

Part 11:

I'm Wrong, You're Wrong

The Top Ten SAT Essay DON'Ts

If you skipped right to this chapter, shame on you. Now, go back to the beginning and start over. You should know better. This chapter is a short one and acts like an overview of the 11 that came before it. If you read anything on this list that you don't understand or worse, don't recognize, go back to that section and go over it again.

Before you read over this condensed version of the last section, see if you can make a list of things you should not do on the SAT essay. When you are done, compare your list to the one on the following page. See how close you came to the "official" list.

Fill this out:

The Top Ten Things I Should Absolutely Not Do on the SAT Essay:

1. ______________________________

2. ______________________________

3. ______________________________

4. ______________________________

5. ______________________________

6. ______________________________

7. ______________________________

8. ______________________________

9. ______________________________

10. ______________________________

How did you do? Were they easy to come up with? How does your list compare to this one?

The SAT Essay "DO-NOT-DO" Top Ten

If you copy any page of this book, this is the one. Make a copy and put it up somewhere where you can see it on a daily basis. If there were crib notes for the SAT, this is it.

1. DO NOT skim the writing prompt. Read it slowly and carefully so that you know exactly to what question(s) you should respond.

2. DO NOT skip writing the outline. It is your roadmap that tells you where to go next at every step of the essay. As you start writing, you will be more than grateful for it.

3. DO NOT write a definition essay. DO NOT write a narrative. This is a persuasive essay that calls on you to convince readers to agree with your point of view.

4. DO NOT forget to have strong, solid and relevant examples of some kind to support your statement. These can be quotes, information learned from history and literature, current events or personal experiences. Make sure each one connects directly and clearly to the question asked in the writing prompt. Remember that the one thing you can do to earn a big, fat ZERO on the essay is to go off topic.

5. DO NOT leave more than one or two lines of the 46 provided blank. Length really does help. However, the space should be filled up with quality writing. If you try to make it look longer through double spacing, large handwriting, extra indentation or repeated information, it will count against you. In addition, do your very best to keep your handwriting legible. If that means printing or writing in all capitals, that's okay. Just make it clear.

6. DO NOT write the information in random order. Make sure the essay has three distinct sections: the introduction, the body and the conclusion. Organization is one of the most important elements graders look for in the essay. Make it clear and obvious and your score will reflect it.

7. DO NOT forget to create a thesis statement for the introduction and a topical sentence for each one of the essay's paragraphs. They are your guideposts.

8. DO NOT use idioms, clichés and slang in your writing if you can avoid it. Sometimes it is hard to recognize them because they are such a part of our language, but it is important.

9. DO NOT turn in the essay until you read it over in your head to check out the flow. You may "hear," "see" or "feel" an error that needs to be corrected.

10. DO NOT forget to proof the essay before you turn it in. Try to save the last one to two minutes of your time for scanning the essay for errors in grammar, spelling and punctuation. Check to make sure that you haven't left out a word by accident or used commonly confused or multiple meaning words incorrectly.

Part 12:

Makin' a List, Checkin' It Twice

Last Minute Checklist

Okay, I was wrong. There are TWO pages in this book you should copy and this is the second one. Post it next to the one in the previous part. When you practice your essays (and you know you will, right?), you also get to score them. Here is a checklist of things to look for (remember the actual scoring guide is in section 2 of the book). Use the box to the left of each number to check those things you did well.

- ❑ You read the writing prompt thoroughly and carefully.
- ❑ You took the time to brainstorm some possible ideas.
- ❑ You created a dependable and effective outline.
- ❑ The introduction related directly (on topic) to what was asked in the writing prompt.
- ❑ The introduction contained the essay's thesis statement.
- ❑ The essay's body contained at least one relevant support for the viewpoint stated in the introduction.
- ❑ The conclusion reflected back to your thesis statement and summarized your points.
- ❑ The essay was organized clearly and logically.
- ❑ You read the essay for flow and made all necessary corrections.
- ❑ You checked the essay for errors in grammar, spelling and punctuation.
- ❑ You avoided using any slang, clichés or idioms in your writing.
- ❑ You stayed within the 25-minute time limit.
- ❑ You filled up virtually every line without resorting to large handwriting.
- ❑ You made your points without repetition.
- ❑ You wrote legibly.

- ☐ You wrote a persuasive essay that was designed to convince readers of your opinion.
- ☐ You paid attention to vocabulary, using complex words when possible.
- ☐ You paid attention to sentence structure, using different kinds (simple, complex and compound) of sentences when possible.
- ☐ You used appropriate transitions throughout the essay to make it flow smoothly.
- ☐ You did the best job you possibly could.

Read It and Weep (Then Improve!)

Highlights: What you will (hopefully) learn in this chapter…

- What a high scoring SAT essay looks like
- How to transform a low scoring essay into a high scoring essay
- Inspiration and examples to help you ace the SAT writing section

Read It and Weep (Then Improve!)

"Destiny is no matter of chance. It is a matter of choice. It is not a thing to be waited for; it is a thing to be achieved."

~ William Jennings Bryan

Okay, take a deep breath. You are done with the how-to part of the book. Now it is time to move on. Put your essay scoring hat on and together, we will look at a bunch of essays written on a specific quote or subject. No, you don't get paid $17 to $22 an hour (hey, neither do I!), but you will get much more familiar with essays and you'll learn what mistakes to avoid.

Pay special attention to the summary boxes following each essay. They highlight the student's strengths and weaknesses, tell how long the essay is and give an overall score between zero and six. After you have read a few and are used to the format, try covering up the boxes and see what good and bad aspects you can point out. What score would you give the essay? Compare it to mine. Would we need a third scorer to come in?

As you read each of these essays, think how you would have answered the same writing prompt had it been on *your* SAT exam. This gives you additional practice in preparing to be the one holding the pencil.

On the following page, you will find the basic essay directions as a reminder of what the writer (and eventually you) will be asked to do for an essay. Then the page(s) will have an essay with a summary box after it. Essays that earned a 1, 2 or 3 will be either completely or partially rewritten to show how they can be improved. Those that score a zero will be clearly highlighted but not revised because it would take a completely different essay altogether to meet minimum requirements.

Note that the essays are numbered but they are randomly organized, so that scores from zero to six are jumbled together in no particular order.

ESSAY #1

> **Assignment:** Do you believe that there is such a thing as destiny? Do you think it is something people can control? Plan and write an essay in which you develop your point of view on the issue. Support your position with reasoning and examples taken from your reading, studies, experience or observations.

Here (underlined) is the statement of the point of view this essay should develop.

(1) <u>I disagree with the statement that destiny is a matter of choice.</u> The idea of having a choice negates the idea of having a predetermined destiny. One's destiny is one's inescapable fate; no amount of personal choice, weighted decision, hard wrought achievement or individual determination can off-set the mighty power of destiny. Destiny is what happens to you, the ways and means that you meet this destiny are simply that: ways and means of meeting destiny. There is no escaping destiny through choice or achievement.

(2) If you are destined to be swept away in a major hurricane, you shall be. If you are destined to die in a small traffic accident, you shall. People survive earthquakes,

Error in capitalization of "world war one."

Use of a quote is relevant.

Shifting between first and third person is somewhat confusing.

Good use of vocabulary with the word "clime."

floods, shootings and fires...to die of heart failure two years later. Soldiers in world war one believed that bullets and "whizbangs" either had your name on them or they did not—you might duck a bullet to die in a blast; you might avoid a blast to be shot by an errant fragment...or you might survive the entire nightmare of war to die, like so many soldiers did, of influenza one year later. As the old saying goes: "when your number is up, your number is up." One dies when one's time is done.

(3) The idea of having a choice in one's destiny implies a hand in the forming of one's destiny—but humans have no hand, have no say, in who we are born to, how we are born, with what faculties we are born with, where we are born and when we come into this world. All these determining factors are put into play without one single choice being given to the human concerned. You may wish to become the greatest artist ever known, but if you are born blind...you cannot be this thing. You may try all your life to become the best high jumper the world has ever seen...and the Olympic games in which you were to show off your achievements may be cancelled due to war or political clime.

(4) All a human can do is wait and see. One may endeavor to become prepared for whatever fate, or destiny, may have in store, but one cannot choose one's destiny.

(5) Some are born kings, some are born beggars, some people achieve the greatness that they knew lurked in their fates, some have this fated greatness thrust upon them—although both greatnesses are equally predestined—no human, believing in the fact of destiny, can do anything to avert this same said destiny.

(6) Belief in destiny means a belief in that which humans cannot know, a predetermined span of existence that one can only wait to experience; notions of choice or achievement have no place within the fatalistic framework of the idea of human destiny.

DONE WELL	**NEEDS WORK**
1. uses a relevant quote	1. a number of punctuation errors
2. clearly states point of view on topic	2. switching between first and third person
3. good use of several vocabulary words	3. too much repetition of word "destiny"
4. stays relatively on topic	4. supporting examples are vague
Overall Score: 3	**Word count: 464**

Okay, what can we improve? Let's look at the first paragraph. It is rather confusing. The point the author is trying to make is somewhat lost because of the repetition of the word "destiny." "Inescapable" is used in the same paragraph as "no escape." On the other hand, there are some great vocabulary terms here that should be retained.

Overall, the paragraph comes across like a student who is trying too hard to fill up all of those lines. The sentences are so complex that the reader ends up saying, "Ah, what was that again?"

ORIGINAL VERSION	REWRITE
I disagree with the statement that destiny is a matter of choice. The idea of having a choice negates the idea of having a predetermined destiny. One's destiny is one's inescapable fate; no amount of personal choice, weighted decision, hard wrought achievement or individual determination can off-set the mighty power of destiny. Destiny is what happens to you, the ways and means that you meet this destiny are simply that: ways and means of meeting destiny. There is no escaping destiny through choice or achievement.	Destiny is not a matter of choice. Instead, I think that one's destiny is inescapable. No amount of personal choice, weighted decision, hard wrought achievement or individual determination can interfere with the mighty power of one's fate. Destiny is simply what happens to a person.

How did that sound instead? The meaning is preserved, but the repetition and confusion are gone. What about the next two paragraphs? The author switched from "one" and "person" to "you," which can be confusing. Either can work, but whichever one the writer chooses must be continued throughout the essay.

ORIGINAL VERSION	REWRITE
If you are destined to be swept away in a major hurricane, you shall be. If you are destined to die in a small traffic accident, you shall. People survive earthquakes, floods, shootings and fires...to die of heart failure two years later. Soldiers in world war one believed that bullets and "whizbangs" either had your name on them or they did not—you might duck a bullet to die in a blast; you might avoid a blast to be shot by an errant fragment...or you might survive the entire nightmare of war to die, like so many soldiers did, of influenza one year later. As the old saying goes : "when your number is up, your number is up." One dies when one's time is done.	If a man is destined to be swept away in a major hurricane, he will be. If a woman is fated to die in a small traffic accident, she will be. People have been known to survive earthquakes, floods, shootings and fires, only to die of heart failure a few years later. Soldiers in World War I believed that bullets either had their names on them or not. They might duck a bullet to die in a blast, or they might avoid a blast only to be shot by an errant fragment. They might even survive the entire nightmare of war to die, like so many soldiers did, of influenza one year later. As the old saying goes, "When your number is up, your number is up."

The idea of having a choice in one's destiny implies a hand in the forming of one's destiny—but humans have no hand, have no say, in who we are born to, how we are born, with what faculties we are born with, where we are born and when we come into this world. All these determining factors are put into play without one single choice being given to the human concerned. You may wish to become the greatest artist ever known, but if you are born blind...you cannot be this thing. You may try all your life to become the best high jumper the world has ever seen...and the Olympic games in which you were to show off your achievements may be cancelled due to war or political clime.	The idea of having a choice in one's destiny implies an element of control, yet humans have no say in who gives birth to them, where or when they are born or with what faculties they enter this world. All of these determining factors are put into play without one single choice being given to the human concerned. A person may want to become the greatest artist ever known, but if he is born blind, it is not possible. Another may try her entire life to become the best high jumper in the world, but then the Olympic Games may be cancelled due to war or political climate.

Let's look at the last part of the essay now. We are combining paragraphs here to make it read smoother, making sentences simpler and eliminating any repetition. You can see that the essay is shorter, but much more precise and tighter overall.

ORIGINAL VERSION	REWRITE
All a human can do is wait and see. One may endeavor to become prepared for whatever fate, or destiny, may have in store, but one cannot choose one's destiny. Some are born kings, some are born beggars, some people achieve the greatness that they knew lurked in their fates, some have this fated greatness thrust upon them—although both greatnesses are equally predestined—no human, believing in the fact of destiny, can do anything to avert this same said destiny. Belief in destiny means a belief in that which humans cannot know, a predetermined span of existence that one can only wait to experience; notions of choice or achievement have no place within the fatalistic framework of the idea of human destiny.	Whether a person is born a king or a beggar; whether they are born with greatness or have it thrust upon them, no one can do anything to avert destiny. Believing in it means accepting an existence that one can only wait to experience. Notions of choice or achievement have no place within the fatalistic framework of the idea of human destiny.

ESSAY #2

Benjamin Franklin once said, "At 20 years of age, the will reigns; at 30, the wit and at 40, the judgment."

Assignment: How do you think this applies to people today and to yourself? Do you agree or disagree with this viewpoint? Plan and write an essay in which you develop your point of view on the issue. Support your position with reasoning and examples taken from your reading, studies, experience or observations.

(1) Benjamin Franklin is often quoted because his wisdom was so timeless. It's interesting to realize that what was true of society in general 200 years ago still applies today, even though the society that we live in is so radically different than that in which Mr. Franklin lived.

Here is the student's point of view. It is introduced later than usual and could be moved up to the first paragraph.

(2) I agree with his assessment. The people that I know who are in their 20's are either in college or are recent college graduates who are trying to find jobs. I think that getting that degree and being able to support yourself and following a career path takes quite a bit of willpower. On the negative side, when you read about crime, the perpetrators are often in their 20's, which indicates that will more than judgment is the motivating factor.

(3) When people get into their 30's, they are in jobs that they will probably hold until they retire. At this time in their lives, they may also be married and raising children, all of which are probably better done with a sense of humor. I think Mr. Franklin also included creativity in his definition of "wit," as by the time you are 30. I would hope that your life experience enables you to think creatively and see many paths that will take you to the same goal.

(4) By the time a person is in his 40's he has experienced a lot, both good and bad, and can anticipate the potential outcome of his actions much better than he could at 20 or 30 years old. Thus, he uses his better judgment. As a newly licensed driver, I know that while my insurance rates reflect the willfulness of 20 year olds rather than the better judgment used by 40 year old drivers, who have some of the lowest insurance rates.

Student ties conclusion to the rest of the essay clearly and strongly.

(5) I think Ben Franklin was a very wise man. As a young person, being willful isn't necessarily a bad thing, and hopefully, by the time I'm in my 40's, I hope I'll be exercising good judgment.

DONE WELL	NEEDS WORK
1. uses three clear examples with clear details	1. transitions between paragraphs would make it read more smoothly
2. conclusion clearly relates back to the main topic	2. point of view statement should be moved up to the first paragraph
3. uses general and personal examples as support to the main idea	3. some vague words like "a lot," "good" and "bad" could use more specific detail
4. stays completely on topic	
Overall Score: 5	**Word count: 333**

ESSAY #3

Funny man Groucho Marx once said, "I find television very educating. Every time somebody turns on the set, I go into the other room and read a book."

Assignment: What do you think about television in today's culture? Is it educational or are you better off leaving the room and picking up a book? Plan and write an essay in which you develop your point of view on the issue. Support your position with reasoning and examples taken from your reading, studies, experience or observations.

Where is the thesis statement for this essay?

This entire paragraph is off topic. It is not addressing the question stated in the prompt.

"And their children" and "And their stereos" are fragments. While grammar is not as high a priority in the essay, an abundance of errors will definitely affect the overall score.

(1) Television is loud. It's so loud that the only messages you get are the ones the producers want you to get. Takes up so much room in your head you're not going to pick up other things. Take commercials for example. All sound recording for television is done with a measuring device that keeps sound at a certain level. Anything on the chart between point A and point B is an acceptable level according to standards and practices. B is next to the red line. Commercial sounds are always recorded at the highest possible level, to get your attention. That's why you can hear the commercials from the bathroom, where you went when the commercial came on. I don't hear the commercials, because I use the mute button on the remote control. I think the mute button is the single most important contribution to the world since chocolate. I'd like to see the mute button improved quite a bit, though. I'd like to see it used in other applications. Perhaps in traffic. Maybe in local discount stores where the noise level is so high it's mind-numbing. I'd like to mute other people. And their children. And their stereos.

This is where the student begins to address the question asked. Terms like "good" and "bad" are so vague that they don't make much impact on the reader.

(2) What do you learn from television? Well, you learn about the world, but only the parts of the world that they want you to see. Small pieces of it. When you see bad things, it's because they aren't making an effort to show you the good things. Good things don't sell programming. And selling programs is how they make money. Money is the most important thing for television people and for most people.

Here the student is attempting to give support to some earlier statements.

(3) If you read a book instead of sitting in front of the television screen, you're only limited by your own interests and desire to learn something. If you sit in front of the television instead, you're only getting the things someone else has decided you should see. This is not good. If you allow them to tell you how to look at the world without thinking for yourself, then you deserve to be ignorant. I think it's better to read a book because a book doesn't just materialize on your shelf. Sometimes you have to go to the library or the book store to get one. At the very least, you have to get up to get it, instead of switching it on from your chair. And if you don't like what you're seeing in the book, you have to get a different book. You can't just push a button to get a different book. That's good for you because you need to move more.

(4) Also, television is like a magician. Magicians pull birds out of the costumes of barely dressed girls and stuff. People watch VERY closely, hoping that something

besides a bird will tumble out, and they miss it when the magician's real assistant is going through the audience and picking pockets. That's how television is. It makes you focus on what they want you to see while bad things go on and they're stealing your brain, your money and your life.

DONE WELL	NEEDS WORK
1. some support for his/her opinion	1. uses vague terms
2. strong analogy (television as a magician) in the conclusion	2. spends far too much time off topic
	3. repetition of terms like "book"
	4. multiple fragmented sentences
Overall Score: 2	**Word count: 515**

How did you feel as you read through this essay? Could you spot the mistakes as you went along? Although it is clear that this student does have some strong opinions about the educational value of television (or the lack thereof), the organization and grammar errors get in the way so much that the message is largely lost. What can we salvage from this essay? Let's find out. We are going to just dump the entire first paragraph because it is too off topic to repair.

ORIGINAL VERSION	REWRITE
What do you learn from television? Well, you learn about the world, but only the parts of the world that they want you to see. Small pieces of it. When you see bad things, it's because they aren't making an effort to show you the good things. Good things don't sell programming. And selling programs is how they make money. Money is the most important thing for television people and for most people.	I do believe that you can learn many things from television, but often they are neither the most important nor are they especially educational. For example, while you may learn about the world from television programs, you must do so from the small pieces that the powers that be have chosen to air. When you are constantly bombarded with negative images, it is because the networks are not making an effort to show you anything positive. After all, good news doesn't sell programming and that is how the channels make their money.

Can you see how all of the original ideas were kept intact but were put in a more organized manner, with much more precise vocabulary? Let's try another paragraph.

ORIGINAL VERSION	REWRITE
If you read a book instead of sitting in front of the television screen, you're only limited by your own interests and desire to learn something. If you sit in front of the television instead, you're only getting the things someone else has decided you should see. This is not good. If you allow them to tell you how to look at the world without thinking for yourself, then you deserve to be ignorant. I think it's better to read a book because a book doesn't just materialize on your shelf. Sometimes you have to go to the library or the book store to get one. At the very least, you have to get up to get it, instead of switching it on from your chair. And if you don't like what you're seeing in the book, you have to get a different book. You can't just push a button to get a different book. That's good for you because you need to move more.	If you take the time to read instead of watch television, you will find that the subject areas available for study are limitless. You can follow your own interests and your inherent desire to learn something new. Television restricts the information to which you have access. Allowing someone else to tell you how to look at the world without thinking for yourself is not wise, and you risk being ignorant. Books can be better tools for learning because they do not simply materialize on your shelf with the push of a button. You have to get up and search for a book, whether it is at a library, bookstore or at least in another room. If you don't like what you select, you can always get a different book.

Some ideas were rearranged here; some vocabulary choices were kept. The essay is getting stronger as it gets tighter and more precise.

ORIGINAL VERSION	REWRITE
Also, television is like a magician. Magicians pull birds out of the costumes of barely dressed girls and stuff. People watch VERY closely, hoping that something besides a bird will tumble out, and they miss it when the magician's real assistant is going through the audience and picking pockets. That's how television is. It makes you focus on what they want you to see while bad things go on and they're stealing your brain, your money and your life.	Television is also like a magician. Everyone has seen the illusion of a magician pulling a bird out of a hat or the costume of a scantily dressed woman. People watch very closely, hoping to spot the way the trick is done. In fact, they are so entranced that they are oblivious to the fact that the other magician's assistant is going through the audience picking pockets. It is the same with television. It makes you focus on what the networks want you to see, while in reality, they are stealing your thoughts, your money and your life.

The student's conclusion was strong, as was the ending analogy, so those were kept. Generic terms like "stuff" and "barely dressed" were changed to words and phrases that were more descriptive or specific. Now the essay has a much better chance of a high score.

ESSAY #4

William Shakespeare is credited with saying, "Some are born great, some achieve greatness and some have greatness thrust upon them."

Assignment: Do you believe there are people who have had greatness thrust upon them in today's culture? Choose at least one person that fits this scenario. Then plan and write an essay in which you develop your point of view on the issue. Support your position with reasoning and examples taken from your reading, studies, experience or observations.

Here is the student's statement of point of view.

(1) Our Nation is facing the largest natural disaster of modern time, Hurricane Katrina. The 200 mph winds, 20 ft. storm surges, relentless rain and massive flooding have been compared to being stuck in a tornado for more then 12 hours. <u>During and following the destruction of Katrina, greatness was thrust upon countless people</u>.

(2) Dr. Nathan Summers decided he would go to the Astrodome and help the other doctors care for the 1000's of people waiting out the hurricane in the old stadium. When he arrived with only a stethoscope in hand he realized he was the only doctor there. He was not going be helping other doctors he was going to be the sol-medical caretaker of over 10,000 people. After realizing the dire situation everyone was in he recruited the help of a security guard and together they looted a near by pharmacy for supplies. He spent 5 days caring for people the best he could. "Mostly, I held their hands and gave them assurance that help was on the way."

(3) Thirty miles away there was a very different man who was quickly discovering his greatness for the first time. Michael Morely was in prison for forgery when Katrina hit. The harsh winds blew the roof off his cell. He quickly climbed the walls to escape, but found himself surrounded by massive amounts of debris with voices calling for help. First he found a prison guard injured from the desk and filing cabinets that had fallen on him. He spent 20 minutes digging him out and then began saving the people from near by buildings. "I think this is the first time in my life, I really helped other people. It felt very good."

This essay does have a number of usage mistakes, for example, spelling out words and punctuation.

(4) Over two thousand miles away in Portland, OR Nastassia Dahl also found greatness bearing down on her. She is a seventeen-year-old home schooler who spent last summer volunteering for the Red Cross. She was called and asked to manage the set up a shelter for 500 refugees coming in from Louisiana. In less then 24 hours the teenager was ordering people around a high school that had been shut down years ago. She had two security guards at her side at all times and dozens of other people coming to her for directions and orders.

The student mentions all three support examples in the conclusion, helping to wrap it up solidly.

(5) Greatness can find people in many situation and circumstances. You don't need a natural disaster to be great. However to be truly great you need to rise to the occasions you find yourself in. As Dr Summer helped people with his warm hand and kind heart, as Michael Morely used his prison escape to save dozens of people instead of himself and as a teenager in OR spent 18 hours a day doing work most adult couldn't handle, others choose to steal luxuries from flooded stores in New Orleans, shot at the very people who were coming to help them or spend hour after hour watching the news reports on there television sets without leaving their couches. Sometimes greatness can find you but you are only great if you choose to invite it in and follow it.

DONE WELL	NEEDS WORK
1. states point of view and relationship to the writing prompt clearly and quickly	1. needs some work on punctuation
2. conclusion clearly relates back to the main topic and ends with very strong statement	2. needs some work on usage (spelling out Oregon, numbers less than ten, etc.)
3. uses very strong, detailed examples and quotes as support for the main idea	3. somewhat longer than what would fit on the allotted lines unless using tiny handwriting
4. stays completely on topic at all times	
Overall Score: 5	**Word count: 515**

This student used a current event as the foundation for the essay. Now, let's look at how another student tackled the same question. How do the two essays compare?

ESSAY #5

(1) I'm sure that Shakespeare's definition of greatness was probably fairly broad. Greatness can include a talent for something like cooking or playing a musical instrument, the ability to problem solve, a knack for dealing with all types of people, being able to remain calm when your instincts are telling you to panic. And that would be a good thing, too, because even though we can't all excel at all things, most of us do have talents and strengths in areas that our friends don't share, so we all have the opportunity to be "great" in our own way.

The student does not state his/her point of view until into the second paragraph. It should be sooner.

(2) In today's culture, there are probably lots of incidents where greatness is thrust upon everyday people, but since they aren't celebrities, or the newspaper reporters don't happen to be there to witness it, these incidents go unnoticed. For example, you might read about an elderly lady whose purse was snatched by some drug addict, yet some Good Samaritan steps in and chases the thief down and recovers the purse, without thinking about his own safety, rather than just calling the police on his cell phone and continuing on with his plans for the day. I'm sure that the person who does such a selfless act will have a chance to experience the gratitude of the old lady whose purse he recovered, and any citizens who happen to witness the event will surely be clapping him on the back and telling him what a great guy he was for doing that good deed. Afterward, the hero might reflect on what a wonderful thing he did, and chances are, when the opportunity presents itself, he'll try to be a helpful person again.

Paragraphs 3 and 4 provide two strong examples of support for the main thesis statement.

(3) For a more specific example of someone who had greatness thrust upon him, I think Bill Clinton is a good example. When he was a young boy his mother married a man who was abusive, beating Bill's mom. When Bill was about 12 years old, he confronted his stepfather, telling him that if he ever laid a hand on his mom again, he'd have to deal with Bill, too. His stepfather backed down, and the physical abuse stopped. From a very poor and abusive home life, Mr. Clinton went on to become a Rhodes Scholar, then President of the United States. I suspect that if he'd had an easier childhood, he might not have developed the drive to achieve all that he did.

(4) A final example of having greatness thrust upon someone would be the firefighters and rescuers who came to help out when the World Trade Center was attacked by terrorists. Those many civil servants started their day thinking that it was going to be like every other day. We heard many stories of incredible heroism as people were lead down or carried down staircases, and taken away from the building before it collapsed. Those who survive that horror are truly heroes in my opinion.

The conclusion relates directly back to the point of view.

(5) So even though my examples include people who had unique opportunities to do great things, I think we can all be great, sometimes even be heroes, in small ways, if we take the time to look for those opportunities to do a kindness for a stranger whenever we can.

DONE WELL	NEEDS WORK
1. uses strong examples of people who have dealt with greatness	1. first paragraph of the essay is unnecessary, does not relate to the rest and could simply be taken out
2. stays completely on topic at all times	2. overuse of the word "example"
	3. third paragraph wanders a bit and is somewhat confusing; words could be taken out to make it sharper
	4. conclusion is only one sentence and is somewhat confusing, best to break it up into two sentences to make point stronger and conclusion complete
Overall Score: 4	**Word count: 533**

This student also used current events as the foundation of her examples, but she uses several, rather than one. How do the two compare to each other?

ESSAY #6

Margaret Mead once said, "Never doubt that a small group of thoughtful, committed citizens can change the world. Indeed it is the only thing that ever has."

Assignment: Do you believe that small groups are responsible for change in today's culture? Plan and write an essay in which you develop your point of view on the issue. Support your position with reasoning and examples taken from your reading, studies, experience or observations.

Here is the position that the student is going to take for this essay.

While this makes a good point, it is written in a confusing manner that leaves the reader asking, "What did you just say?"

(1) I do not agree with the statements that one should never doubt that a small group of thoughtful, committed citizens can change the world and that it is indeed the only thing that ever has. The world, that is this space we occupy that is also occupied by non-living and/or non-human things, exists not solely in relation to human beings. The world exists in and of itself, and the world has changed in many ways since the so-called 'big bang' put this universe into existence. It is only for the last few thousand years that humans (let alone humans actually defined as "citizens") have held enough sway to commit any sort of changes upon it.

Here the student writes statements that support the main idea. However, they are not developed and need to be expanded.

(2) This is not to say that thoughtful and committed groups of citizens have not changed the world in any way, for they have. The Egyptians forever changed the face of northern Africa, the Chinese forever altered the landscape of Asia, Greenpeace members have enlightened people to the dangers of over-fishing, over-polluting and over-harvesting the world's rainforests, thus the effective ecology movement of the twentieth century was born. All of these changes to the world have been monumental and long lasting. But! These planet altering shifts at the hands of humans are not the only changes that have ever re-dedicated the world. Nature itself is always at play in this regard.

Excellent use of vocabulary words with "indelible," "epochs" and "cached."

(3) Asteroids hitting the earth cause great craters, holes in the surface of the planet that are as distinct and as indelible as human-created walls and temples. Fires that raged thousands of years ago are still evidenced by their charcoal deposits found cached deep within the very ground we stand upon, changing the chemical make up of this ground forever. Shifts to and from ice ages to warmer epochs cause enormous changes in the world—from sea levels to the distribution of life itself upon this planet. Time itself changes the world—and with time, those natural planetary actions that come about with time: erosion, volcanic disturbances, seismic activities, wind patterns, all contribute to changing this world. Each of these natural changes is as distinct and long lasting as any change wrought by small groups of thoughtful and committed citizens.

(4) Thus, in conclusion, I say that thoughtful and committed groups of citizens are not the only thing that ever have changed this world; they make up a part of life that has caused great changes, but they are not the only thing that changes this world. Nature, and all the natural forces that that term encompasses, also changes this world. Indeed, nature changes the world far more and has done so for far longer.

DONE WELL	NEEDS WORK
1. states point of view and relationship to the writing prompt clearly and quickly	1. point of view is simply a repeat of the writing prompt and should be changed to be more original/student's own words.
2. conclusion clearly relates back to the main topic and ends with very strong statement	2. thesis statement needs to reflect that this student disagrees because…
3. good use of vocabulary	3. could improve on punctuation
4. strong details with examples	
Overall Score: 5	**Word count: 438**

ESSAY #7

William James was credited with saying, "The greatest discovery of my generation is that a human being can alter his life by altering his attitudes of mind."

Assignment: Do you agree or disagree with this statement? Can people alter their lives simply by changing their attitudes? Plan and write an essay in which you develop your point of view on the issue. Support your position with reasoning and examples taken from your reading, studies, experience or observations.

Here is the student's point of view. It is very clear.

(1) I emphatically disagree with this statement. I believe that what is, is, and altering attitudes will not change it. A human being is trapped by many circumstances, among them: time, space, physical being, the need for food and water, and fate itself, which dictate that no matter how a human may attempt to alter his thoughts, he simply cannot alter his life.

Student uses two strong examples for support.

(2) A wise woman living in thirteenth century England could not alter the facts that she, being a female, would never know the right to attend Oxford University, no matter how much she altered her own personal attitude toward her femaleness. A person afflicted with giganticism will always be viewed by the thronging masses as a spectacle, a stranger, a freak, and no amount of personal attitude change will alter the way in which such a large person will live—for it is his physical being that dictates the manner in which he may live his life, and nothing more or less.

This sentence is too long and rather confusing. Needs to broken up and explained with more details.

(3) We may, as humans, try to overcome our own selves—courting fate as we take off for mountain climbing expeditions without enough supplies, sailing adventures without adequate fresh water, winter hikes without warm enough clothing, etcetera—but in the end, our lives are altered not by the attitudes we have brought with us to our lives, but by, instead, the way we live our lives around the limitations life itself imposes upon us. We cannot alter anything of our lives, we can but adapt ourselves to life's realities, and this has nothing whatsoever to do with altering attitudes of mind and everything to do with being ever mindful of what life is truly made of.

Conclusion needs more than one sentence to make it complete.

(4) There is no greater mistake to be made than to think that one's attitude in life is all that it will take to alter life itself.

DONE WELL	NEEDS WORK
1. states point of view and relationship to the writing prompt clearly and quickly	1. very long sentences can make it hard to understand what is being said
2. strong examples to support main point of view	2. rather short; could have used development of ideas
3. good use of vocabulary	3. conclusion needed at least another sentence to flesh it out and make it a complete paragraph
4. conclusion relates directly to the writing prompt	
Overall Score: 4	**Word count: 304**

The following essays are three examples of extremely well-written essays. Compare them. While they center on the same quote, they take three uniquely different perspectives. One relates the quote to war, one to the overuse of the world's natural resources and the other to a global, national and personal level. Which one do you like the best? What scores would you give each one? Why? What would you have written in response to the same quote? You can use these as models for your practice essays.

ESSAYS #8-10

A comic strip character from the 1940s named Pogo Possum once said, "We have met the enemy and he is us."

Assignment: What do you think Pogo meant with this quote? How does it apply to the world today? Plan and write an essay in which you develop your point of view on the issue. Support your position with reasoning and examples taken from your reading, studies, experience or observations.

(1) Somewhere in the world, it seems, there are always people at war. This has been true through times past and is certainly true in our world today. It seems that people are always looking for reasons to fight each other.

(2) Where in this does the expression "We have met the enemy and he is us" fit in? <u>This is true no matter if the conflict is local or across the sea.</u> The reason for this is that we are all people. Our differences are less than our similarities. Take, first, a "local" dispute, or a civil war. In a civil war, brother fights brother, friend fights friend and neighbor fights neighbors. If we are not these people, then who are we? These are groups of people who have the same backgrounds. These people have been raised with common sets of values and morals. In a civil war, we are the enemy.

(3) Next, consider a foreign war. In this situation, we're fighting people who often look different from us, have different religion and are most definitely not our families. Are we still the enemy? Yes, in more ways than one. First, in the sense that sometimes we are the aggressors and, second, in the sense that we are all still human—and these things make us the enemy.

(4) Consider the current war in the Middle East. We, Americans, are off fighting in another land. We have decided we know what is right and we are fighting for it. We've invaded them. We are the enemy.

(5) Now, even if we weren't being aggressors in this situation, does that mean that we aren't the enemy? No, because the enemy is human and so are we. We mourn for the loss of our people's lives. So do they. We want our families and friends to be safe and happy. So do they. We need to eat, drink, and have shelter. So do they. On the most basic levels, we are the same - humans. If we are fighting each other, we are the enemy.

(6) There is no time like the present to consider the true costs of war. One of these costs is what it makes people become. We become killers, mourners, savages. We become the enemy.

DONE WELL	NEEDS WORK
1. point of view is in the second paragraph but the introduction leads naturally to it	
2. excellent use of vocabulary and transitions (first, next, now)	
3. strong organization, moving from local to foreign wars and repetition of "we are the enemy" makes overall essay stronger	
4. strong and passionate conclusion relates directly to the writing prompt	
Overall Score: 6	**Word count: 370**

This essay is basically flawless. If you are going to imitate any essay during your practice sessions, this would be one of them. The student writes exactly what is being asked from beginning to end, and includes transitions, strong vocabulary and most of all, passion and support of a strong opinion.

Now, let's take a look at another essay on the same topic. How do you respond to it in comparison to the one above? Note how it is based on the same quote but takes a completely different slant.

Essay #9

(1) Pogo once said, "We have met the enemy and he is us." Today, we Americans are facing the harshest of truths about our inner enemy. We build our oversized mansions on unstable lands. We drive cars that spew toxins into the very air we breathe. We fertilize our lawns with chemicals whose run-off poisons the waterways we enjoy and the fish we eat. Why is it we are so shortsighted in our use of our lives?

(2) Our nation has been blessed with natural resources beyond equal in the world. Our lands are fertile, our water plentiful, and our American ability to work and prosper unrivaled. But each time we upgrade our technology, we give away a little piece of the environment that spawned our natural production. Massive automated agri-business churns out food in unprecedented quantities. But the hormones we pump into our livestock now, and the pesticides we must use to fight off pestilence seeps into our food supply making the products less wholesome for our bodies. We are our own worst enemy when we give up health and natural environmental beauty for a shortcut to wealth and prosperity. But is wealth and prosperity really all it's cracked up to be?

(3) Wealth for its own sake is a hollow attribute, according to Christian doctrine, which proclaims all wealth must come from God. The Bible says, "The love of money is a root of all kinds of evil, for which some have strayed from the faith in their greediness, and pierced themselves through with many sorrows" (I Timothy 6:10). Speaking strictly from a religious view, the "love of money" drives us to disregard our best interests in the pursuit of bigger, better, faster and more efficient use of our natural resources. Unfortunately we can't have it both ways: We can't continue to go against the natural cycle of our world and expect the environment to sustain its health.

(4) Pogo's comment about our being our own enemy will continue to be true as long as we place a higher value on the easiest way to succeed while disregarding that which brought us to this place in history.

DONE WELL	NEEDS WORK
1. point of view clearly stated in the beginning	1. conclusion could be slightly longer (more than one sentence)
2. good use of relevant Bible quote	2. overall essay could be a bit longer, on the shorter side
3. support examples shown in first paragraph and then expanded	
4. excellent use of vocabulary	
Overall score: 5	**Word count: 355**

Again, this is an example of a very well-written essay. Use it as a model for yours.

Essay #10

(1) When Pogo said, "We have met the enemy and he is us" I think that he was trying to say that we are our own worst enemy. He might have been speaking globally, nationally, or personally, but there's certainly truth in his statement in all of those applications.

(2) On a global level, well, just look at the nuclear arms race. The United States doesn't want any other nations to have the same level of nuclear weaponry as it has, especially nations that historically haven't been the best of friends with the U.S., like North Korea. If you look at it from the North Korean's perspective, of course they want nuclear weapons to protect themselves from the United States, and why should the U.S. have the power to tell another nation what kinds of weapons they can or cannot have? So both nations are stockpiling weapons, and finding newer, better ways to blow up their enemies. Maybe if we all just got rid of the nuclear weapons altogether, we'd all sleep a lot better at night. But, would the U.S. be willing to take a giant step like that? Of course not. The U.S. won't cooperate with other nations, and it wonders why it's losing support from nations that have historically been allies. We are our own worst enemy.

(3) On a national level, we could be a very strong nation, and yet partisan politics rule. When budgets are passed, our legislators make sure that their states are given special funding, also known as "pork," for federal projects which often are relatively unimportant, and at worst may be totally unnecessary. People are going hungry, many people are without health care, people are un- or underemployed, and yet federal dollars are going to fund these pork projects. Just think of how much greater we could be as a nation if all of those federal dollars went to help real people in real need. Just think of how much stronger and cohesive we could be if we could see beyond the needs of each state, and look at the bigger picture, and pull together as a united nation.

(4) On a personal level, it's been said that we are our own worst critic, and that's probably true. We're always comparing ourselves with everyone around us: Who has the best clothes, who drives the best car, who lives in the biggest house, who has the biggest TV or the newest electronic gadget? When we spend so much time focusing on what everyone around us is doing or wearing or driving, we're not really spending any time figuring out how to make our own lives better from a non-materialistic perspective. We're not thinking about how rewarding it would be to, say, tutor a school kid who's having trouble in an area we're good in. We're not taking the time to make long range goals when we're worrying about short term luxuries, that probably won't really make us happy anyway, and which will be out of style or no longer the coolest, newest thing in only a few months. Why do we do this to ourselves? We're our own worst enemy.

DONE WELL	NEEDS WORK
1. point of view clearly stated in the beginning	1. a little too casual with slang in places (for example, first sentence in the second paragraph or fourth sentence in the last paragraph)
2. maintains first person (we, us) throughout the essay	2. this is longer than what would fit in the typical test booklet and would need to be edited down
3. support examples shown in first paragraph and then expanded in each separate paragraph	3. could use a more independent conclusion
4. excellent use of vocabulary and connection of quote to the conclusion	
Overall score: 5	**Word count: 523**

ESSAY #11

World famous author J.R.R. Tolkien (as in The Lord of the Rings) once stated that, "All who wander are not lost."

Assignment: Do you think wandering is a sign of being lost? Is wandering a positive or negative part of life? Plan and write an essay in which you develop your point of view on the issue. Support your position with reasoning and examples taken from your reading, studies, experience or observations.

Instead of just stating an opinion, this student decides to analyze the question being asked. This can work if it is done well.

(1) To answer "Do I agree with JRR Tolkien that all who wander are not lost," I would have to deconstruct the question to see what its core meaning really is. First ill start with the maybe strongest word from the sentence, Lost. To understand what a wander is by JRR Tolkien's standards you must first understand what lost means. From prior knowledge and personal experiences, I would say that a ruff definition of lost is the unwilling ignorance of ones whereabouts. Therefore, to be wandering and lost would be like aimlessly meandering in search of some place you might recognize in some form of foreign territory.

Here is where the student finally writes the thesis statement.

(2) So I guess I should answer the question can one wonder and know where they are. The nature of wondering for me does not have a direct connection with the concept of being lost. I can choose to wander around the garden in my back yard and know exactly where I am.

The student struggles with commonly confused words like "were" and "where," as well as "wonder" and "wander."

There are a number of grammar mistakes in this essay, enough to affect the overall grade. Here, the student uses "your" instead of "you're" and mixes up first and third person.

(3) And so, in those technical ways yes one can wander without being lost. If you where to think of the word lost in a broader sense, not only applying to the body, is it still true? I personally wonder to find something, or to see something. Sometimes I wander just to keep moving in some sort of desperate race against some invisible thing waiting to pounce if I sit still too long. If someone feels the need to wander (assuming if you know where your going you have to make a conscious decision to wander) that there is something missing. In other words, something is lost. For example, the feeling of contentment with just sitting and looking is lost. Then wandering around the garden would be a way to alleviate the need to fill that hole of unfuffiledness.

There are multiple spelling errors in this essay that detract from the overall presentation, and hence, affect the score.

(4) When i think of wandering i think of sad lonley people walking aimlessly around a dark city unaware of there surrounding but somehow searching. They are not searching for anything conciously more searching for some unknown to fill the driveing need to e sated. My feeling on the word wandering are purly my own emotions surrounding the word and in no way reflect the overall ecsepted meaning. This tests question was wether or not i agreed with the quote, and i think i do in the physical sence.

(5) Wandering can be done intentionaly as a choice, and i belive is most often done in such a way. Since it is a choice to wander you either know your surrounding, or you are willingly walking without a good understanding of were you are. You are willingly unaware, or unknowledgeable of your surroundings, the fact that you

or willing in this activity means you are not "lost" but in some other state. So not all that wander are lost. Ones who wander are always in search though, for something be it tangible or not. In that situation, the wanderer is not lost but it missing something and that makes all the difference.

DONE WELL	NEEDS WORK
1. good use of some vocabulary words	1. multiple spelling and grammar errors
2. fairly strong closing statement in the conclusion	2. lack of organization
3. decent length	3. problems with commonly confused words
	4. switching between first and third person
Overall score: 1	**Word count: 496**

What are your comments on this one? You can tell the student gave the prompt some serious thought. However, the errors in word usage, punctuation and spelling are a real problem, as are the continuous confusion of "where" and "were" and "wonder" and "wander." The mistakes interfere with the reader's ability to comprehend the essay. Lack of organization contributes to an overall feeling of rambling. It's time to do some serious rewriting to see what can be saved in this one.

Although the technique of analyzing the quote in the first paragraph is interesting, it tends to be confusing. Let's take it out completely, start with the thesis statement, combine the next two paragraphs and then see what happens. I am going to cut out several of the sentences that just do not add anything to the overall essay.

ORIGINAL VERSION	REWRITE
So I guess I should answer the question can one wonder and know where they are. The nature of wondering for me does not have a direct connection with the concept of being lost. I can choose to wander around the garden in my back yard and know exactly where I am.	The nature of wandering does not have a direct connection with the concept of being lost, in my opinion. I can choose to wander around the garden of my backyard and yet, know exactly where I am. Personally, I wander in order to find or see something. Other times I wander simply to keep moving in some sort of desperate race against some invisible thing waiting to pounce if I sit still too long. Perhaps if I feel the need to wander, it is partially because I feel something is missing.

And so, in those technical ways yes one can wander without being lost. If you where to think of the word lost in a broader sense, not only applying to the body, is it still true? I personally wonder to find something, or to see something. Sometimes I wander just to keep moving in some sort of desperate race against some invisible thing waiting to pounce if I sit still too long. If someone feels the need to wander (assuming if you know where your going you have to make a conscious decision to wander) that there is something missing. In other words, something is lost. For example, the feeling of contentment with just sitting and looking is lost. Then wandering around the garden would be a way to alleviate the need to fill that hole of unfuffiledness.	Wandering through the garden could then become the best way to alleviate that emptiness.

As you can see, a good portion of the essay has been eliminated. It simply does not make sense; it rambles, repeats and does not support the thesis statement. Even rewritten, this one would most likely not make more than a 2 or 3.

ORIGINAL VERSION	REWRITE
When i think of wandering i think of sad lonley people walking aimlessly around a dark city unaware of there surrounding but somehow searching. They are not searching for anything conciously more searching for some unknown to fill the driveing need to e sated. My feeling on the word wandering are purly my own emotions surrounding the word and in no way reflect the overall ecsepted meaning.	When I think about wandering, I picture sad, lonely people walking aimlessly around a dark city, unaware of their surroundings yet still searching. Perhaps they are looking for the unknown in an attempt to fill a driving need to be sated. This is not how I feel, however.

This tests question was wether or not i agreed with the quote, and i think i do in the physical sence. Wandering can be done intentionaly as a choice, and i belive is most often done in such a way. Since it is a choice to wander you either know your surrounding, or you are willingly walking without a good understanding of were you are. You are willingly unaware, or unknowledgeable of your surroundings, the fact that you or willing in this activity means you are not "lost" but in some other state. So not all that wander are lost. Ones who wander are always in search though, for something be it tangible or not. In that situation, the wanderer is not lost but it missing something and that makes all the difference.	Wandering intentionally is a matter of choice, whether in familiar or unfamiliar surroundings. Not all who wander are lost. Those who do so are always in search of something though, tangible or otherwise. In this case, the wanderer is not at all lost but is missing something, and that makes all of the difference.

Even rewritten, this essay is incomplete. It does not have enough support and its conclusion is weak and confusing. The average test scorer would need some serious chocolate and therapy by the end of this one.

ESSAY #12

The military leader and historical figure George S. Patton once said, "Success is how high you bounce when you hit bottom."

Assignment: Do you agree or disagree with this statement? What is your definition of success? Plan and write an essay in which you develop your point of view on the issue. Support your position with reasoning and examples taken from your reading, studies, experience or observations.

Here are the examples the student is going to develop in the following paragraphs. The key to improving these would be to make them complete sentences rather than fragments.

In paragraph 2, notice the use of first person here. However, this changes back and forth between first and third later within the essay.

Paragraph 4 is where the student begins to expand on the original thesis statement.

In paragraphs 5 and 6 the student is now expanding on the comment about Presidents in the first paragraph.

(1) George S. Patton once said, "Success is how high you bounce when you hit bottom." Examples of this feeling can be seen all over, in lots of aspects in our world. From a young child struggling to read, to several presidents of the United States.

(2) Many of us yell, "success!" when we get an "A" on a hard math quiz or someone playing sports when they hit a home run. For some these are true examples of success; for others they are merely achievements. Real success is in the eye of the beholder or, in this case, the achiever.

(3) When you accomplish something, you have succeeded. but if it wasn't much of a struggle to do it, if it didn't take much work or sweat or late nights then I feel it is just an achievement. Success is a strong word, indicating some kind of victory.

(4) For the child learning to read that struggles and tries and practices every day but keeps at it, his achievement of finally reading is truly a "success." For someone that reading, or other schoolwork comes easily for they don't recognize their triumph as such a big deal.

(5) In the movie "Pearl Harbor" the President is telling his staff how to react to the Japanese invasion. They tell him it can't be done. He then struggles to stand from his wheelchair under their protests. He says, "Don't tell me it can't be done!" They are suddenly very busy doing as he asked. An ordinary man standing would not have had that big an impact on their actions.

(6) Many presidents, captains of industry, and people in the community inspire me the same way. Presidents that were born into wealthy families involved in politics often feel the world owes them success. They expect it. They might even put some effort into it, but the Presidents that struggled to home educate themselves, the one that spent several commitments in a mental institution, or overcame physical or family tragedies are way more inspiring and demonstrate success in their achievements.

(7) If someone comes from "the bottom" and works hard to get where they are going they aren't just showing a mere achievement, that they accomplished something. It is those individuals that rise from the ashes like a Phoenix to a wonderful reality, whose journey is the farthest, that can say they truly succeeded. If things are easy for you, you might not even notice when you achieve something. Or appreci-

ate it. I think those are often the people that show it off the most, too. True success is often not just in the eye, but also in the heart, of the beholder, and much more inspiring to us who watch the flight out of the ashes of depression, drug addiction, financial ruin or poverty, or being a political nobody and, like a superball with wings, bounce into the clouds like Harry Potter's golden snitch.

DONE WELL	NEEDS WORK
1. good thesis statement	1. switching from first to second and third person and slang terms
2. relevant historical example(s)	2. several spelling and punctuation errors
	3. several fragments scattered throughout
	4. conclusion is somewhat confusing and introduces new concepts
Overall score: 3	**Word count: 484**

There are many good points in this essay but they are somewhat lost in the muddle of fragments and switching from one person to another. Let's see what can be done with it.

ORIGINAL VERSION	REWRITE
George S. Patton once said, "Success is how high you bounce when you hit bottom." Examples of this feeling can be seen all over, in lots of aspects in our world. From a young child struggling to read, to several presidents of the United States. Many of us yell, "success!" when we get an "A" on a hard math quiz or someone playing sports when they hit a home run. For some these are true examples of success; for others they are merely achievements. Real success is in the eye of the beholder or, in this case, the achiever.	George S. Patton once said, "Success is how high you bounce when you hit bottom." Examples of this sentiment can be seen all over the world, from young children struggling to read to several U.S. Presidents. Many students feel they have succeeded when they get an A on a math quiz or when they hit a home run. For some, these are true example of success, while for others, they are merely achievements. Real success is in the eye of the achiever.

When you accomplish something, you have succeeded. but if it wasn't much of a struggle to do it, if it didn't take much work or sweat or late nights then I feel it is just an achievement. Success is a strong word, indicating some kind of victory. For the child learning to read that struggles and tries and practices every day but keeps at it, his achievement of finally reading is truly a "success." For someone that reading, or other schoolwork comes easily for they don't recognize their triumph as such a big deal.	When people accomplish something, they have succeeded; but if there was no struggle—if it didn't take hours of toil and sweat on late nights—then it is simply an achievement, not a success. For example, if a child learning to read must try very hard and practice daily, his ability to read is truly a success. For someone else who learned how to read easily and quickly, it is not the same degree of triumph.

Do you see how the essay fits together better once the "we," "you" and "they" are merged into all third person? Unnecessary words are taken out and vague vocabulary is replaced with words that are specific.

ORIGINAL VERSION	**REWRITE**
In the movie Pearl Harbor the President is telling his staff how to react to the Japanese invasion. They tell him it can't be done. He then struggles to stand from his wheelchair under their protests. He says, "Don't tell <u>me</u> it can't be done!" They are suddenly very busy doing as he asked. An ordinary man standing would not have had that big an impact on their actions. Many presidents, captains of industry, and people in the community inspire me the same way. Presidents that were born into wealthy families involved in politics often feel the world owes them success. They expect it. They might even put some effort into it, but the Presidents that struggled to home educate themselves, the one that spent several commitments in a mental institution, or overcame physical or family tragedies are way more inspiring and demonstrate success in their achievements.	In the movie "Pearl Harbor," President Franklin D. Roosevelt asks his staff how to respond to the Japanese invasion. They have no answers for him. He then struggles to stand from his wheelchair, despite their protests. "Don't tell <u>me</u> it can't be done!" he shouts. Suddenly, his staff gets busy doing as he asks. An ordinary man simply standing up and saying the same thing would never have had such a huge impact on people. Many Presidents are inspirational like this. For instance, Presidents that were born into wealthy, political families feel that the world owes them success. They expect it. But the Presidents that struggled to home educate themselves or overcame physical or family tragedies are far more inspiring and truly demonstrate success through their achievements.

What changes did you spot here? One of the primary improvements was to name the U.S. President being quoted. Chances are if you knew what he said, when he said it and that he was in a wheelchair, you'd remember his name as well. If you didn't, you could have said "the President at that time" or something along those lines. Notice I cut out the reference to "captains of industry and people in the community." Can you guess why? Look back at the thesis statement. The two examples mentioned were children learning to read–and United States Presidents. By sticking to Presidential examples, the thesis statement is reinforced.

Let's go through the ending of the essay now.

ORIGINAL VERSION	REWRITE
If someone comes from "the bottom" and works hard to get where they are going they aren't just showing a mere achievement, that they accomplished something. It is those individuals that rise from the ashes like a Phoenix to a wonderful reality, whose journey is the farthest, that can say they truly succeeded. If things are easy for you, you might not even notice when you achieve something. Or appreciate it. I think those are often the people that show it off the most, too. True success is often not just in the eye, but also in the heart, of the beholder, and much more inspiring to us who watch the flight out of the ashes of depression, drug addiction, financial ruin or poverty, or being a political nobody and, like a superball with wings, bounce into the clouds like Harry Potter's golden snitch.	If someone comes from the "bottom" and works hard to climb back up, he isn't just showing a mere achievement. It is those individuals who rise from the ashes like a phoenix, or whose journey is the farthest, that can say they have honestly succeeded. True success is not just in the eye, but also in the heart, and it is much more inspiring to others who watch the flight out of the ashes of tragedy and adversity into victory.

A number of things were taken out of this portion of the essay. Statements like, "If things are easy for you, you might not even notice when you achieve something. Or appreciate it," have already been covered earlier and there is no need to repeat them now. The last statement of the essay is a strong one but is lost among too many words and complicated by the Harry Potter reference. By cutting out the extra and focusing on the main message, that ending sentence is much stronger and so is the rest of the essay for it.

ESSAY #13

President Ronald Reagan was quoted as saying, "You can tell a lot about a fellow's character by his way of eating jellybeans."

Assignment: Do you agree or disagree with this statement? What do you think is the best judge of a person's character? Plan and write an essay in which you develop your point of view on the issue. Support your position with reasoning and examples taken from your reading, studies, experience or observations.

The student has a strong and clear thesis statement.

(1) The best way to judge a person's character is through observation. Observation will show you how this person acts, thinks, works and feels as he goes about his life so you can make an informed judgment about his character. Observing the way he eats jellybeans is one example of such observation.

Here are the ways that the student is supporting the thesis statement.

(2) If a person shares his jellybeans, or saves some for somebody else, you can judge that that person is considerate. If a person eats them fast, gobbling them, offering them to no one and sharing them with no one, you can judge that person to be selfish. If a person hoards jellybeans while another goes hungry you can judge that person to be mean. If a person charges a quarter for each jellybean he "shares" with another, that person is petty and miserly. Eating the jellybeans nicely, one by one, will lead you to judge that that person has nice manners. Eating the jellybeans with an open mouth, stuffing them in, chewing them badly and letting pieces of jellybean fall onto his shirt would make you judge that person to have no manners at all.

(3) Also, the type of jellybeans eaten will give you clues as to how judge a person. Eating cheap 'corn syrup' jellybeans can be judged as something that an unsophisticated person would do. But eating expensive "jelly belly" beans can be judged as a cultured person's choice.

(4) If a person only eats one certain color of jellybean, you can judge that he is fussy. If a person doesn't care at all about what color jellybean he eats, you can judge him to be easy going and carefree.

(5) Continually wiping his hands between jellybeans will let you judge a person as finicky and sensitive, but eating jellybeans with dirty hands will let you judge him as oafish and ignorant. Eating jellybeans with normally clean hands, and wiping them only if they become overly sticky, will let the observer judge that the person is moderate and reasonable in all things.

These sentences tie the conclusion back to the rest of the essay and thesis statement.

(6) The way that people behave with small things, in insignificant situations such as eating jellybeans, is the way that these people will usually behave with larger things, and in more significant situations. The way a person eats a jellybean will tell a great amount about the kind of person he is. It is as reasonable to judge a person on how he eats jellybeans as it is on how he conducts himself in any other area of his life.

What did you think of this essay? It is a very good one that you can use for a model. Throughout the entire presentation, the student stayed on topic and supported the thesis statement. (Who knew there was this much to write about jellybeans!) Good use of vocabulary also played a large part in the overall score.

DONE WELL	NEEDS WORK
1. good, strong thesis statement right at the start	1. slightly wordy here and there
2. strong and relevant examples	
3. completely on topic throughout the essay	
4. good use of vocabulary words	
Overall score: 5	**Word count: 425**

ESSAY #14

Someone once said, "Stupid is forever, ignorance can be fixed."

Assignment: Do you agree or disagree with this statement? What is the difference between stupidity and ignorance? Plan and write an essay in which you develop your point of view on the issue. Support your position with reasoning and examples taken from your reading, studies, experience or observations.

The student immediately states the thesis statement for the essay.

(1) The differences between stupidity and ignorance are many. Stupidity is the state of being unable to become intelligent. Ignorance is the state of being not informed. Stupidity is complete; ignorance can be partial. Stupidity does not know of its own stupidity. Ignorance sometimes does and sometimes does not know of its own ignorance. Stupidity does not desire to be made different. Ignorance sometimes does and sometimes does not desire to be made different.

(2) Stupidity is total. A person is stupid or he is not. Stupid people do not become great at one thing, but not at other things. Stupid people do not achieve greatness in any areas of their lives. They are too stupid to strive for greatness, although sometimes greatness may be thrust upon them.

(3) Stupid people do not know that they are stupid. They perceive the world from their own dim, thickness. They think that other people are either "good" or "bad," which means that other people are either acceptable to them or not, they lump all people that they do not understand into "good" or "bad" based on popular opinion and not on personal judgment. Stupid people do not have judgment, stupid people have opinions.

(4) Stupid people do not wish to change. They stupidly accept the life they have been born into. They do not question what they think is "good" or "bad" about their lives, they just live. Some things make them happy, some things make them sad, but they do not think deeply.

Unignorant is not an actual word. If it were, the student would be using it correctly, however.

(5) Ignorant people are people who have the intelligence to change from being ignorant to being informed. Ignorant people who have the intelligence to change and do not, remain ignorant. Ignorant people who have the intelligence to change and do so are called educated, talented, refined or unignorant.

(6) Ignorant people are aware that there are things they need to learn. The desire and the ability to learn will make these ignorant people become unignorant. Ignorant people see the world from many points of view, they will understand that there are many opinions and many ways of living, they just don't understand them. They will strive to understand them if they are to become unignorant. They do not see the world by standards of "black or white," they judge and think deeply about what they see and learn.

(7) Ignorant people can be quite talented in one or two areas of their lives, but woefully uninformed in others. Ignorant people understand that they are ignorant of some things. Ignorant people usually wish to change. Ignorance is not a good personality trait, they understand. They question life, they question how they live. Ignorance is not irrevocable; it is simply an obstacle blocking an intelligent brain from realizing its potential.

This example from theatre helps to support and illustrate the student's main point.

(8) The movie "My Fair Lady" aptly illustrates the differences between ignorance and stupidity. Eliza Doolittle, the heroine, is ignorant, she becomes very educated. She changes, through her learning, from a street urchin to a genteel lady. She wants to change and she does. She is able to because she is ignorant, not stupid. Her father, though, is actually a stupid man and he never changes at all, he is happy not to change.

(9) Stupidity and ignorance are quite different. Stupidity can only ever be stupidity. Ignorance can change to unignorance. Stupidity is inescapable, ignorance is not.

DONE WELL	NEEDS WORK
1. good, strong thesis statement right at the start	1. slightly wordy here and there (and "unignorance" is not a real word)
2. strong and relevant examples	2. transitions for the paragraphs would be helpful for the flow
3. completely on topic throughout the essay	3. several places where semi-colons would improve the flow and prevent run-ons
4. conclusion ties in directly to the thesis statement and the prompt	4. so long it probably wouldn't fit on the lines provided
Overall score: 4	**Word count: 548**

ESSAY #15

Albert Camus had a unique way of defining friendship. He wrote, "Don't walk behind me, I may not lead. Don't walk in front of me, I may not follow. Just walk beside me and be my friend."

Assignment: **Do you agree or disagree with this statement? What is your definition of a good friend? Plan and write an essay in which you develop your point of view on the issue. Support your position with reasoning and examples taken from your reading, studies, experience or observations.**

The student clearly states the thesis statement and connects it to the writing prompt.

(1) A friend is a person you like, and who likes you, in all aspects of your being. A friend is well matched, well suited and well fitted to be your companion. As the above quotation states, "Don't walk behind....don't walk in front...just walk beside me and be my friend"—a friend doesn't lead or be led, a friend walks with a friend.

The student starts using "you" instead of staying with third person.

(2) Anyone who walks agreeably beside you, in any sense of the word, whether it is helping you chop onions for a big company dinner, whether it is cheering you while you bring your first paintings to a big show in the city, whether it is sitting next to you and telling you that it doesn't matter what the world thinks, so long as you are happy, that person is a friend.

(3) Friends appreciate what is special about each other without trying to change each other. Friends will not abandon friendships for petty reasons, such as squabbles, misunderstandings or accidentally hurt feelings. Friends will like each other despite small grievances or differences. There is so much agreeability to a friendship that it can suffer small blows and trivial set backs, sometimes being made stronger for them.

(4) Friends are happy for each other's success, but do not need any for themselves. Friends are sorry for each other's mishaps. Friends do not need to ask for help between themselves, for they will help each other without asking. Friends do not lord this help over each other. Friends help each other because it is agreeable to do so.

(5) Many people confuse friends with mentors or guides. Phrases like "A real friend wouldn't let you do something like that" turn the term friend from meaning "happy companionship" to meaning "co-responsible caretaker" and take friendship from being about walking with, to being about leading or being led.

This is a strong and relevant literary example to use.

(6) A friend doesn't even have to be a good person. In Henry IVth part one, Prince Hal is friends with many unsavory types, among them the rascal, Falstaff. Yet, they are good companions, they enjoy each other's company. They do not lead each other, nor are they led by each other. They simply are themselves, and like each other's friendship that way.

(7) Friendship can be not responsible, or not particularly careful. Friends can experience danger, intrigue, adventure and non-responsible behaviors together. That is often what makes up some friendships. These friends do not lead, nor are led by each other. They get along well, they are evenly matched in personality, they like each other. They are friends even though they let each other do dangerous things.

Here the student slips back into first person again.

(8) Friends do not ask anything of us but for us to be ourselves, for us to walk with, not behind or in front of, them. Not to lead, not to follow, just to walk, agreeably, side by side. That alone is the essence of friendship.

DONE WELL	NEEDS WORK
1. good, strong thesis statement right at the start	1. slips from first to third person and back again
2. strong literary example to support the thesis statement	2. repetition of the word "friend" gives a slightly monotonous tone to it; synonyms would help
3. completely on topic throughout the essay	3. semi colons between independent clauses are needed in several places
4. conclusion ties in directly to the thesis statement and the prompt	
Overall score: 5	**Word count: 474**

ESSAY #16

Max Nordau, German author and physician once stated, "Civilization is built on a number of ultimate principles…respect for human life, the punishment of crimes against property and persons, the equality of all good citizens before the law…or, in a word, justice."

Assignment: Do you agree or disagree with this statement? Do you think our culture is a just one? Does our civilization do what is listed in this quote? Plan and write an essay in which you develop your point of view on the issue. Support your position with reasoning and examples taken from your reading, studies, experience or observations.

The thesis statement is clearly stated and connected to the writing prompt.

(1) If a just civilization must observe a certain number of ultimate principles, outlined by the quotation as: respect for human life, the punishment of crimes against property and persons and the equality of all good citizens before the law, <u>then the civilization that we find ourselves in the midst of is not a just one.</u>

An excellent use of vocabulary words.

(2) Punishment of crimes against property and persons is not completely observed by this civilization. Pollution, deforestation, toxic foods are all crimes against humans, and against property (such as trees) of the planet we live on, yet the people that create these conditions continue, unscathed. Such impunity then creates an unjust civilization, according to the quotation.

(3) The equality of all good citizens before the law can not be observed in the governance of this civilization. For example, rich good citizens have access to much better arbitrators of the law than do poor good citizens, thus they are not afforded real equality before the law. The inequality of this is very unjust, making the civilization which fosters such a state of imbalance unjust as well, as judged by the quotation.

(4) Respect for human life is not much observed by the civilization of which we are part. War continues to this very minute, homeless children go hungry nightly, medical help is not freely offered to all and jails still enforce the death penalty upon prisoners. If respect for lives of humans is the quotation's criteria for a just civilization, then we are not living in a just civilization.

The conclusion sums up the prompt and the examples mentioned in the essay.

(5) Because the civilization in which we are living does not follow the quotation's specific principles of respect for human life, punishment of certain crimes and equality of the good before its own law, I conclude that, according to the quotation, this civilization we find ourselves in is not a just one.

DONE WELL	NEEDS WORK
1. good, strong thesis statement right at the start	1. with the repetition of some words, synonyms might be helpful
2. excellent use of vocabulary from beginning to end	2. the conclusion is somewhat repetitive
3. completely on topic throughout the essay	
4. strong, relevant examples	
Overall score: 5	**Word count: 303**

What did you think as you read through this essay? Did you notice the use of vocabulary? The examples are strong and clear. Could you tell that this student really thought about what he wanted to say and that there was passion behind those statements? This is a good essay to study because it is rather short but still manages to competently cover the introduction, body and conclusion.

ESSAY #17

Helen Keller, a role model for courage and perseverance, once stated, "Character cannot be developed in ease and quiet. Only through experience of trial and suffering can the soul be strengthened, ambition inspired and success achieved."

Assignment: What do you think is the key to developing character? Is it what Helen Keller stated or something else? Plan and write an essay in which you develop your point of view on the issue. Support your position with reasoning and examples taken from your reading, studies, experience or observations.

(1) Helen Keller was an amazing woman, really she was. I cannot imagine what it would be like to live my life without being able to see, hear or talk. Can you? It seems like it would be so lonely, dark and scary. It sure is a good thing that Annie Sullivan came along and taught her sign language. I have watched the movie "The Miracle Worker" a dozen times. It's really good. The best movie ever, in my opinion. The old one with someone named Patty Duke is my favorite. The newer one was made by Disney. They didn't do a very good job at all.

(2) When I was little, I would imagine being Helen Keller. Isn't that silly? I would put on a blindfold. I would stuff cotton balls in my ears. I would refuse to speak. It drove my Mom crazy. Stumbling around the rooms, bruising my shins and knocking things over.

(3) Actually, Helen Keller kind of inspired me. I have decided that I want to be a sign language teacher when I go on to college. I have already taken several classes at the local community college. Did really good too. The teacher said I would be a great instructor one day. That's good because they get paid well and there are always openings. My friend's brother is deaf and his parents are always looking for a sign language teacher to help him out in school. Must be a real pain to try and keep up on things if you aren't sure what people are saying.

(4) Helen Keller was a fascinating person and I just wish she hadn't died before I was born. I guess I will just have to be content reading about her and watching those movies that I mentioned above. She knew everything there was to know about developing character, she truly did. I hope I can do as well as she did and I can talk, see and hear!

STOP RIGHT HERE. Before I tell you what was done well (little to nothing) and what needs works (virtually everything), can you spot the number one mistake this student made? Was it a lack of any thesis statement? No. Was it the missing examples or essay format? No. Was it too long or too short? No. Was it fragments or run-ons? No. Was it slang terms? No. Was it the misspelled words? No. Keep thinking. Read the assignment over again and then look at the essay. This essay gets a score of ZERO because ("Think, think, think" as Winnie the Pooh would say.)

Did you get it? This essay gets a big fat ZERO because it is COMPLETELY OFF TOPIC. It never once addressed the question within the actual assignment (what gives a person character). Instead, the student glanced at the name in the quote and immediately started writing about the person. There was no time spent reading it carefully, brainstorming or making an outline. Even if all of these mistakes were corrected, the essay would still get a lousy zero because it is totally (say it with me, please) OFF TOPIC. Heck, I'm not even going to tell you what it did well because it would be like searching for a needle in a haystack–and that is being rather optimistic!

ESSAY #18

There is a saying that states, "It is not enough to prepare our children for the world; we must also prepare the world for our children."

Assignment: What do you think it means to prepare the world for children? How can families best do this? Plan and write an essay in which you develop your point of view on the issue. Support your position with reasoning and examples taken from your reading, studies, experience or observations.

Here is the student's extended thesis statement.

(1) While many parents take the time to prepare their children for the world, that is not sufficient, in my opinion. The world is a precarious state between the war, environmental issues and homelessness. How can parents safely send their children out into a place like this?

Good analogy to clarify the previous sentence.

(2) First, I believe that children should be sheltered from the horrors of war until they are emotionally mature enough to handle the information. This age can vary from child to child, of course. Watching the news and hearing about repeated bombings, weapons and threats is often too much for a young person to handle. While there is little a parent can do as an individual to change the war itself, he or she can at least not make it a part of a child's daily life. Instead, I feel they should protect their children by teaching them that the world is a wonderful place but precautions must be taken. Maybe they could point out it is a little like riding a bike. It is exciting and fun but you have to be careful.

Each paragraph (1-3) relates directly back to the examples listed in the introduction. This is an excellent example of clear organization.

(3) Next, the world needs to have adequate resources to support the needs of children as they grow into adults. This means an increased pressure to recycle, avoid using toxic products and limiting the amount of resources used, such as gasoline. Teaching children about the importance of these lifestyle choices is essential; doing what you can as the adult role model is even more so. Children imitate what they see, especially when parents are not looking.

(4) Finally, the issue of homelessness can be difficult. If you live in small towns, you many not see many examples of this. If you live in a big city like I do, however, it is all around you, on every busy traffic corner and highway entrance. I think it is a good idea to talk with your children about how you want to handle the issue of homelessness. For example, my family and I work once a month in a local shelter, filling plates and doing dishes. We also carry coupons for free meals at shelters in our car to hand out to some people.

(5) Although it is very difficult to make a true difference in global issues, talking to your children about each one and taking a clear position on them is important. This way, parents can help prepare their children for the world—and vice versa.

What do you think about this one? What strikes you the most? Compare it to the previous essay. This one stays ON TOPIC and shows excellent organization. It's a good one to use as a model for your essay.

DONE WELL	NEEDS WORK
1. good, strong thesis statement that directly relates to the assignment	1. a little work is needed on switching from first to third person in a few places
2. good use of transitions (first, next and finally) and vocabulary	2. in a few places it is unclear which nouns the pronouns refer to, and this can be confusing to the reader
3. completely on topic throughout the essay	
4. conclusion related directly to the points made throughout the essay	
Overall score: 5	**Word count: 402**

ESSAY #19

Malcolm X once said, "The media's the most powerful entity on earth. They have the power to make the innocent guilty and to make the guilty innocent, and that's power. Because they control the minds of the masses."

Assignment: Do you think the media has great power in today's culture? Does it truly control the minds of the people? Plan and write an essay in which you develop your point of view on the issue. Support your position with reasoning and examples taken from your reading, studies, experience or observations.

Here is the thesis statement. Notice, however, that the student is just rewriting the prompt rather than using his own words to rephrase the topic.

(1) <u>Yes, I think the media has great power in today's culture and it controls the mind of the people. Malcolm X was right</u>. Newspapers, television and radio have become far too powerful in this country. It is very obvious to me.

These would be good examples except that the student does not give enough detail. If you don't recall enough points of information, don't attempt to use the examples. Come up with something you know better.

(2) People no longer think for themselves. They let others do it for them. This is wrong. It results in bad things. Many times people who committed a crime are written about and then said to be guilty even before the judge says it. Look what happened with OJ Simpson and Scott Peterson. They are perfect examples of what Malcolm X meant when he said they make the innocent guilty and the guilty innocent. That's what I heard, at least.

(3) If the magazines say a fashion is hot, then people wear it. Even if they don't like how it looks on them. Then, another magazine will say the fashion is not hot, so people stop wearing it. That is just stupid.

Do you see how the student has double spaced between paragraphs? This is usually done to make the essay look longer.

(4) I recently read a magazine article in *Sports Illustrated* about a football player who was accused of taking steroids and other drugs. Later they found it was not true but it was too late. His career was over. I thought that was just terrible.

The student uses a relevant example here to back up his opinion.

(5) So yes, I must agree that the media has great power in today's culture. It truly does control the minds of the people. Malcolm X definitely knew what he was talking about.

DONE WELL	NEEDS WORK
1. thesis statement is stated right at the beginning of the essay	1. obvious attempt to make the short essay look longer
2. stays relatively on topic throughout the essay	2. examples are too briefly mentioned and need far more detail to be supportive
	3. the introduction and conclusion are both repeats of the writing prompt and should be rewritten in the student's own words
	4. many vague terms like "bad" and "wrong" and slang like "hot"
Overall score: 3	**Word count: 237**

There is some thought to this essay but it runs out pretty quickly. Let's see what we can do to bump it up a point or two.

ORIGINAL VERSION	REWRITE
Yes, I think the media has great power in today's culture and it controls the mind of the people. Malcolm X was right. Newspapers, television and radio have become far too powerful in this country. It is very obvious to me. People no longer think for themselves. They let others do it for them. This is wrong. It results in bad things. Many times people who committed a crime are written about and then said to be guilty even before the judge says it. Look what happened with OJ Simpson and Scott Peterson. They are perfect examples of what Malcolm X meant when he said they make the innocent guilty and the guilty innocent. That's what I heard, at least.	I truly do believe that the media holds tremendous power in current culture. Newspapers, magazines, television and radio are incredibly influential in the United States and examples in justice, popular culture and even sports can be found everywhere. In my opinion, people no longer think for themselves. They let the media do it for them and this can result in a great deal of confusion over what the truth actually is. For example, look at what happened with O.J. Simpson and Scott Peterson. Both were deemed guilty by the general public long before the judge delivered a sentence. This was because of the media's coverage of the crimes, arrests and the trials that followed.

What are the main differences you see between these examples? The vague words have been replaced, the examples have been expanded, repetition is deleted and useless sentences like "That's what I heard, at least" have been eliminated. The thesis statement is clear and it directs where the rest of the essay will go. Let's tackle the rest of it now:

ORIGINAL VERSION	**REWRITE**
If the magazines say a fashion is hot, then people wear it. Even if they don't like how it looks on them. Then, another magazine will say the fashion is not hot, so people stop wearing it. That is just stupid.	Another example can be found in popular magazines and tabloids. If a specific fashion is suddenly the new trend, then people wear it. When another article warns people that the style is now "so five minutes ago," people quit wearing it. They do this regardless of whether the style is flattering or comfortable. That seems ridiculous to me.
I recently read a magazine article in Sports Illustrated about a football player who was accused of taking steroids and other drugs. Later they found it was not true but it was too late. His career was over. I thought that was just terrible.	The media has also influenced the sports world. I recently read an article in Sports Illustrated which told of a football player who had been accused of using steroids and other drugs. Later, it was clear that these were false allegations, but by then it was too late. His career was ruined. I felt that was terribly unfair.
So yes, I must agree that the media has great power in today's culture. It truly does control the minds of the people. Malcolm X definitely knew what he was talking about.	I do believe that the media has too much influence on people's actions and thoughts today. It seems to touch every area from what we wear to how we judge another person. In my opinion, that is tragic.

As you read through the rewritten version, does the point of view seem stronger now? It also sounds more like the student's honest opinion, with clear support, than just a repeat of the prompt and lots of double spacing to fill up those 46 lines.

ESSAY #20

Everyone follows some kind of pathway in life. Poet Robert Frost once wrote, "Two roads diverged in a wood and I—I took the one less traveled by, and that has made all the difference." A related proverb says, "Do not go where the path may lead, go instead where there is no path and leave a trail."

Assignment: Which pathway do you believe is the best to follow? Is it the one where others go, or a distinct and undiscovered one? What makes the difference for you? Plan and write an essay in which you develop your point of view on the issue. Support your position with reasoning and examples taken from your reading, studies, experience or observations.

The point of view is stated clearly and right on topic with the assignment.

(1) People my age almost obliviously and obsessively follow the most traveled path. It seems to be hardwired into teenagers' brains that fitting in is paramount, regardless of personal preferences, interests or leanings. Following that common pathway, however, is a big mistake in my opinion. By doing so, we betray our own individuality.

Look at the words in paragraphs 2-4 that the student uses to maintain the path analogy: footprints, directions, detours and trails.

(2) When people blindly walk in the footsteps of others, as so many people my age tend to do, then they forget how to listen to their own opinions. Suddenly, they stop choosing what clothes to wear, what words to say, what attitudes to carry and what friends to have until they make sure they are all the "right" choices. Unfortunately, "right" in this case does not imply what each individual believes is best, but what the "in crowd" determines to be best. I have seen this happen repeatedly throughout my years in high school. Each time, I am further disappointed in my generation.

(3) Forging your own path is never the easy choice, but to me, it is the wisest one. By creating a path where none existed before, you get the chance to explore and discover things that no one else has had the chance to yet. Instead of listening to other's directions of where and when to turn, you can take your own detours, never knowing what treasure waits around the next corner.

(4) All of my life, I have fought for the right to forge my own trails. Being the only one on the route can sometimes be quite lonely, but I also get the unique opportunity to get to know myself better within the silence. Every now and then, something amazing happens. I look up and find, to my delight, another traveler running adjacent to my pathway. Those people often become my dearest friends or at least play a pivotal role in my life.

Here is a direct tie to the quote and the assignment.

(5) Robert Frost was a wise man to realize that the road less traveled is the better one. I hope that I can follow his philosophy closely and conversely, honor him by never following in his exact footsteps.

DONE WELL	NEEDS WORK
1. thesis statement is stated right at the beginning of the essay and directly relates to the prompt	
2. stays completely on topic throughout the essay and maintains pathway metaphor	
3. uses strong examples and vocabulary	
4. conclusion ties directly to the quote and helps sum up the major points made	
Overall score: 6	**Word count: 346**

What can I say about this essay other than imitate it? Give it your full attention! It is one of those rare excellent essays that earned a perfect score. Look to see what is done well because that is the best way to learn how to do it yourself.

ESSAY #21

Martha Washington, mother to President George Washington, once stated, "I am still determined to be cheerful and happy, in whatever situation I may be; for I have also learned from experience that the greater part of our happiness or misery depends upon our dispositions, and not upon our circumstances."

Assignment: Do you believe that our happiness or unhappiness primarily depends upon our mind set, rather than the circumstances that surround us? Plan and write an essay in which you develop your point of view on the issue. Support your position with reasoning and examples taken from your reading, studies, experience or observations.

The student has a thesis statement that gives his point of view, but it is the same as the writing prompt.

(1) I do agree that a person's happiness depends on his mind set and not on the circumstances surrounding us. I think that is an important idea. Martha Washington was right, although I always thought she was George's wife, not his mother. Anyway, what she said was true. Your mood is usually a decision rather than a reaction to something around you.

There are a number of fragments here, plus the student is starting to go off topic.

(2) I am happy most of the time but then certain things get me down. Like my parents or my little sister. Sometimes my friends and usually school. I get through it okay though. I spent a lot of time reading. I like listening to my music too. Recently I have been taking guitar lessons so that I can learn to make my own music. That will be cool.

The student is trying to figure out how to conclude the essay. He is already out of things to say.

(3) After thinking about it, I believe that my mood is too influenced by others. I don't know if that is a good thing or not. Maybe I could learn something from Martha Washington. I think I will make a concentrated effort to work on ignoring the things around me even more now that I have given it some thought.

DONE WELL	NEEDS WORK
1. does take a stance on the topic	1. thesis statement is word for word the same as the writing prompt
	2. essay is far too short and uses slang terms
	3. no examples are developed to support the thesis statement
	4. shifts from one person to another
Overall score: 1	**Word count: 188**

What did you feel that you learned about this student after reading this essay? Did you get some kind of insight into the writer's assessment of happiness and how he believes people find it? Not really. It is too muddled. This one will take some major rewriting and even then, it will not rise to a score much more than a 2 or a 3–tops.

ORIGINAL VERSION	REWRITE
I do agree that a person's happiness depends on his mind set and not on the circumstances surrounding us. I think that is an important idea. Martha Washington was right, although I always thought she was George's wife, not his mother. Anyway, what she said was true. Your mood is usually a decision rather than a reaction to something around you.	I agree that an individual's state of mind depends more on attitude than environment, as Martha Washington stated. It makes sense to me that my mood is more a decision that I make rather than a reaction to what is going on around me.

Is this better? Some. It's still far from brilliant but there is not much to work with here. Let's wrap it up.

ORIGINAL VERSION	REWRITE
I am happy most of the time but then certain things get me down. Like my parents or my little sister. Sometimes my friends and usually school. I get through it okay though. I spent a lot of time reading. I like listening to my music too. Recently I have been taking guitar lessons so that I can learn to make my own music. That will be cool. After thinking about it, I believe that my mood is too influenced by others. I don't know if that is a good thing or not. Maybe I could learn something from Martha Washington. I think I will make a concentrated effort to work on ignoring the things around me even more now that I have given it some thought.	Although I tend to be happy most of the time, there are things that depress me. Sometimes I don't get along with my parents, my little sister or my friends. Now and then, school makes me unhappy too. I cope with it all, however, by spending time reading and listening to music. I realize that my mood is influenced by others, so perhaps I should pay closer attention to what Martha Washington once said. As she reminded us all, the key is in choosing to be happy rather than letting others make that choice for us.

It's not brilliant, but at least it makes more sense and stays on topic far better. Can you think of some other ways the student could have addressed this question? Perhaps he could have told of a time in his life where a conscious decision to remain happy, calm or amused was made, despite surroundings that might have influenced him to react otherwise. What other ideas can you come up with? What was your initial response to the quote when you first read it? I am sure you are getting better and better at creating a solid response in your head–something this student obviously did NOT do.

ESSAY #22

Antoine de Saint-Exupery, author of *The Little Prince*, once wrote, "If you want to build a boat, do not drum up people to collect wood or assign them tasks or work but rather teach them to long for the endless immensity of the sea."

Assignment: What do you believe is the best way to motivate people to get something accomplished? Plan and write an essay in which you develop your point of view on the issue. Support your position with reasoning and examples taken from your reading, studies, experience or observations.

The student's point of view is very clear and strong in this essay. You can tell quickly that he is talking from personal experience.

(1) Motivating people is challenging. Just ask any boss or manager. Although a few people may be motivated by money or other rewards, that is not very dependable. The best person to have for a job is someone who is self-motivated, who does a job because that is simply the right thing to do. That kind of person can be very hard to find. I know! I know because my family has their own business and I have watched my father struggle to find competent and reliable employees year after year.

Here the student refers back directly to the quote and ties it in with what he is writing. That makes the essay stronger.

"You know what I mean?" needs to be omitted. It fills up space but has no substance.

(2) I believe there is only one way to show employees the importance of motivation. As the quote states above, if you want people to build a boat, you have to demonstrate a good reason for them to do so. They have to realize that by learning a skill, their lives will be better for it in some way. A simple paycheck is not enough to do that. It is too common and can be found at almost any job. You know what I mean? With this example, those that learn to build a boat will then be able to explore the endless mystery of the sea. For the employer, this means that he has to find a way to motivate his employees such that they see the benefits of it.

This paragraph needs more expansion. The conclusion came too soon and too abruptly, as if the student tired of writing and just stopped.

(3) With my family business, my father has done this with some of his employees. It does not work for all of them, of course. Just a few. Those employees are his best ones. Besides offering them insurance and stuff, my dad also tracks how much each person sells. He does this on his computer. For every percentage of sales above average each employee does, he turns it into days of paid vacation. The better they become at sales, the more time they get to spend with their families. This gives them a reason to do better; they see the perks. Now doesn't that make a lot of sense? That is what motivation is all about.

DONE WELL	NEEDS WORK
1. clear statement of the student's point of view	1. vague terms like "stuff"
2. relevant personal experience examples	2. asking the reader unnecessary questions
3. good use of vocabulary in several areas	3. ending feels too abrupt and not thought out
	4. rather short; could have used more details
Overall score: 4	**Word count: 335**

To me, this essay was like a great book with a lousy ending. It started out wonderfully. It had a clear thesis statement and good examples to back up the point of view. However, about two-thirds of the way through it, it felt like the student gave up and just tried to finish it quickly. Perhaps he was down to the last minute and was in a panic. Whatever the reason, it made what could easily have been a 5 point essay drop down to a 4.

ESSAY #23

President Dwight D. Eisenhower once said, "Don't join the book burners. Don't think that you are going to conceal thoughts by concealing evidence that they ever existed."

Assignment: Do you think censorship protects or deprives the public from ideas? Plan and write an essay in which you develop your point of view on the issue. Support your position with reasoning and examples taken from your reading, studies, experience or observations.

The thesis statement comes at the end of the first paragraph, but it is there and it is clear.

(1) Censorship is wrong. It really is. How can someone else tell me what I should or should not read or watch? That is my decision alone. Like the president said, getting rid of the material or not letting someone see it will not make it disappear. In fact, in my opinion, I think that censorship violates one of the human rights like they talked about in the Constitution. I think it is the one they call Freedom of Speech. <u>It definitely deprives the public of important ideas.</u>

A number of spelling and grammatical errors make this paragraph harder to understand.

(2) Every year, a list of the most censored books comes out. These are the books that many schools or teachers have not been allowed to share with students. Somehow the ideas in them are supposed to be bad for us or something. How can an idea be bad? Isn't it what you do with the idea? I was lucky tho. I had a really cool English teacher last year. She brought the list. Handed it out to us. Told us to look it over carefully and to never, ever, under any circumstances, read a single one of them. Then she did something neat. She winked at us. We new right away she meant we should read them.

Slang and misspelled words get in the way and impede the essay's flow.

(3) I was amazed at what was on the list. Classics like *Tom Sawyer* and *Huck Finn* by Mark Twain. How could classics be on the banned list? *Harry Potter* was on their to and that really ticked me off. Those books are the best ones to come out in like forever. I have read all of them at least twice. My favorite character is Professor Snape. I still cannot figure out whether he is a good guy or a bad guy.

(4) When one person decides what is right to see or read for another person, then something is wrong with this world. It should be up to the individual to choose. I firmly am against censorship. After all, if it was put into place, maybe you wouldn't be able to read an essay such as mine speaking out against it! That would be crummy.

DONE WELL	NEEDS WORK
1. thesis statement takes a stance on the issue	1. slang terms that should be replaced with better vocabulary words
2. a good example (experience with English teacher)	2. third paragraph completely loses focus on the topic
	3. misspelled words and grammar errors make the essay harder to comprehend
	4. conclusion needs to be stronger
Overall score: 2	**Word count: 348**

This one had potential but the student got lost along the way. In the third paragraph she stopped focusing on the idea of whether censorship is right or wrong and instead dwelled on whether Professor Snape is a good guy or bad guy in the Harry Potter books. (Gotta admit, I'm trying to figure that one out too.) Losing focus and veering off topic were contributing factors in the essay's low score. Let's see if we can bump that number up a bit.

ORIGINAL VERSION	REWRITE
Censorship is wrong. It really is. How can someone else tell me what I should or should not read or watch? That is my decision alone. Like the president said, getting rid of the material or not letting someone see it will not make it disappear. In fact, in my opinion, I think that censorship violates one of the human rights like they talked about in the Constitution. I think it is the one they call Freedom of Speech. It definitely deprives the public of important ideas.	Censorship is wrong and it definitely deprives the public of important ideas. How can anyone presume to tell me what I should or should not read or watch? That is my decision. As President Eisenhower said, destroying ideas will not make them disappear. They will live on in people's minds. In my opinion, censorship is actually a violation of the Constitution's Freedom of Speech.

Every year, a list of the most censored books comes out. These are the books that many schools or teachers have not been allowed to share with students. Somehow the ideas in them are supposed to be bad for us or something. How can an idea be bad? Isn't it what you do with the idea? I was lucky tho. I had a really cool English teacher last year. She brought the list. Handed it out to us. Told us to look it over carefully and to never, ever, under any circumstances, read a single one of them. Then she did something neat. She winked at us. We new right away she meant we should read them.	Several years ago I found out that that a list of censored books is issued annually. These are the books that teachers and schools are not allowed to use in the classroom. Supposedly the ideas found in them are dangerous for students to know. I don't understand how an idea can be dangerous; it is what you do with the idea that makes the difference. I was fortunate that I had an English teacher who was also strongly against censorship. When the annual list was published, she made copies and gave each student one. Then, she instructed us to look it over carefully and never, ever read a single title on it; but as she said it, she winked. We knew immediately that that meant we should read all of them!

Do you see how some sentences were blended together while others were completely eliminated? Sentence variety is important. It makes the essay less choppy. Study those examples to see how it is done. You can do it too!

ORIGINAL VERSION	REWRITE
I was amazed at what was on the list. Classics like <u>Tom Sawyer</u> and <u>Huck Finn</u> by Mark Twain. How could classics be on the banned list? <u>Harry Potter</u> was on their to and that really ticked me off. Those books are the best ones to come out in like forever. I have read all of them at least twice. My favorite character is Professor Snape. I still cannot figure out whether he is a good guy or a bad guy.	I was amazed at what books I found on that list of banned books. <u>Tom Sawyer</u> and <u>Huck Finn</u> were there. I never expected to see classics on the list! The <u>Harry Potter</u> series was on it too and that really irritated me. I believe that those books are the best ones to be published in years. They have interested more kids in reading than any other books I know.

When one person decides what is right to see or read for another person, then something is wrong with this world. It should be up to the individual to choose. I firmly am against censorship. After all, if it was put into place, maybe you wouldn't be able to read an essay such as mine speaking out against it! That would be crummy.	When one person has the right to decide what is okay for another person to read or watch, then something is terribly wrong in this culture. It should be an individual decision. After all, if censorship were commonplace, you might not be allowed to read an essay like mine that speaks out against it!

The off-topic information was removed and a few points were expanded. Keeping the unique comment in the conclusion gave the ending an interesting twist and remained right on topic at the same time.

ESSAY #24

Winston Churchill was reported to say, "The optimist sees opportunity in every danger; the pessimist sees danger in every opportunity." On the other hand, author James Branch Cabell says, "The optimist proclaims that we live in the best of all possible worlds; and the pessimist fears this is true."

Assignment: Do you consider yourself an optimist or a pessimist? How does it affect how you look at life on a daily basis? Plan and write an essay in which you develop your point of view on the issue. Support your position with reasoning and examples taken from your reading, studies, experience or observations.

The student does point out that she is basically an optimist.

(1) The optimist looks on the happy side. Other people don't. They see the bad parts of life. I think I am a little of both. I see the great parts but the lousy parts are still there too.

She uses a number of vague words in the essay like "good" and "a lot."

(2) Every day, I try to think only about the best parts of the day. Maybe I did good on a test. Maybe my boyfriend told me I looked really good. He likes it a lot when I wear that baby blue shirt with the big red heart on it. Of course, sometimes things happen that make it hard to think happy.

This is definitely veering off topic here.

(3) That happened the other day. It was crappy. My best friend was mad at me. She said I copied off of her math homework and I didn't. I was just seeing if I had the right answers or not. We had a big fight in the cafeteria. She called me some nasty names that I can't write here. It was really embarrassing. It was hard for me to look on the bright side then, I can tell you.

The student is trying to bring in an example from current events, but it is so vague that it is confusing.

(4) Sometimes life makes it really hard to be happy. I mean, look at those people in New Orleans. Some of them lost everything they had. Families were separated. It was terrible. How can you look on the bright side then?

(5) I do think it is important to be an optimist. I want to live in the best of all possible worlds. But then, doesn't everyone?

DONE WELL	NEEDS WORK
1. does state point of view	1. slang and misspelled words
	2. vague terms
	3. veers off topic half way through the essay
	4. weak examples and too short
Overall score: 1	**Word count: 241**

I imagine you knew by the second paragraph that this was one essay that needed help. The intention is there, but the student cannot seem to maintain any kind of organized thought.

ORIGINAL VERSION	REWRITE
The optimist looks on the happy side. Other people don't. They see the bad parts of life. I think I am a little of both. I see the great parts but the lousy parts are still there too. Every day, I try to think only about the best parts of the day. Maybe I did good on a test. Maybe my boyfriend told me I looked really good. He likes it a lot when I wear that baby blue shirt with the big red heart on it. Of course, sometimes things happen that make it hard to think happy.	The optimist is clearly someone who manages to look on the positive side of things, while a pessimist focuses on the opposite qualities of life. A pessimist certainly sees the glass half empty, rather than half full. I tend to focus on the happier moments of life, but I always remember that the sad moments are a part of life also. Everyday, I work to concentrate on what has gone well. Perhaps I have earned a good grade on a test or my boyfriend compliments me. Other days, finding those high points is more difficult.

Things look a little better now, but the essay still has a long way to go. Let's take a look at the last half of it.

ORIGINAL VERSION	REWRITE
That happened the other day. It was crappy. My best friend was mad at me. She said I copied off of her math homework and I didn't. I was just seeing if I had the right answers or not. We had a big fight in the cafeteria. She called me some nasty names that I can't write here. It was really embarrassing. It was hard for me to look on the bright side then, I can tell you.	For example, the other day was really difficult and I had a hard time maintaining an optimistic attitude. My best friend was upset with me because she felt I had copied some of her homework. Actually, I was just comparing our answers to see if I had done the problems correctly. She did not believe me and we had a big fight in the cafeteria. It was embarrassing and I struggled to find a positive way to view the situation.

Sometimes life makes it really hard to be happy. I mean, look at those people in New Orleans. Some of them lost everything they had. Families were separated. It was terrible. How can you look on the bright side then? I do think it is important to be an optimist. I want to live in the best of all possible worlds. But then, doesn't everyone?	Another example of people working hard to find hope in trying circumstances can be found in New Orleans. So many people there have had their lives disrupted and devastated due to the power of Hurricane Katrina. They have lost their homes, all of their belongings and even their families! I certainly do feel that it is important to remain an optimist whenever possible. It helps to think that we are, as the quote says, living in the best possible world.

Better? You bet…and I'm not just being optimistic.

ESSAY #25

Sir Walter Scott once stated, "He that climbs the tall tree has won the right to the fruit."

Assignment: Do you agree or disagree with this metaphor that the fruit belongs to those that climb the tree, or should the fruit be freely given to everyone? Plan and write an essay in which you develop your point of view on the issue. Support your position with reasoning and examples taken from your reading, studies, experience or observations.

(1) I do believe that the person who puts out the effort is that one that deserves to enjoy the results of that effort.

The thesis statement is clear and shows the point of view. It should be expanded, however, since paragraphs should be at least three sentences long.

(2) The man or woman who accumulates money to buy a rundown house and, through their own efforts, improve this property and sell it for a profit, deserves to enjoy it. No one else has any "right" to a share of it, in my opinion.

(3) In the story, "The Ants and the Grasshopper," for example, the ants all work hard, while the grasshopper gives no work or life energy, so he deserves nothing.

The student has three examples to back up his point. One is a current example, one is literary and the other is personal. All three directly relate to the writing prompt.

(4) I mow lawns in the summer time while my friends are goofing off. Later, I have money in my pockets. I can buy things I want while my friends look at me with envy. I earned it and my friends did not and have no right to enjoy it.

(5) Some think that the people who have wealth <u>should</u> share it, thinking that there is some kind of natural or moral law that says they have a right to the share. Answer? No! A person who has more may choose to share the wealth but is under no obligation to do so.

(6) Some think the government should tax the wealthy to give to the poor but this is only another example of saying that they have the right to the fruit of someone else's labors.

(7) If those who put out the effort find that more and more of their reward is taken and given to someone who didn't earn it, much of their incentive will disappear.

Here the student refers back to his original point of view and the writing prompt. It needs another sentence to make the conclusion complete, however.

DONE WELL	NEEDS WORK
1. thesis statement takes a stance on the issue	1. sentences are too short, as are the paragraphs
2. several good examples to strengthen the main point of the essay	2. paragraphs are underdeveloped
	3. far too short, needs more expansion on ideas presented
	4. conclusion needs to be longer and more detailed
Overall score: 3	**Word count: 260**

This essay has potential. The examples are relevant and illustrate the student's point of view. However, he sped through his arguments and did not take enough time to develop his paragraphs. By fleshing out the writing with more details, this essay could have earned a 4 and possibly a 5. Let's see what we can add to it.

ORIGINAL VERSION	REWRITE
I do believe that the person who puts out the effort is the one that deserves to enjoy the results of that effort. The man or woman who accumulates money to buy a rundown house and, through their own efforts, improve this property and sell it for a profit, deserves to enjoy it. No one else has any "right" to a share of it, in my opinion. In the story, "The Ants and the Grasshopper," for example, the ants all work hard, while the grasshopper gives no work or life energy, so he deserves nothing.	I do believe that the person who puts forth the effort to achieve is the one that deserves to enjoy the result of his work. While some may think that selfish or unfair, it is not. For example, the man or woman who accumulates enough money to purchase a rundown house and, through their efforts, improve it and sell it for a profit, deserve to enjoy what they have accomplished. No one else has any right to a share of it, in my personal opinion. Another example is the old children's story, "The Ants and the Grasshopper." In this tale, the ants work hard all summer to prepare for winter, while the lazy grasshopper simply watches. He offers nothing: no work, no life energy. When cold weather arrives, he finds himself in trouble. Despite his hardship, he deserves what he contributed—nothing.

You can see that I kept all of the student's examples but developed them so that the essay is longer and the points are easier to relate to the thesis statement. Let's do that with the rest of the essay and see how it turns out.

ORIGINAL VERSION	REWRITE
I mow lawns in the summer time while my friends are goofing off. Later, I have money in my pockets. I can buy things I want while my friends look at me with envy. I earned it and my friends did not and have no right to enjoy it. Some think that the people who have wealth should share it, thinking that there is some kind of natural or moral law that says they have a right to the share. Answer? No! A person who has more may choose to share the wealth but is under no obligation to do so. Some think the government should tax the wealthy to give to the poor but this is only another example of saying that they have the right to the fruit of someone else's labors. If those who put out the effort find that more and more of their reward is taken and given to someone who didn't earn it, much of their incentive will disappear.	I have strong opinions on job issues that are effort related because I have won the right to the fruit of my own labor. I mow lawns every summer while the rest of my friends are relaxing and having fun. After I work hard, I have money in my pockets which allows me to buy the things I want. My friends envy me, but I earned it, not them, so it is not their right to enjoy it. Some people think that the wealthy should share their money with those that are not. It is as if they believe there is a natural or moral law that demands it. My answer to that is NO. A person who has more may certainly choose to share it but is under no obligation to do so. Some politicians support legislation that would cause the government to tax the wealthy in order to share with the poor. I do not agree; this is only another example of people having the right to the fruit of someone else's labors. Such laws seem completely unfair. If those who actually put forth the effort to succeed discover that more and more of their rewards are being given to those who did not earn it, much of their incentive is bound to disappear. Why wouldn't it? The motivation to achieve is gone; the point of the climb is irrelevant because the fruit is almost gone.

Now the essay is much longer and each point is the same but expanded and developed. It has good organization with solid examples and would likely earn at least a four.

ESSAY #26

Scientist Charles Darwin once stated, "It is not the strongest of the species that survive, nor the most intelligent but the one most responsive to change."

Assignment: What do you think is the key to survival for mankind? Is it strength or intelligence, or is it as Darwin said, the ability to cope with change? Or is it something completely different? Plan and write an essay in which you develop your point of view on the issue. Support your position with reasoning and examples taken from your reading, studies, experience or observations.

(1) Charles Darwin spent his life attempting to discover exactly what determined both the survival of the human species, as well as its origins. In fact, his name is synonymous with the then ground breaking concept of evolution. He spent almost all of his life studying numerous kinds of plants and animals to see how they changed over long periods of time. His results set the world afire with a brand new paradigm of thought. After he published his research, the world would never again be the same.

(2) Darwin's ideas were not popular at the time that he presented them and oddly enough, they are not all that popular today either. The concepts behind it are at direct odds with the philosophy that the human race, as well as everything else on the planet, was created by God. This particular theory is referred to as creation science, although evolutionists, as Darwin's followers are called, do not truly consider it any type of science.

(3) The constant argument between the creationists and the evolutionists has been ongoing for years and will not likely be settled any time soon either. People on both sides of the fence are equally passionate and can argue persuasively and powerfully. The topic never quite fades away from interest either. Multiple books promoting each point of view are published regularly; debates are held in auditoriums and broadcast across many radio stations. They have even entered the courtroom on more than one occasion as schools fought bitterly over whether creation or evolution should be taught to students in textbooks or the classroom.

(4) Darwin would probably be surprised and flattered that his controversial ideas created such a domino effect of interest in the science world, even all of these years after his death. His perspectives on the origins and survival of life on earth were not only unique but truly intriguing and unexpectedly divisive.

So what score do you think this essay should get? It's well thought out, has excellent sentence variety and extraordinary vocabulary. There are no grammar errors, the words are all spelled correctly and the information is even historically correct. What do you think? A 5? Maybe even the much coveted 6? Well, would you believe that the author of this very intelligently written essay would walk away with a zero? Yup, that big, fat old zero. I bet that by now you know why too…you got it! It is completely and utterly OFF TOPIC. It tells you all about Darwin and the controversy his research has created but never once does it address the assignment: *what is the key to survival for mankind? Is it intelligence, strength or the ability to cope with change?* If I were the scorer, I would be distraught (probably pacing around the room and calling up a friend to vent for awhile) giving such a wonderfully written essay a zero, but I would be compelled to do it because those are the rules. If the essay is off topic, the score is ZIP. Please remember that.

ESSAY #27

Writer and humorist Bill Vaughan once stated, "Suburbia is where the developer bull dozes out the trees then names the streets after them."

Assignment: What is Mr. Vaughan trying to say about what suburbia actually is in this country? Do you agree or disagree with his witty comment? Plan and write an essay in which you develop your point of view on the issue. Support your position with reasoning and examples taken from your reading, studies, experience or observations.

This is the student's viewpoint on what the quote meant for him. It includes some strong vocabulary.

(1) I believe that Mr. Vaughan is saying that suburbia is a facsimile, a pale representation of the real world. The people who move into this environment think this is what the real world is like, not knowing what the world was like before.

(2) Before development, the area may have been rich with different plants. There may have been any variety of trees, young seedlings, rotting logs and stumps. Native Americans may have rested, hunted and lived under those trees. Many kinds of animals may have lived under these trees. Who know how many creatures passed through? Some of these trees may have been many hundreds of years old.

(3) The very land itself is usually changed with time. Hills are leveled; low areas are filled; ponds are drained for more land to be developed; sewers, drains, and pipes are buried and wires are strung. Land is divided and subdivided. Each lot looks like another. Often even the houses are indistinguishable, one from another.

This paragraph has a good point, but it needs to be expanded with additional detail.

(4) The developer has taken a natural area, one that has likely changed little in thousands or even millions of years and in months has changed it so that it looks similar to most any of endless suburbs throughout the country.

(5) What was once a thing of beauty is now where people may eat, sleep and raise families, but it is a pale existence. As Melanie once sang in a popular song, "Pave paradise; put up a parking lot."

DONE WELL	NEEDS WORK
1. thesis statement takes a clear stance on the issue	1. introduction needs to be expanded so the point of view is stronger and easier to understand
2. some good use of vocabulary	2. needs reorganization to make each example stronger
	3. conclusion has a relevant quote but it needs more information to support it
	4. too short so needs additional detail to flesh out the ideas
Overall score: 3	**Word count: 240**

Like the last essay, this one has potential. You can tell that the student is passionate about the topic. The key to making this good essay an outstanding one is expanding it, adding details and making each example stronger. As it is (about 240 words), the essay is short and many lines will be empty. Let's work on filling them up a little bit more.

ORIGINAL VERSION	REWRITE
I believe that Mr. Vaughan is saying that suburbia is a facsimile, a pale representation of the real world. The people who move into this environment think this is what the real world is like, not knowing what the world was like before. Before development, the area may have been rich with different plants. There may have been any variety of trees, young seedlings, rotting logs and stumps. Native Americans may have rested, hunted and lived under those trees. Many kinds of animals may have lived under these trees. Who know how many creatures passed through? Some of these trees may have been many hundreds of years old.	I believe that Mr. Vaughan was saying that suburbia is actually a facsimile, or a pale representation of the real world. Like him, I think that most people living in today's environment have no idea what the world used to be like. Before the majority of this country's land was developed, much of it was rich with different plants. There were a variety of trees, from young seedlings to rotting logs and stumps. Some were hundreds of years old. Native Americans and animals may well have rested, hunted and lived under some of these trees. Who knows how many different creatures passed through the forests or fields in which they grew!

What do you think of the changes I made? We lost some words, which is a problem, but it reads more smoothly and the points are clearer.

ORIGINAL VERSION	REWRITE
The very land itself is usually changed with time. Hills are leveled; low areas are filled; ponds are drained for more land to be developed; sewers, drains, and pipes are buried and wires are strung. Land is divided and subdivided. Each lot looks like another. Often even the houses are indistinguishable, one from another. The developer has taken a natural area, one that has likely changed little in thousands or even millions of years and in months has changed it so that it looks similar to most any of endless suburbs throughout the country. What was once a thing of beauty is now where people may eat, sleep and raise families, but it is a pale existence. As Melanie once sang in a popular song, "Pave paradise; put up a parking lot."	Time brought countless changes to the land. Nature was pushed out as mankind took control of all the wide open spaces. Hills were leveled; low areas filled; ponds drained; sewers, drains and pipes buried and wires strung. The large land lots were divided and subdivided. After a while, one lot looked just like the other. Individuality disappeared. Houses were built and within a few years, they were also indistinguishable one from another. Developers of all kinds took natural areas that were virtually unchanged over the course of thousands, or even millions, of years and in a matter of months, turned it into something that looked like any of the other endless suburbs throughout the country. In my opinion, this destroyed pure beauty and replaced it with modern ugliness. As the popular music artist Melanie once sang in a song from the 1970s, people tend to "Pave paradise; put up a parking lot." What was once a thing of splendor is now where people may indeed eat, sleep, raise their families—or park their cars—but in comparison, it is a truly pale existence. It is a clear facsimile of what once was and will never exist again.

This is better–most likely a score of 4 and with some more work, a 5. The student needed to give more thought to each point, adding details to fill out the essay. Now it is closer to the ideal word count; from 240 to a little over 300. The conclusion is also much stronger after revision because it relates back to the original quote and ties in the example just mentioned (the song lyrics).

ESSAY #28

Some of the most brilliant men in the world had to fail multiple times before they succeeded. Albert Einstein said, "Anyone who has never made a mistake has never tried anything new," while Thomas Edison said, "I have not failed. I've just found 10,000 ways that won't work."

Assignment: What do you think mistakes teach us? What is the primary lesson of failure? Plan and write an essay in which you develop your point of view on the issue. Support your position with reasoning and examples taken from your reading, studies, experience or observations.

The point of view is here but lost in the confusion of the paragraph.

(1) Everyone makes mistakes. It is part of being a human. You make them all the time. They are not any fun. If I really try though, I can learn from them. I think that's the lesson maybe.

This is the first example and it is a relevant one. There is little to no sentence variety.

(2) This one time, I made the mistake of telling a secret. I shouldn't have done it. It hurt my friend. She didn't like me anymore. Not friends at all now. I still miss her. You learn not to tell secrets.

Both of these paragraphs have relevant examples but they are lost amid fragments and misspellings.

(3) Then once, when I was at camp, I took something from the cabin. It was not mine. The whole camp got in trouble. We could not go on the horse riding trip we were supposed to go on. It was the main reeson I had gone to camp in the first place. That was a lousy lesson.

(4) Just last week, I learned this hard lesson again. I told my parents I would take care of my younger brother and then I forgot. I hung out with friends instead. By the time I got home, my brother had been home alone for two hours. He was upset. It had been scary. I felt rotten. So much for being a good big sister.

(5) Mistakes are awful. But I learned good things from them. Trust and honor and risponsibility. Good stuff. That's the lesson.

DONE WELL	NEEDS WORK
1. thesis statement is clear and relates directly to the writing prompt	1. switching between first and third person
2. uses three relevant examples for support	2. multiple misspellings and slang terms
	3. little sentence variety
	4. too short so needs additional detail to flesh out the ideas
Overall score: 2	**Word count: 218**

This student has good intentions and has pinpointed the answer to the writing prompts. However, there are so many other errors that you lose sight of that quickly.

ORIGINAL VERSION	REWRITE
Everyone makes mistakes. It is part of being a human. You make them all the time. They are not any fun. <u>If I really try though, I can learn from them. I think that's the lesson maybe.</u> This one time, I made the mistake of telling a secret. I shouldn't have done it. It hurt my friend. She didn't like me anymore. Not friends at all now. I still miss her. You learn not to tell secrets.	I believe that everyone makes mistakes because it is simply a part of being human. As the old saying goes, "To err is human; to forgive divine." Mistakes are rarely fun but they can often contain a lesson. If I can learn from failure, it makes the mistake more valuable. Once, I made the mistake of telling one of my friend's secrets. I should never have done it. It hurt my friend's feelings and it eventually ended our friendship because she no longer trusted me. I miss her and I have since learned the importance of keeping a secret.

This is much better. Ideas are tied together in a more organized manner and a saying was added to give support to the thesis statement.

ORIGINAL VERSION	REWRITE
Then once, when I was at camp, I took something from the cabin. It was not mine. The whole camp got in trouble. We could not go on the horse riding trip we were supposed to go on. It was the main reeson I had gone to camp in the first place. That was a lousy lesson.	Another example happened at camp. I stole something from one of the cabins. The entire camp was punished for it, and the horse riding trip was cancelled. The horse riding excursion was the main reason I had gone to this camp and I was incredibly disappointed. I also felt guilty because others were punished for what I did. It was a hard lesson.

Just last week, I learned this hard lesson again. I told my parents I would take care of my younger brother and then I forgot. I hung out with friends instead. By the time I got home, my brother had been home alone for two hours. He was upset. It had been scary. I felt rotten. So much for being a good big sister. Mistakes are awful. But I learned good things from them. Trust and honor and risponsibility. Good stuff. That's the lesson.	I made yet another big mistake last week. I told my parents that I would take care of my younger brother while they were gone for the evening and I forgot because I was out with my friends. By the time I got home, my brother had been home alone for almost two hours and he was quite upset. He was frightened and I felt absolutely terrible. I certainly was not a good sister that day. Mistakes are awful but they usually contain important lessons like trust, honor and responsibility. If I can just remember my past mistakes and failures, I am sure to not repeat them in the future.

This is a much stronger essay and the examples are easier to understand. Misspelled words, grammar errors, vague examples and slang have all been removed. Aren't you impressed?

ESSAY #29

Nelson Mandela once wrote, "There is nothing like returning to a place that remains unchanged to find the ways in which you yourself have altered."

Assignment: As time passes, things change. Do you believe the most changes are in your environment or within yourself? Plan and write an essay in which you develop your point of view on the issue. Support your position with reasoning and examples taken from your reading, studies, experience or observations.

The thesis statement is clear on the author's point of view. The student switches from first to third person here.

(1) I think that Nelson Mandela was right but I only realized it in the last few months of my life. Although you change with each passing day, it happens slowly so most of us do not even notice it. We change on the outside. We change on the inside too. We do it far more than any of the places we visit too.

These are strong and relevant examples to support the student's opinions. (Paragraphs 2-3)

(2) When I started my senior year in high school, I decided to go back and visit some of my junior high teachers. I missed some of them. I was shocked when I got there. It was so small. It really was. The hallways, classrooms and desks seemed tiny. I thought they must have shrunk. They didn't. I guess I just grew.

(3) It was the same last summer when my parents and I went back to visit the town I had lived in when I was only six years old. Now I know what the old saying, "You can't go home again" means. The whole town seemed different to me. It was as if I was seeing it through new eyes. It was definitely smaller. It was boring. Some of the places I had liked the best now seemed kind of silly. My relatives that still lived there seemed smaller than I remembered. I guess that was also because I had grown.

The conclusion starts to fall apart and ends rather limply. It should be rewritten to make a stronger last impression.

(4) The lesson about how much I had changed was really proven to me later. A couple of old friends came to see me while I was in town. When they saw me, they said, Wow. You look so different. You have gotten so big. In fact, you really look a lot like your mother now. That was startling to hear. It is also when I really realized all of the many changes that have occurred on the outside and inside of me. The environment was the same as it always was. The contrast between the two was harsh. I am not sure I liked it. Maybe it is just part of growing up.

DONE WELL	NEEDS WORK
1. thesis statement is clear and relates directly to the writing prompt	1. switching between first and third person
2. uses three relevant examples for support	2. multiple misspellings and slang terms
3. the conclusion restates the original thesis statement and relates directly to the prompt	3. little sentence variety
	4. too short so needs additional detail to flesh out the ideas
Overall score: 4	**Word count: 337**

The student kept his focus on the writing prompt and came up with three relevant and strong examples for support. There were some usage issues, but overall this was a decent essay.

ESSAY #30

The journalist Elmer Davis once wrote, "One of the things that is wrong with America is that everybody who has done anything at all in his own field is expected to be an authority on every subject under the sun."

Assignment: Experts and authorities are highly valued by society. Do you believe that an expert in one area is unfairly expected to be an authority in a diverse number of fields? Plan and write an essay in which you develop your point of view on the issue. Support your position with reasoning and examples taken from your reading, studies, experience or observations.

(1) There is no question that an "expert" in a certain subject is a prized asset to society. <u>However, it would be a mistake and even dangerous to assume that someone accomplished in one area is therefore automatically an authority in all aspects of life.</u> Yet, such assumptions are made every day and often have disastrous results.

(2) My uncle is an accomplished surgeon and within my family is rightfully held in very high regard. However, there is a tendency for family members to expect my uncle to be an expert in areas that have nothing to do with medicine. For example, when my father was looking for investment advice he naturally turned to my uncle. My uncle gladly explained which investments were promising and which to avoid and I remember my father feeling very confident as he dutifully followed the advice. It wasn't too long before that elation turned to regret. While my uncle is indeed a skilled physician he apparently is not an investment adviser. Blindly following that advice cost by father money but it also taught him a valuable lesson about the dangers of assuming that an authority in one area is also an expert in everything.

(3) In my daily life I find that I must constantly struggle to avoid making the same mistake. It is human nature to seek out accomplished individuals and expect that their expertise extends beyond their own fields. I've found myself seeking relationship advice not from friends with stable relationships but from those who I respected for their skills on the basketball court. I've asked for computer buying tips not from someone who is a thrifty shopper but from a classmate who is a gifted computer programmer. In most of these occasions while the advice I received was well meaning it turned out to be misleading and in some cases plain wrong.

(4) None of this is to suggest that experts can only speak on their chosen fields. Instead it is us—the seekers of advice—that must be vigilant and carefully weigh what we are told. At all times we must avoid assuming that just because a person is an expert that all of his or her advice will be infallibly authoritative. No doubt that Mr. Davis, himself a respected writer, not only realized this but also experienced it as people sought him out for professional advice on areas that had nothing to do with writing.

DONE WELL	NEEDS WORK
1. clear and well written thesis statement that addresses the writing prompt	1. main point could have been strengthened with an additional example outside of personal experiences
2. good use of examples that clearly support the thesis statement	2. some repeated use of certain words and phrases
3. thoughtful conclusion that also ties back to the writing prompt	
Overall score: 5	**Word count: 399**

Overall, this is an excellent essay that advances the student's contention and does not stray from the assignment.

ESSAY PRACTICE TIME

ESSAY PRACTICE TIME

Aha! You thought you were done with this portion, didn't you? You were all ready to kick back and say, "Enough of those darn essays. After 30 of them, I feel like an expert." Well, here is your chance to prove it. You've rested long enough while I critiqued and rewrote all of these essays and heaven knows, I've worked hard.

It's time to switch roles. I'm going to sit back, put my feet up and maybe watch a few old episodes of "Friends." You pick up your pen or pencil and tackle at least one of these practice essays. (You know you should do all of them, right? I don't have to tell you, do I?) Don't worry about your time limits right now; just get familiar with the process. Work on each stage and see how you do. I know you'd rather surf the net, call a friend or even clean your room more than you want to do these practice essays, but when test day rolls around, you will be thanking me profusely (sending money, chocolate or flowers is also allowed).

Ready? Great. Have fun! (Now come on, I STILL don't hear that cheering!)

Practice Essay #1

> Singer Eddie Cantor once said, "Slow down and enjoy life. It's not only the scenery you will miss by going too fast—you also miss the sense of where you are going and why."
>
> **Assignment:** Do you agree or disagree with this statement? Will you miss something by going too fast or will your speed help you to accomplish more? Plan and write an essay in which you develop your point of view on the issue. Support your position with reasoning and examples taken from your reading, studies, experience or observations.

MAKING A DECISION

Choose one and check it:

__ I agree completely with this quote.

__ I agree with this quote but with reservations.

__ I disagree completely with this quote.

__ I disagree with this quote but with reservations.

BRAINSTORM

Use this space to quickly brainstorm a few ideas on how to approach this essay.

THESIS STATEMENT

Use these lines to write out your thesis statement.

OUTLINE

Don't worry about complete sentences or any other little details. Just fill this out with some basic thoughts or ideas.

Introduction:

Body:

Example 1:

Example 2:

Example 3:

Conclusion: ____________________

____

Okay. Those are the basics. Now it is time to actually write the essay. There are 46 lines here. Fill 'em up!

Practice Essay #2

The famous and respected scientist Albert Einstein was quoted as saying, "There are only two ways to live your life. One is though nothing is a miracle. The other is as though everything is a miracle."

Assignment: Which of these two perspectives do you think is correct? How can you live your life in such a way to make this your own philosophy? Plan and write an essay in which you develop your point of view on the issue. Support your position with reasoning and examples taken from your reading, studies, experience or observations.

MAKING A DECISION

Choose one and check it:

__ Nothing in life is a miracle.

__ Everything in life is a miracle.

__ Neither of the above but something different.

BRAINSTORM

Use this space to quickly brainstorm a few ideas on how to approach this essay.

___

___

___

THESIS STATEMENT

Use these lines to write out your thesis statement.

___

___

___

___

OUTLINE

Don't worry about complete sentences or any other little details. Just fill this out with some basic thoughts or ideas.

Introduction:

___

___

Body:

Example 1: ________________________

Example 2: ________________________

Example 3: ________________________

Conclusion: ________________________

Again, those are the basics. Now it is time to actually write the essay. There are 46 lines here. Fill 'em up!

Practice Essay #3

(Okay, sorry, but I love what this guy says, so here is another one.)

> Albert Einstein once said, "Imagination is more important than knowledge, for knowledge is limited while imagination embraces the entire world."
>
> **Assignment:** Do you agree or disagree with this statement? What do you think is more important in life: imagination or knowledge? Plan and write an essay in which you develop your point of view on the issue. Support your position with reasoning and examples taken from your reading, studies, experience or observations.

MAKING A DECISION

Choose one and check it:

__ Imagination is more important.

__ Knowledge is more important.

__ Neither of the above but something different.

BRAINSTORM

Use this space to quickly brainstorm a few ideas on how to approach this essay.

____

____

____

THESIS STATEMENT

Use these lines to write out your thesis statement.

____

____

____

____

OUTLINE

Don't worry about complete sentences or any other little details. Just fill this out with some basic thoughts or ideas.

Introduction:

Body:

Example 1:

Example 2:

Example 3:

Conclusion:

Again, those are the basics. Now it is time to actually write the essay. There are 46 lines here. Fill 'em up!

Practice Essay #4

An author named Henri Nouwen once wrote, "When we honestly ask ourselves which person in our lives means the most to us, we often find that it is those who, instead of giving advice, solutions or cures, have chosen rather to share our pain and touch our wounds with a warm and tender hand. The friend who can be silent with us in a moment of despair or confusion, who can stay with us in an hour of grief and bereavement, who can tolerate not knowing, not curing, not healing and face with us the reality of our powerlessness, that is a friend who cares."

Assignment: What do you think makes a truly good friend? What qualities do you look for in a friend or what qualities do you have that make you a good friend? Do you agree with the qualities listed in this quote or do you give importance to other ones? Plan and write an essay in which you develop your point of view on the issue. Support your position with reasoning and examples taken from your reading, studies, experience or observations.

MAKING A DECISION

Choose one and check it:

__ I agree with the quote.

__ I disagree with the quote.

__ Neither of the above but something different.

BRAINSTORM

Use this space to quickly brainstorm a few ideas on how to approach this essay.

____

____

____

THESIS STATEMENT

Use these lines to write out your thesis statement.

____

____

____

____

OUTLINE

Don't worry about complete sentences or any other little details. Just fill this out with some basic thoughts or ideas.

Introduction: ______________________________

____

____

Body:

Example 1: ______________________________

____

____

Example 2: ______________________________

____

____

Example 3: ______________________________

____

____

Conclusion: ______________________________

____

Okay. There are those basics again. Now it is time to actually write the essay. There are 46 lines here. Fill 'em up!

____

____

____

____

____

____

____

____

Eeenie, Meenie, Miney, Mo... The Multiple Choice Portion of the SAT

Highlights: What you will (hopefully) learn in this chapter...

- How to ace the multiple choice questions
- Key strategies to identifying sentence errors
- The best way to answer the improve sentences and improve paragraph questions
- When and how to guess wisely

Eeenie, Meenie, Miney, Mo... The Multiple Choice Portion of the SAT

Have you ever heard the statement, "I've got good news and bad news"? Always take the bad news first; that way you can end on a high note with the good stuff. So, here is the bad news: the part of the SAT that tests to see how well you grasp the many intricacies of the English language is the multiple choice section. For this portion, you are given 35 minutes to answer a total of 60 questions. They are broken down in this way:

30 questions on identifying sentence errors

18 sentences on improving sentences

12 questions on improving paragraphs

Now, the good news is that you are NOT tested on any of the following:

- the definition of any grammatical terms
- punctuation
- capitalization
- spelling

(Cheering? Cheering? Do I hear it? Sigh. Nope.)

Before we begin to tackle each section and the different knowledge and strategies that they involve, I want you to imagine something else for a moment. Ready?

You came home from school today to discover that your favorite ________ (insert term here: could be book, candy, CD, sweater–whatever you want) has disappeared. You search and search but to no avail. It is simply gone. Quickly, your suspicious mind turns to the other people in the house. Could your sister have snuck it out of your room? Did your brother hide it? Did your mother accidentally put it away somewhere? Did your best friend borrow it without asking first? Where the heck did it go?

To figure out this mystery, you decide to use the much underappreciated but highly effective method of (drum roll and dramatic soundtrack, please) *the process of elimination.* This simply means that you are going to use all of the clues and knowledge that you have in order to figure out the right answer by FIRST finding all the wrong answers. In this case, that means the dastardly culprit who purloined your ________. (Ah, those vocab words. Ya gotta love 'em–and look 'em up.)

So, could it have been your sister? Ah…no! It could not. Your _______ only came up missing today and your sister has been at summer camp since Wednesday morning. She is innocent (of this, at least). Your sister can be eliminated from the possible suspect list.

Could it have been your little brother? Think, think. No! It couldn't be him because he spent the night at his best friend Austin's house. He isn't back yet. Check him off the list.

Suspicion turns to your mother now. Could she have come into your room and (oh, the horror!) cleaned it? You look around. Dirty laundry still on the floor; desk still covered in papers and last night's midnight snack; dresser drawers all still hanging open; cracker crumbs still all over your sheets. Nope, she hasn't been in here. Her name is off the list.

This leaves…your best friend Adam. Aha! He was over last night for a couple of hours. That gives him access. He loves your _______ and often gazes at it longingly. That gives him motivation. Quickly, you dash to the phone and give him a call. "Hey! Do you have my _______?" you demand fiercely. Filled with regret and remorse, he admits to the crime and promises to bring it right back to you. You hang up feeling totally vindicated because you figured out the puzzle. You did it through the process of elimination (POE) and guess what? You can do this on the SAT multiple choice questions too (You knew I would eventually connect these two thoughts, right?).

Am I telling you to guess on some of these questions? Ummm, yes. Of course it is better if you know the answer because you are smart and clever and attentive and learned every grammar and writing lesson your teachers ever taught you, but in the case of being completely stumped on an item, GUESS, but guess WISELY.

Look at it this way: If you leave the question blank, you lose an entire point. You have no chance of gaining anything other than one of those fat zeroes we don't like. If you guess, however, you at least have a 25 percent chance of being right (four possibilities and one is right). Now, I am not telling you to just blindly close your eyes and pick a circle to fill in. That is where the "wisely" part of the directions comes in. With the process of elimination, do what you did in the scenario we just went through: look at the information you have, and start eliminating those obvious answers you know are wrong (as in the sister, brother and mom). From the ones that are left (Adam), choose. If you eliminate one, your chances of getting the right answer are 25 percent. If you can eliminate two, it skyrockets to a 50 percent chance. Not bad!

Let's put this valuable piece of information together with several others (officially all known as "test approaches"). You just learned about POE. Here is another test strategy: ***answer the easy questions first***. Doesn't that make sense? Read through the questions and when you know the answer immediately, fill in those little ovals, and then forget about those questions.

The next step is to ***read the ones that are left*** and determine if (a) you probably know the answer and just need to think about it for a moment or (b) you don't have a clue what the answer is and wouldn't if you had until the 22nd century to mull it over. The ones you don't know at all, simply leave alone. Concentrate on the others that are left. Time is of the essence and there is no point on blowing it all on figuring out one question when you could be answering ten. If you still have time left after answering the questions you knew, ***go back and start guessing wisely on the rest.***

Strategy time is over; now let's move on to looking at the three main kinds of questions you will encounter. We will investigate what knowledge these questions are testing, how to approach each one using POE and other exciting fun things that will make this a real page-turner. (Yeah, right.) Please note that I will explain how these questions will be designed and what you are expected to do and know to answer them correctly.

Following a look at the questions, there will be a quote from one of the actual SATs to show you an example of how the instructions are worded. This may seem repetitive but the SAT directions can be confusing. When you are on a tight time schedule, even instructions can easily feel overwhelming. By explaining them twice and in two different manners, you will be familiar with what you are supposed to do before you even get to the test.

After becoming familiar with the SAT directions, we will look at some samples of each type of question. Then at the end, you get the chance (lucky bums!) to try your hand at answering some of them to make sure you understood what we just covered. I promise not to grade them.

> **IMPORTANT CLUE:** Approximately 20 percent of *error identification* and *improving sentences* questions CONTAIN NO ERROR AT ALL. Do not be afraid to choose that answer because you could very well be right.

Identifying Sentence Errors

One-third of the questions asked in the section on identifying sentence errors will be on spotting a mistake in how a sentence is written. Again, remember that the good news is the error will not be in punctuation, spelling or capitalization. Instead it will be a mistake in grammar or usage. Keep in mind that there is only one error, so if you found one, you're done with that question. You do not have to state what the error is; just be able to spot an error if it is there or recognize that there are no errors in the sentence. It isn't rocket science or brain surgery, right? Let's analyze a few and then practice to make sure you've got it. (Ah, c'mon, you knew I would be using the "P" word again, didn't you?)

These questions (according to the College Board web site) are designed to measure your ability to:

- recognize faults in usage
- recognize effective sentences that follow the conventions of standard written English

You will be given a sentence that will either contain ONE error or NO error. This sentence will have five parts underlined. Each underlined section will be labeled A, B, C, D and (I bet you have already guessed this!) E. The "E" section of the sentence says "No error" and it is the one you choose if the sentence has (duh!) no error.

Here is how the actual directions on the test will read for this specific portion:

> "The following sentences test your ability to recognize grammar and usage errors. Each sentence contains either a single error or no error at all. No sentence contains more than one error. The error, if there is one, is underlined and lettered. If the sentence contains an error, select the one underlined part that must be changed to make the sentence correct. If the sentence is correct, select choice E. In choosing answers, follow the requirements of standard written English."

Let's look at an example. It will make everything easier to understand.

The other students (A) and her (B) automatically headed to the classroom (C)
when the school bell rang (D). No error (E).

Here is how to approach the question. (1) Read the entire thing from first to last word. (2) Pay extra attention to the underlined portions of the sentence (A-D). Remember that the error will be in one of them, if there is one. In this case, the choices are:

A. other students

B. her

C. headed to the classroom

D. rang

Did any of them pop up at you as incorrect? If so, terrific. You get another 20 SAT lottery points. If not, don't worry. That is what this section is all about. (And, hey, it makes me feel needed!)

Let's take each possible answer. The phrase "other students" is correct. The word "other" modifies "students." You can see that "her" is the problem. It is the wrong pronoun for this sentence. Would you say, "Her automatically headed for the classroom"? It doesn't sound right, does it? This choice is the number one suspect, but let's check C and D as well. The phrase "headed to the classroom" is the action of the students and it is correct. The verb "rang" is past tense, which matches "headed," so it is correct as well. As you eliminate each choice (POE!), the chance of picking the right answer increases. In this case, the answer is B.

Since that one was so much fun, let's try another one. (I could tell you were hoping I would say that.)

> The beautiful (A) cheerleaders were responsible for improving morale, (B) encouraging the team, to entertain the fans (C) and distracting the players (D) on the opposite team. No error. (E)

Did you spot any error in this one? Your choices are these:

A. beautiful

B. for improving morale

C. to entertain the fans

D. distracting the players

E. no error

If you think there is a mistake, choice E is not an option. Let's look at A. "Beautiful" is an adjective that modifies "cheerleaders." It is used correctly. Next, there are three phrases to check. Do you notice a difference in them? Take another look. See how two of the three start with verbs that end in "-ing," while the third one starts with "to"? I could give you the fancy names that go with that (like parallelism and such) but the point is that they don't match. The phrase "to entertain the fans" should actually be "entertaining the fans." You don't have to fix it; just find it. The answer is C.

Yes, yes, if you insist, we will do one more.

> At the television station (A), reporters shuffled through papers, (B) hurried through phone calls (C) and wrote multiple interoffice emails (D). No error. (E)

Read it over. What grabs your attention? Again, the choices are:

A. television station

B. shuffled through papers

C. hurried through phone calls

D. wrote multiple interoffice emails

E. no error

"Television" is the adjective modifying "station," so it is okay. The other three phrases start with verbs. Are all of them in past tense? Shuffled...hurried...wrote...yep, those are all past tense. So guess what? The answer to this one is E. There is no error.

How do you feel about questions about identifying sentence errors now? Better? I hope so. Much to your boundless joy and delight, I will be ending this section with sample questions for you to try. So make sure you understand each type before you get to all that fun that is just waiting ahead.

Improving Sentences

The second section of multiple choice questions focuses on improving sentences. There are 18 of these. All of them are similar to the section we just covered. In the error identification questions, you had to figure out if there was a mistake and if there was, which underlined part was at fault. Your job ended there. This portion takes it one step further. You will look for the error and then choose the multiple choice option that best corrects it. You want to make sure the sentence reads well with no awkwardness. In the Identifying Sentence Errors section, option E meant there was no error in the sentence. That will be different in these questions. Option A will be a repeat of the underlined portion. Choosing A means that there is no error. Is your head swimming? Don't despair. We will go through examples and it will all become clear.

Once again, according to those fun-filled people at the College Board, these questions will measure your ability to:

- recognize and correct faults in usage and sentence structure

- recognize effective sentences that follow the conventions of standard written English

These questions will include errors in grammar, choice of words, sentence construction and punctuation. Yeah, yeah, I said you weren't going to be tested on punctuation, and I was telling the truth. The only punctuation questions are ones that alter the basic structure of the sentence. By rearranging the words, the punctuation may sometimes have to be changed as well. So, see? I didn't lie to you, really!

Here is how the test's directions will most likely be phrased:

> "The following sentences test correctness and effectiveness of expression. Part of each sentence or the entire sentence is underlined; beneath each sentence are five ways of phrasing the underlined material. Choice A repeats the original phrasing; the other four choices are different. If you think the original phrasing produces a better sentence than any of the alternatives, select Choice A; if not, select one of the other choices.

"In making your selection, follow the requirements of standard written English; that is, pay attention to grammar, choice of words, sentence construction and punctuation. Your selection should result in the most effective sentence—clear and precise, without awkwardness or ambiguity."

Let's take a look at some sample sentences. Hopefully, they will make everything clearer. Remember that the directions are the same. Read the whole sentence over and see if you spot a mistake. Eliminate the ones you know aren't right and make the best choice from there.

Arthur Conan Doyle did not actually like the character of Sherlock Holmes he created because he was anxious to write the story that included his demise.

A. because he was anxious to write the story that included his demise.

B. at the time he was anxious to write the story that included his demise.

C. although he was anxious to write the story that included his demise.

D. and he was anxious to write the story that included his demise.

E. when he was anxious to write the story that included his demise.

What happened when you read this sentence the first time? Did you feel/hear/see that something was amiss? There are two ideas in this sentence that are joined together by the word "because." That implies some kind of cause and effect, which is not true. Doyle did not dislike Holmes *because* he wanted to write about his death. That eliminates the original version of the sentence, repeated as Choice A.

Now what about choices B, C, D and E? Choice B introduces the phrase "at the time." This does not link the ideas together logically, so choice B is out. Choice C uses the conjunction "although" and implies a contradiction when none is needed. Choice C is eliminated. Choice D connects the two ideas with "and." This indicates that the two ideas are equal in importance–which they are. Choice D is a possibility. This leaves Choice E and the connection of "when." This implies the two ideas occurred simultaneously which also doesn't make sense. Choice E is out and Choice D wins.

Was that tons of fun or what? We simply must try another one, don't you think?

The big screen television at Julia's house is both larger and more high-tech than Kevin's house.

A. larger and more high-tech than Kevin's house.

B. larger and high-techer than Kevin's house.

C. larger and more high-tech than the big screen television in Kevin's house.

D. larger and more high-tech than Kevin's.

E. larger and more high-tech than the one at Kevin's house.

Here is a case of what is called *faulty comparison.* In the example, the houses are not being compared; it is big screen televisions, right? That certainly is not clear in the sample sentence; choice A is out. Choice B is wrong because "high-techer" is not a real word. It's out. Choice C is pretty wordy; repeating "big screen television" seems unnecessary but it does make the sentence clearer, so it is a possibility. Choice D leaves everything up to imagination. Larger and more high-tech than Kevin's what? So, now we have choice E. It makes sense because it adds the words "the one." *The big screen television at Julia's house is both larger and more high-tech than the one at Kevin's house.* Choice E is the winner.

And now, one more, just for your personal home entertainment...

Recognized and adored by thousands of female fans nationwide, the limousine pulled up and the actor voted sexiest man on the planet stepped out.

A. the limousine pulled up and the actor voted sexiest man on the planet stepped out.

B. the actor voted sexiest man on the planet stepped out of the limousine.

C. it pulled up and the actor voted sexiest man on the planet stepped out.

D. voted sexiest man on the planet, the actor stepped out of the limousine.

E. stepping out of the limousine, the actor voted the sexiest man on the planet.

The problem with this sentence is a *dangling modifier*–and no, you don't need to know the term but you should know how to recognize one. A phrase is a group of words. A phrase that *modifies* simply means that it gives extra details about something. When a phrase modifies something, it should be right next to what it modifies. If it isn't, then it is a *dangling* modifier.

Read the underlined phrase again. What does it modify or give details about? The limousine? No. The actor? Yes. In the example, the modifier is right next to limousine and unless it is some kind of truly original car, it is not likely adored and recognized by thousands of female fans. Knowing this, look at the choices again. You know A is wrong. Option B is possible since it moved "the actor" next to the modifying phrase. Choice C replaces "the limousine" with "it." This only muddles things more. C is out. In D, the words are simply scrambled and make no sense, while in choice E, it is even worse. The answer to this one is B.

How did you feel about this sample question? Are you ready for what the improving sentences portion of the SAT will require you to do now? I hope so because as you already know, some practice samples will be coming up soon.

Improving Paragraphs

This section includes a dozen questions about improving entire paragraphs of writing. These are the equivalent of about three paragraphs of a student's rough draft. Areas that should be rewritten will be indicated. You will be asked to read the passage and then select the best answers to the questions that pertain to the selection.

You will be asked to find and correct problems with the entire passage, a paragraph or an individual sentence or phrase. Questions will focus on sentence structure, usage issues, expression and style, word choice, faulty emphasis and flawed organization or illogical development. (Whew!) Without a doubt, this is the most time consuming of the sections because there are multiple paragraphs instead of single sentences. There is no "no error" or "fine as is" type option with these items either. If it is being questioned, it has an error in it.

Our dear friends at the College Board state that this type of question will measure your ability to:

- edit and revise sentences in the context of a paragraph or entire essay
- organize and develop paragraphs in a coherent and logical manner
- apply the conventions of standard written English

The actual directions for this portion of the test will read something like this:

> "The following passage is an early draft of an essay. Some parts of the passage need to be rewritten. Read the passage and select the best answers for the questions that follow. Some questions are about particular sentences or parts of sentences and ask you to improve sentence structure or word choice. Other questions ask you to consider organization and development. In choosing answers, follow the requirements of standard written English."

Looking at the entire passage, you will quickly see that the sentences are numbered so it is easy to see where each one fits within the essay. Now here is an area where the judges are split on what is better to do. Some SAT experts say that you should read the entire passage from beginning to end before attempting to answer any of the questions. Others say that this is a waste of precious time and instead, you should go straight to the questions. Whichever strategy you choose to implement, it is safe to say that if one of the questions asks about something regarding the essay as a whole, you should read it through quickly.

Remember that you are not responsible for understanding anything in a given passage. It could be about the latest neurology technique or how to test mosquitoes for West Nile virus; you don't have to comprehend a bit of it. You only have to recognize writing errors.

Here is an example of the kind of passage on the SAT. Following it will be the types of questions asked. Those questions tend to be one of three types: (1) Revision; (2) Combination or (3) Content. Don't start shaking your head at me already! Patience, my child, and I will explain each one to you.

> **REVISION** means you will be asked about a sentence that has some kind of grammatical error in it, much like the ones in identifying errors and improving sentences. You will fix the sentence so that it is easier to read and understand. Revisions must follow the rules of "standard written English."
>
> **COMBINATION** questions ask you to join two sentences together in the way that makes the most sense, doesn't lose any meaning and is still grammatically correct. Many times this is done by choosing the appropriate conjunction. To help, here are the most common ones in this handy-dandy little chart. (I know; I am so good to you.)

Coordinating Conjunctions:

for	and	nor	but	or	yet	so

Correlative Conjunctions:

both/and	either/or	neither/nor	not only/but also	whether/or

Subordinating Conjunctions:

after	as if	although	as long as	as though	as soon as	as
because	before	even though	if	in order that	since	so, so that
though	till	when, whenever	unless	until	where, wherever	

CONTENT questions deal with the presentation of subject matter. That means that you will be asked to determine what changes could be made to a sentence so that the meaning is made clear. You may be asked to add a necessary, clarifying sentence to the passage, eliminate an unnecessary or confusing sentence from the passage or locate the main idea of the passage overall (which means you would probably need to scan the whole thing really fast).

You have the theories; now let's put them into practice with a few sample questions.

First, here is the essay where the errors will be found:

> (1) Today's image of the Native American is a fuzzy, and usually inaccurate, one. (2) Legends and tales often paint one of two portraits of this race: either the kindly, gentle chief who is one with the earth and his people or the vicious, drunken savage out to destroy anything in his path. (3) Like all of the stereotypes that exist in any culture, it has glimmers of truth, buried under layers of myths and misconceptions.
>
> (4) Following the history of the many different Native Americans tribes is a sobering journey. (5) It cannot help but alter the outlook of those who always wanted to be the cowboy when it was time to play. (6) Indians were the "bad guys." (7) History shows that there were multiple bad guys when it came to the claiming of land throughout the United States. (8) Promises were made and broken on both sides; treaties often were not worth the paper they were written on. (9) Revenge ran rampant on both the white man and the Native American sides. (10) Peacekeepers existed on either side of the issues and most of them, whether American, European or Native American, was swept aside by powerful forces beyond their control.
>
> (11) As Europe and then the United States marched across the nation in search of new lands to conquer, explore and settle, the Native Americans were often the victims of their enthusiasm and passion. (12) From those first curious explorers, through the settlers after the Civil War and the miners hoping for gold, people invaded lands where others already lived and tried to find a way to call it their own. (13) The Native American people, like other minority races, have suffered at the hands of men who saw it as their right and duty to expand their environment and change it to suit their needs. (14) That inherent drive resulted in incredible triumphs and horrific losses, in moments of glory and moments of heartbreak and in this nation becoming what it is—from the grand to the immoral.

1. In context, which of the following is the best revision of sentence 3 (reproduced below)?

Like all of the stereotypes that exist in any culture, it has glimmers of truth, buried under layers of myths and misconceptions.

(A) Like all of the stereotypes that exist in any culture, these two extremes have glimmers of truth, buried under layers of myths and misconceptions.

(B) Like all of the stereotypes that exist in any culture, Native Americans have glimmers of truth, buried under layers of myths and misconceptions.

(C) Like all of the stereotypes that exist in any culture, savages have glimmers of truth, buried under layers of myths and misconceptions.

(D) Like all of the stereotypes that exist in any culture, stereotypes have glimmers of truth, buried under layers of myths and misconceptions.

(E) Like all of the stereotypes that exist in any culture, glimmers of truth, buried under layers of myths and misconceptions.

Answer Analysis: This is an example of the type of question where you are being asked to revise what the student originally wrote. The problem with this sentence is the pronoun. Remember when we talked about pronouns...the ones where you were not sure what noun they represented? This is one of those. The word "it" is vague; the reader is not sure what it means. In choice A, the word has been replaced with "these two extremes," referring to the previous sentence. This certainly makes the sentence easier to understand. In choice B "it" was replaced with "Native Americans," but the sentence does not make sense. With choice C "it" has been replaced with "savages" and that does not make any sense either. Choice D takes the pronoun out and puts "stereotypes" in its place, which makes the sentence both repetitive and confusing. Choice E takes out the pronoun but makes no replacement, leaving a non-grammatical and puzzling statement. The correct answer then is A.

2. In context, which word should be placed at the beginning of sentence 7 if it were combined with sentence 6 (reproduced below)?

Indians were the "bad guys." History shows that there were multiple bad guys when it came to the claiming of land throughout the United States.

(A) Because

(B) Subsequently

(C) However

(D) Unless

(E) Whether

Answer Analysis: This is a combination question. To make sure that you understand this question, re-read sentence 6 to see how the two sentences connect. Choice A is "because," a conjunction that implies cause and effect, so that does not work. Choice B's "subsequently" implies one event occurs after another like a time sequence, so that does not work. "However" in choice C implies a contrast, which makes sense. Choice D is putting a qualifier on the previous sentence and that is illogical, while choice E implies one thing happens regardless of another; again, puzzling and does not make sense. The correct answer is C.

3. The author's main point in writing this essay is to:

(A) show that Native Americans are completely different from the usual stereotypes

(B) analyze why the Native Americans were pushed out of their lands so violently

(C) discuss how the country developed and the role of the Native Americans in it

(D) prove that the Europeans were wrong to invade the Native American's lands

(E) describe the multiple treaties that were created for the Native American people

Answer Analysis: This is a content question. It is asking you to figure out the main point of the entire essay. If you have not read the entire thing yet, now is the time to do it. Look at the essay as a whole to see what main idea the author is trying to share. Choice A is incorrect because the essay is not attempting to show how Native Americans vary from the usual stereotype. That is mentioned but the entire piece goes far beyond that. Choice B is also incorrect since there is no analysis mentioned anywhere in the essay. With choice C, the verb is "discuss" which seems appropriate, as does the topic of how the country developed and the role of the Native Americans. In choice D, the verb "prove" should immediately clue you that it is a wrong answer since nothing is proven within the scope of this essay. Choice E is also incorrect because, although treaties are briefly mentioned, they are not talked about in any detail. The correct answer is C.

4. In context, which of the following represents the best way to revise and combine sentences 5 and 6 (reproduced below)?

It cannot help but alter the outlook of those who always wanted to be the cowboy when it was time to play. Indians were the "bad guys."

(A) It cannot help but alter the outlook of those who always wanted to be the cowboy when it was time to play, yet the Indians were the "bad guys."

(B) It cannot help but alter the outlook of those who always wanted to be the cowboy when it was time to play, because, after all, the Indians were the "bad guys."

(C) It cannot help but alter the outlook of those who always wanted to be the cowboy when it was time to play, although the Indians were the "bad guys."

(D) It cannot help but alter the outlook of those who always wanted to be the cowboy when it was time to play and the Indians were the "bad guys."

(E) It cannot help but alter the outlook of those who always wanted to be the cowboy when it was time to play since, as if, the Indians were the "bad guys."

Answer Analysis: This is a combination question. You are being asked to blend together two sentences into one without changing the meaning and in the process, making it read smoother. In choice A, the two statements are combined with the word "yet." This implies contrast which does not fit with the meaning of the sentence. In B, "because, after all" is added which means the first part of the sentence results in the second part. This makes sense. Choice C uses the word "although" which also implies some kind of contrast, but it is not a good answer since it alters the meaning. With choice D, the sentences are connected with "and" which makes them equal in importance but does not show the correct relationship between them. In E, "since, as if" simply does not make grammatical sense because two subordinate conjunctions should not be used where only one is needed. Choice B is the correct answer.

5. Which of the following represents the best revision, in context, of the underlined part of sentence 10 (reproduced below)?

Peacekeepers existed on either side of the issues and most of them, whether American, European or Native American, was swept aside by powerful forces beyond their control.

(A) if they happened to be American, European or Native American, was swept aside

(B) despite being American or European or Native American, was all swept aside

(C) regardless of whether they were American, European or Native American, were swept aside

(D) although American, European or Native American, was swept aside

(E) whether American, European or Native American, were swept aside

Answer Analysis: Here we are back to a revision question. You are supposed to find the mistake in the underlined portion of the sentence and then select the best correction. First, read over that part and see if any mistakes pop up for you. The clue is in the verb tense of the "hidden" clause: *most of them... was swept aside by powerful forces beyond their control.* Finding the clause gets a little tricky because of the phrase that is slipped between the subject and the verb. In this case, it helps to mentally eliminate the words between the commas (the phrase, *whether American, European or Native American,*) and focus on the interrupted clause. Look at the subject of the clause: *most.* It is a plural pronoun, which means the verb has to be plural as well. The verb "was" is singular. Thus, the correct choice is E, which keeps the rest of the sentence intact and changes the verb to the correct tense so that it is in agreement with the subject.

6. The logical flow of the passage as a whole would be most improved by adding the following sentence between which of the essay's lines?

It is a pattern that is seen throughout the history of every culture on the planet and while that makes it a common one, it does not make it a noble one.

(A) Between lines 2 and 3

(B) Between lines 4 and 5

(C) Between lines 9 and 10

(D) Between lines 10 and 11

(E) Between lines 13 and 14

Answer Analysis: This is a content question. You are being asked to add information to make the passage clearer. Again, this is the type of question that requires you to be familiar with the entire piece. You will not be able to figure out where extra information should go unless you know how the passage is organized. In this case, the additional sentence gives information about a pattern that has been repeated throughout history. The only place where that makes sense–where a pattern is clearly inferred–is choice E, between lines 13 and 14. If you try putting the new sentence between the sentences in the other choices, it will not make any sense.

This brings us to the end of the instruction section for the multiple choice writing questions. Now I ask you, was that enormous fun or what? My guess is that you will want to read it all over again since you enjoyed it so much. Right? Okay, don't answer that.

Anyway, you are now ready for the last part of the book–and then you will be done. Do you feel smug? Proud? Impressed with yourself? You should! I am proud of you!

Before you get too carried away, however, you need to complete this very last portion. It has sample test questions over the three kinds we just spent 6,000 words going over: error identification, improving sentences and improving paragraphs. If you find yourself struggling with some of them, go back and re-read the part that tells you how to approach and respond to them.

Before starting this section, get up and take a break. Get a drink, stretch, hit the bathroom, grab a snack and find a comfortable spot (not necessarily in that order). Be relaxed and confident before beginning. Remember those positive affirmations we talked about wayyyyyy back in the beginning? Approach these questions believing that you will do a good job. There's no pressure here, no grades, no time clocks. Just think about the questions and do your best. When you are done, read the answers and the reasons behind them. Make sure you understand why you missed some. Learn from these practice drills so that the next time you encounter these types of questions (i.e. on the SAT day!), you are prepared to be right.

All right, deep breath. Sharp pencil (or pen). I have total confidence in you, so let's get started.

Error Identification Questions

The following sentences test your ability to recognize grammar and usage errors. Each sentence contains either a single error or no error at all. No sentence contains more than one error. The error, if there is one, is underlined and lettered. If the sentence contains an error, select the one underlined part that must be changed to make the sentence correct. If the sentence is correct, select choice E. In choosing answers, follow the requirements of standard written English.

1. According to the public library's records (A), there weren't no books (B) that hadn't been checked out (C) at least twice that year (D). No error (E).

2. Reading about the plight of Hester's imprisonment in *The Scarlet*
A

Letter literally made my skin crawl as I imagined the suffering
B C

she experienced. No error.
D E

3. Realizing that everyone in the house was asleep, Kathryn
A

descended the spiral staircase as quiet as she possibly could.
B C D

No error.
E

4. Flying through the air, the circus audience cheered at the
A B

acrobats' bravery, elegance, and skill. No error.
C D E

5. The publishing phenomenon of J.K. Rowling's *Harry Potter* books
A B

was quite unexpected and completely unprecedented. No error.
C D E

Answer Key:

1. B. This sentence includes a double negative. The phrase "weren't no books" should be "weren't any books."

2. B. The phrase "made my skin crawl" is an idiom and should be replaced.

3. C. Grammar error. The word "quiet" modifies the verb "descended" so it should be written as an adverb, or "quietly."

4. A. This is a dangling modifier. It is modifying "acrobats," not "audience."

5. E. This sentence is completely correct. There is no error.

Improving Sentences

The following sentences test correctness and effectiveness of expression. Part of each sentence or the entire sentence is underlined; beneath each sentence are five ways of phrasing the underlined material. Choice A repeats the original phrasing; the other four choices are different. If you think the original phrasing produces a better sentence than any of the alternatives, select Choice A; if not, select one of the other choices.

In making your selection, follow the requirements of standard written English; that is, pay attention to grammar, choice of words, sentence construction and punctuation. Your selection should result in the most effective sentence—clear and precise, without awkwardness or ambiguity.

1. The issue of <u>animals that are kept in zoos is</u> something that animal rights' activists like to debate at length at public protests.

A. animals that are kept in zoos is

B. zoo animals are

C. zoos, animals are

D. animals, kept in zoos, are

E. animal that are kept in zoos are

2. <u>Lucy was amazed to discover her missing car keys she'd been searching for getting ready for work that morning</u>.

A. Lucy was amazed to discover her missing car keys she'd been searching for getting ready for work that morning.

B. Getting ready for work that morning, Lucy was amazed to discover her missing car keys.

C. Amazed, Lucy discovered her missing car keys that morning getting ready for work.

D. To her amazement that morning, Lucy discovered her missing car keys getting ready for work.

E. Discovering her missing car keys, Lucy was amazed getting ready for work that morning.

3. Televisions which were not available to consumers until the 1950s revolutionized the way American families looked at entertainment.

A. Televisions which were not available to consumers until the 1950s

B. Televisions not available to consumers until the 1950s

C. Televisions, which were not available to consumers until the 1950s,

D. Televisions, until the 1950s not available to consumers

E. Televisions, consumers were not available until the 1950s,

4. Plunging into the ocean, the dolphins were clearly delighted to be back in their natural home.

A. Plunging into the ocean, the dolphins

B. The ocean, plunging in, the dolphins

C. The dolphins, into the ocean plunging,

D. As the dolphins plunged into the ocean

E. When the dolphins plunging into the ocean

5. Cosmetic surgery is growing in popularity the non-invasive approaches are the most demanded procedures of all.

A. popularity the non-invasive

B. popularity, the non-invasive

C. popularity the, non-invasive

D. popularity; the non-invasive

E. popularity: the non-invasive

Answer Key:

1. A. The word "issue" is the subject. Since it is just one issue – not plural – then the verb should be "is" so that the subject and verb are in agreement. Watch out for the prepositional phrase "of animals." The word "animals" cannot be the subject. It is the object of the preposition. Therefore, the sentence is correct as is.

2. B. "Getting ready for work that morning" should modify Lucy and needs to be shifted next to her name. The placement of the phrase in some of the other choices leads the reader to believe that the keys are "getting ready for work that morning" and that simply isn't logical.

3. C. The clause "which were not available to consumers until the 1950s" is dependent and should be set off by commas. To double-check the comma placement, read the portion that is left outside the commas: *Televisions...revolutionized the way American families looked at entertainment.* If what is left makes a simple sentence, then you have correctly placed the commas around the nonessential clause.

4. A. There is no error. "Plunging into the ocean" modifies dolphins and is in the proper place in the sentence.

5. D. This sentence is comprised of two independent clauses: *Cosmetic surgery is growing in popularity* and *the non-invasive approaches are the most demanded procedures of all.* There is no conjunction to tie them together. In fact, each clause could stand on its own as a simple sentence. That is what makes them "independent." Two independent clauses need to be joined by a semi colon.

Improving Paragraphs

The following passage is an early draft of an essay. Some parts of the passage need to be rewritten.

Read the passage and select the best answers for the questions that follow. Some questions are about particular sentences or parts of sentences and ask you to improve sentence structure or word choice. Other questions ask you to consider organization and development. In choosing answers, follow the requirements of standard written English.

(1) Feathered creatures make their nests out of whatever it can find from twigs and leaves to string and hair. (2) Whether small and sheltered or large and complex, birds' nests are one of nature's most interesting types of homes.

(3) The weaverbird's nests are unlike others. (4) Sociable weavers build a thatched roof style nest with individual chambers. (5) Others construct a funnel-shaped one. (6) Hanging from a branch, the funnel nest is skinny at the top, then widens into a ball-shape. (7) The bottom part is long and narrow again so snakes cannot get inside. (8) Sharp pieces of grass into the entrance so anything that tries to sneak inside will get a piercing surprise. (9) The center of the nest, where babies hatch, has crisscrossed grass stems to prevent eggs from rolling out.

(10) The building process is a slow one and varied depending on the type of weavers. (11) Sociable weavers push straw into place one at a time like people making thatched roofs. (12) Others weave a nest together with knots that would be the envy of any Boy Scout! (13) Some species use slipknots and half hitches, while others use reversed winding and spiral coils—and all by instinct! (14) When finished, these nests can reach 25 feet long, 15 feet wide and four feet high. (15) Earning their name of sociable, weavers enjoy company, and share their nests with up to 300 birds!

1. In context, which of the following represents the best way to revise and combine sentences 4 and 5 (reproduced below)?

Sociable weavers build a thatched roof style nest with individual chambers. Others construct a funnel-shaped one.

(A) Sociable weavers build a thatched roof style nest with individual chambers, because others construct a funnel-shaped one.

(B) Sociable weavers build a thatched roof style nest with individual chambers, unless others construct a funnel-shaped one.

(C) Sociable weavers build a thatched roof style nest with individual chambers, while others construct a funnel-shaped one.

(D) Sociable weavers build a thatched roof style nest with individual chambers, whether others construct a funnel-shaped one.

(E) Sociable weavers build a thatched roof style nest with individual chambers, if others construct a funnel-shaped one.

2. In context, which of the following is the best revision of sentence 1 (reproduced below)?

Feathered creatures make their nests out of whatever it can find from twigs and leaves to string and hair.

(A) Feathered creatures make their nests out of whatever he can find from twigs and leaves to string and hair.

(B) Feathered creatures make their nests out of whatever they can find from twigs and leaves to string and hair.

(C) Feathered creatures make their nests out of whatever you can find from twigs and leaves to string and hair.

(D) Feathered creatures make their nests out of whatever I can find from twigs and leaves to string and hair.

(E) Feathered creatures make their nests out of whatever us can find from twigs and leaves to string and hair.

3. In context, which of the following is the best revision of sentence 8 (reproduced below)?

Sharp pieces of grass into the entrance so anything that tries to sneak inside will get a piercing surprise.

(A) Sharp pieces of grass, into the entrance, so anything that tries to sneak inside will get a piercing surprise.

(B) Sharp pieces of grass into the entrance; anything that tries to sneak inside will get a piercing surprise.

(C) Sharp pieces of grass into the entrance so anything, which tries to sneak inside, will get a piercing surprise.

(D) Sharp pieces of grass are woven into the entrance so anything that tries to sneak inside will get a piercing surprise.

(E) Sharp pieces of grass woven into the entrance so anything that tries to sneak inside will get a piercing surprise.

4. In context, which of the following is the best revision of sentence 10 (reproduced below)?

The building process is a slow one and varied depending on the type of weavers.

(A) The building process is a slow one and varies depending on the type of weavers.

(B) The building process was a slow one and varies depending on the type of weavers.

(C) The building process is a slow one; varies depending on the type of weavers.

(D) The building process is a slow one, subsequently, it varies on the type of weavers.

(E) The building process is a slow one, it varied, on the type of weavers.

5. The writer's main reason or purpose in this essay is to

(A) analyze the contents of most birds' nests

(B) predict how many species of birds build funnel-shaped nests

(C) describe how the weaver birds build their unique nests

(D) prove that weaver birds make the most intricate nests of any species

(E) show how animals make safe places to live out in the wilderness

Answer Key:

1. C. The subordinate conjunction "while" is the only choice that joins the two sentences and keeps the meaning intact.

2. B. The pronoun needs to match "creatures" and "their" so the only correct answer is "they."

3. D. The sentence is a fragment; it is missing the verb and must have "are woven" to be complete.

4. A. The verb tenses need to be consistent, so "varied" should be replaced with "varies" to agree with "is."

5. C. This essay focuses on the development of the weaver bird's nest.

How did you do? What was your score? I hope you amazed yourself with your brilliance!

HELP! I Have Less than a Week to Study

Highlights: What you will (hopefully) learn in this chapter...

- Key study strategies to prepare for the SAT in one week
- Use the powerful "process of elimination" strategy to boost your score
- Don't waste valuable time reading the directions

Procrastination is the bad habit of putting off until the day after what should have been done the day before yesterday.

~ Napoleon Hill

HELP! I Have Less than a Week to Study ... What Do I Need to Know Right NOW?

A week? A week! You are taking the SAT in a week?! What the heck have you been DOING all this time? (I'm probably better off not knowing the answer to that one!) Well, I hope you are a fast reader and a quick learner because you have apparently put test prep so far down on your "to do" list that it is perilously close to completely falling off. You probably do not have time to sit down and read this book leisurely as I designed it, so now we will go straight to the extremely abridged version. This is Ace the SAT Essay on three double espressos.

Below are the TOP SIX things you need to know well before walking in to take the SAT.

(1) Be familiar with the expectations and the format of the test ahead of time so that it will not surprise or confuse you.

The more you know about what the test is like, the more prepared you will be. You will be ready to attack the test because you know what it is going to ask of you before you pick up that #2 pencil. So here are the basics of what it will contain:

- 60 multiple-choice questions over (a) identification of sentence errors, (b) improvement of sentences and (c) improvement of paragraphs (more on that down the list).

- One timed essay based on a writing prompt that is provided. You are given 45 lines to construct your essay and you have 25 minutes from beginning to end to get it done.

(2) The essay is a relatively new addition to the SAT and is designed to test a student's ability to communicate well. Here are the basic requirements:

- You are writing an opinion essay, so it needs to be persuasive or convincing.

- There are NO right or wrong opinions on your essay. You are being graded on your ability to write, not on your personal perspectives on any issue.

- The essay will not be judged on punctuation, spelling or grammar.

- The prompt you are given is often a quote or just an opinion on a current or global issue. You are asked to agree or disagree with it.

- The appearance of your essay is important. You do not want cross outs, scratch outs, arrows or insertions. If you need to take something out, put one simple line through it. If you need to add something, use an insertion mark (^). You also want to use your best possible handwriting. Making your essay hard to read can potentially lower your score, so be neat.

- Using better than average (Superlative? Exemplary? Exceptional?) vocabulary will make your essay more impressive. Avoid using clichés, idioms and slang (Not sure what these are? That's why you need to read the rest of the book!).

■ Remember that the people who are being paid to read and evaluate your essay spend less than a few minutes on it. If you make it clean and neat, it makes their job easier and could help you receive a higher score.

(3) Practicing writing essays is one of the best steps you can take for test preparation.

■ There is a reason that the expression "Practice makes perfect" is such a common one. It's because it is TRUE. Practicing your ability to write an essay for the whole six or seven days you have left is a terrific way to improve your skills quickly.

■ It should be obvious, but do not, I repeat, do not practice writing your essays on your computer. You can type much faster than you can write by hand and so your timing will be completely off. You need to know how much you can write in 25 minutes by hand. The average essay runs between 300 and 500 words so you should aim for a solid 400. Practicing shows you how to manage your time well. Many students spend so much time thinking about what they are going to write that they run out of time to actually do it. Practice and this will not happen to you.

■ By doing several trial runs at essay writing, you will adjust to coming up with an opinion quickly, writing in a set amount of time and doing it by hand rather than using a computer.

(4) Get familiar with writing prompts and how best to respond to them.

■ Your essay will be based on a writing prompt. It will be scored from 0 to 6 points. You know what earns you a zero? It isn't writing too short an essay. It's not that you make a lot of spelling errors. It's that you write on the WRONG topic. So please, please read that prompt carefully and make sure you actually are addressing the question they are asking. It can be any opinion you want, but it has to be valid.

■ All essays need three parts: an introduction, a body and a conclusion. This includes your SAT essay. It needs a beginning, a middle and an end. Typically, you state your opinion about the prompt in the beginning, use supporting examples in the middle and draw it all to a close at the end.

■ The support you use for your opinion is quite important. Just stating an opinion certainly isn't enough–you have to show why you agree or disagree with the prompt. To do this, you need to refer to a variety of resources including these: personal experience, history, political, literature, current events, science, art, sports and quotes. Don't worry if you can't remember where you read something or if you have forgotten part of a quote. Just say something like "In history class, I recently learned…", "According to a magazine article I read last month…", "I know that steroids have been mentioned frequently in the news lately…" or "My Aunt Kimberly once told me long ago that…" and then fill in the information. This gets your point across, illustrates and supports your perspective and yet doesn't demand that you remember the exact source and words used in your examples.

(5) Choices, choices–preparing for the multiple-choice section of the SAT.

Now, let's spend a little time talking about the multiple-choice section. As I stated before, there are a total of 60 questions in this portion. You need to know ahead of time what they are (and are not) testing so that you won't have to take time to read the instructions a few times over.

■ The first 30 questions are called identifying sentence errors. Each question has a sentence and within that sentence, there are four word(s) underlined. They are marked A, B, C and D. At the end of each sentence is E, which stands for no error (and about 20 percent of the questions in the multiple-choice sections have no errors in them at all). Your mission, should you choose to accept it (said in a dramatic voice reminiscent of the original "Mission Impossible" series–not the ones with Tom Cruise) is to read the sentence and figure out what is wrong with it, if anything. Then you narrow it down to which underlined word(s) is the error. Each sentence will contain ONE error only (it might not have any, but it will never have two). Good news–you don't have to say WHY it is wrong. You don't have to FIX the error. You just have to find out which one it is and mark A, B, C, D or E. (Wanna know more? Check out the examples and explanations in Chapter 5.)

■ The next 18 questions are called improving sentences. These are somewhat similar to the first set of questions, but these ask a little more of you. Each one presents a sentence with only one underlined portion. Choices A, B, C, D and E repeat this underlined portion and you have to choose which one is correct. If it is correct as is–no error–then you choose option A. If there is a mistake, however, you must figure out if it has been repaired in B, C, or D. Examples galore can also be found in Chapter 5.

■ The last set of 12 questions is improving paragraphs. This is where, for a moment, you get to experience what it is like to be your English teacher. You read someone else's rough draft (at least one to three paragraphs of it) and pinpoint where the errors are. You will be asked to look at parts of sentences and entire sentences that have mistakes that need repair, as well as consider the entire paragraph or essay to make decisions about what is out of place or needs better organization. You will be asked questions that focus on (1) Revision, (2) Combination and (3) Content. In revision, you will have a sentence that contains a grammatical error and you have to pick the correct option (A, B, C, D or E) that fixes it. (There are no "no error" options in this category of questions.) For combination questions, you are asked to join two sentences together in the best way while retaining meaning and remaining grammatically correct. The third possibility is content and often involves the entire passage as a whole. You are asked to determine whether a sentence is confusing, missing, misplaced, etc. Often you will be able to find this almost instinctively because you will be reading the rough draft and "something" will jump out at you as "feeling" or "sounding" wrong. These are times to listen to your gut because most likely that is just where the error is.

(6) Remember your friend POE at all times.

No, I don't mean Edgar Allan–although hey, that man could WRITE. He really creeped me out in his short story "The Tell Tale Heart" when . . . oops, sorry. I digress (look it up!). Anyway, this time POE stands for "process of elimination" and it will help you greatly in the multiple-choice portion of the SAT. It falls back on the idea that years of English grammar lessons have piled up in your subconscious so that when you read a test question and then read its answers, something internally recognizes the error. There is this BLIP inside and if you listen to it, it MAY (please don't write the publisher and say that Tamra Orr said this BLIP was always right!!), it MAY help you find the correct answer quickly.

Along with this blip, you are using POE. (How many times have you ever read that statement in your life? I am betting this was a first!) Simply put, you look at the available options (A, B, C, D and E) and immediately eliminate any of those that you just know are not the right answers. Sometimes they will jump out at you and other times, they may all look right or wrong and you will have to look at each one a little longer. As you read each choice, cross out the ones you KNOW are wrong and then you will be left with fewer options. It will be easier to (shhhhhhh! I did NOT tell you this) guess at the right answer. I mean, let's be honest, in a perfect world, chocolate would flow from drinking fountains, every outfit we liked would fit, our wallets would never be empty and everyone would like us–plus we would be SURE of every correct answer on the SAT; but sadly, Utopia isn't here so there are times that yes, you will have to guess the right answer. At least, using POE, you can, to spin off a certain Indiana Jones movie line and later soda commercial, "Guess wisely."

So, there you go. That is what you need to know if you only have one week to prepare for the SAT.

Why are you still sitting here looking at this page?

Stop reading now, you fool. You only have ONE WEEK.

GO.

Quit reading this part which has no intrinsic value whatsoever and go study all those wonderful things I took my precious time to tell you about to prepare you for the SAT. Otherwise, you make me feel completely unneeded and ignored.

HELP! I Am Taking the SAT in 24 Hours

Highlights: What you will (hopefully) learn in this chapter…

- 10 tips that will help you with only 24 hours to prepare
- Strategies for smart guessing

HELP! I Am Taking the SAT in 24 Hours ... What Am I Going to do NOW?

Procrastination is one of the most common and deadliest of diseases and its toll on success and happiness is heavy.

~ Wayne Gretzky

Okay, call me psychic...are you the same person who goes shopping for that extra special gift for someone you love at 6 p.m. on Christmas Eve? Do you read the CliffsNotes of the book as you walk down the hall to take the test over it? Do you race through the front door of your house at 11:59 if your curfew is midnight? (Just a hunch, mind you.)

If you are taking the SAT tomorrow and this is the first official "studying" you have done (and let's face it, at best this is skimming and scanning, not studying), then let's go over the top ten points to know. If the previous pages were the Ace the SAT Essay book on three espressos, this is Ace the SAT Essay at supersonic speed (just listen for the BOOM when you break the sound barrier).

Top Ten Things to Know Before You Take the SAT

10. The English portion of the test consists of one essay and 60 multiple-choice questions. The multiple-choice questions each have five options (A through E).

9. The essay will NOT be scored on punctuation, grammar or spelling. It will be scored on a scale from 0 to 6 on how well you can communicate your opinion in response to a writing prompt. Whether you agree or disagree with the statement in the prompt is irrelevant. It is your ability to write your opinion and support it that is being tested.

8. You have 25 minutes to write your essay, so you have to think and plan fast. Make sure your essay has an introduction (where you state your opinion), a body (where you add support such as details and examples) and an ending (where you draw it all to a conclusion).

7. Your essay should be done in your best handwriting and be as free of cross outs and insertions as possible. If you need to include them, make them neat. There are 46 lines to fill out. Fill out as many as possible but don't cheat by writing big or skipping lines.

6. The second half of the test is a set of 60 multiple-choice questions. The first 30 are on identifying sentence errors. The next 18 are on improving sentences. The last 12 are on improving paragraphs.

5. Always answer the easiest questions first so you get as many filled in as possible. Your time will go much faster than you think it will, so the faster you can move, the better.

4. Use POE, the process of elimination, when choosing an answer. Eliminate the answers you know (or are at least pretty sure) are wrong and see what you have left. This narrows the choices and increases your chances of getting it right.

3. When you read the essays to answer the improving paragraphs questions, focus on the first sentence of each paragraph. It will, most times, tell you the subject of that paragraph, making it easier to quickly locate whatever section you are being asked about. Don't waste precious seconds scanning the paragraphs repeatedly.

2. Remember that about 20 percent of the identifying sentence errors and improving sentences questions contain NO ERROR at all in them.

1. If you fail the SAT, it is not an ELE (extinction level event) although it can feel like it at the time. It means you have some work to do and some options to explore. Please do not have a meltdown.

BONUS: Do not, do NOT stay up all night and cram for this test. It just means your brain will be too tired to do much of anything correctly the next day. You will benefit far more from getting a solid night's sleep and eating a healthy breakfast than you will by staying up, guzzling coffee, munching on M & M's (although they are tasty!) and trying to study.

Twenty-four hours minus eight hours of sleep leaves 16 hours. Use it wisely. Use this book. (Buy copies for ALL of your friends or cousins or neighbors or teachers or people you meet in the library.)

Practice Tests with Answers

Highlights: What you will (hopefully) learn in this chapter…

- Get real experience with three practice tests with answers and explanations
- See both good and bad essay answer examples
- Practice choosing the "best" answer which is not always the "right" answer

Practice Test #1

Identifying Sentence Errors

The following sentences test your ability to recognize grammar and usage errors. Each sentence contains either a single error or no error at all. No sentence contains more than one error. The error, if there is one, is underlined and lettered. If the sentence contains an error, select the one underlined part that must be changed to make the sentence correct. If the sentence is correct, select choice E. In choosing answers, follow the requirements of standard written English.

1. Based on the hospital's records (A), there weren't no accident victims (B) with the last name of Smith or Henderson treated (C) in the emergency room that night (D). No error (E).

2. The entire football team (A) and him (B) ran directly (C) onto the field as the huge crowd of fans noisily cheered and called (D) out each one of their names. No error (E).

3. The new school computers are (A) to be used only for doing research for homework (B) assignments, writing school papers or creating graphics (C) for reports and not to check (D) your email. No error (E).

4. I sat down (A) to write my English (B) book report and after writing and throwing away a half dozen introductions, I decided to cut to the chase (C) and just explain my opinion (D) of the novel. No error (E).

5. After her mother told her (A) that she (B) had a soufflé in the oven, Crystal did (C) her best to walk soft (D) throughout the rest of the house. No error (E).

6. Tomorrow morning (A) Joseph will pick you up at the train station at noon and then he will take you (B) over to your cousin's (C) house and you had dinner (D) with the rest of the family. No error (E).

7. The ocean looks unusually active (A) today thanks to the high winds; the surf (B) is pounding the sandy shore (C) with real force so tomorrow there might be (D) seashells all over the place. No error (E).

8. Wearing roller skates (A), the customers at the drive-in restaurant marveled (B) at how well the waiters zoomed (C) from place to place without stumbling or spilling (D) a single drop. No error (E).

9. Lisa could not believe (A) it when the morning radio report stated (B) that there wouldn't be no school (C) that day because of the extreme wind chill (D). No error (E).

10. My mother told me (A) at dinner last night that the handwriting was on the wall (B) and I should confess before things went any further (C) than (D) they already had. No error. (E)

11. Mrs. Hudson was (A) the substitute teacher for the week and surprisingly (B), all of the students made a decision (C) to treat her decently (D) for a change. No error. (E)

12. The two students was planning (A) on sneaking out and spending (B) the afternoon at the lake but at the last minute, their (C) history teacher caught them (D) putting on suntan lotion. No error (E).

13. Mr. and Mrs. Cooper were going on vacation (A) but before they left (B), they hired someone to take care of their pets, water their plants (C), collect the mail and watch over our house (D). No error (E).

14. Kevin was hired yesterday and already he is expected to know how to use the cash
A B
register, how to turn the security system on and off, how to handle customer complaints
C
and keeping the bathrooms clean. No error.
D E

15. The elephants were introduced to their new habitats at the zoo and although most of
A B
them seemed to take little notice, one elephant ferocious pounded the ground with its
C D
huge feet. No error.
E

16. The speaker for the charity event was running an hour behind yet the patrons were
A B C
getting anxious and irritable. No error.
D E

17. Aware that everyone's eyes were on her, Stephanie stopped at the end of the diving
A B
board and took a deep breath before she attempted the double somersault. No error.
C D E

18. Hopping from lily pad to lily pad, the little girls were fascinated by the show the
A B
frogs were putting on for them in the pond. No error.
C D E

19. The principal decided to participate in the school's performance of "Arsenic and Old
A B
Lace" so he was gave the role of the crazy brother. No error.
C D E

20. The new teacher spoke very careful because she did not want to risk hurting
A B C
anyone's feelings. No error.
D E

21. The orchestra began playing the overture and Sheila felt the goose bumps popping
A B C
up all over her arms and legs. No error.
D E

22. Mrs. Connors kept trying to teach Liam how to do the fox trot but no matter how
A B
many times she reminded he, he continued to step on her feet. No error.
C D E

23. The rock concert was so loud that my ears felt like it was going to explode so I
A B
quickly grabbed the soft ear plugs from my purse and shoved them in. No error.
C D E

24. Whipping around the corner, the steaming hot cup of coffee spilled all over my
A B C
brand new ivory blouse, staining it permanently. No error.
D E

25. Unless the television was playing quite loudly, I was still able to hear the telephone
A B C
ringing nonstop in the kitchen. No error.
D E

26. Although my brother swears that he has seen Sasquatch up close,
A B
I don't believe that no such thing exists except in people's overactive imaginations and
C D
science fiction novels. No error.
E

27. The brand new security guard checked the front door one more time before starting
A B
his rounds again. No error.
C D E

28. Running to my front door, my glasses fell off my head and landed somewhere
A B C
behind the couch in the living room. No error.
D E

29. Erin closed her eyes and took several deep breaths before picking up his pencil and
A B
starting the first question on the history final. No error.
C D E

30. The construction crew arrived first thing in the morning and they immediately
A B
began working on the house's new basement. No error.
C D E

Answer Key:

1. B. This is an example of a double negative and should read "there were no accident victims" or "there weren't any accident victims."

2. B. The problem here is the pronoun. A pronoun in objective case is the wrong choice; it must be nominative case. You would not say "Him ran directly onto the field." It should be "he." (Other nominative case pronouns are I, you, he/she/it, we, you, they.)

3. D. This is example of an error in parallelism. All of the examples in the sentence end in –ing so "not to check" should be "not for checking."

4. C. "Cut to the chase" is an idiom which should be replaced with a better choice of words.

5. D. "soft" should be in adverb form since it modifies "walk" and so it should be "softly."

6. D. This is an example of the wrong verb tense. Everything in the sentence takes place in the future, so this should read "you will have dinner."

7. E. There is no error in this sentence.

8. A. This is a dangling modifier. It should be modifying waiters and not the customers. The way the phrase is placed, it looks like the customers are wearing the roller skates, and we know that isn't correct.

9. C. This sentence has a double negative. It should read "would be no school."

10. B. "handwriting on the wall" is an idiom that should be replaced.

11. E. There is no error in this sentence.

12. A. Since the subject is plural, the verb needs to be in agreement. It should read "were planning."

13. D. This is an error in pronoun usage. It should be "their" house (3rd person usage) and not "our" (2nd person). (1st person denotes the person or people talking; 2nd person refers to the person being spoken to; and 3rd person denotes the individual or people being talked about. All the pronouns in a sentence should be in the same person.)

14. D. This is an error in parallelism. Every other example is phrased "how to" so it should read "how to keep the bathrooms clean."

15. D. "ferocious" is being used an as adverb so it should be "ferociously" .

16. B. This coordinating conjunction is used improperly which makes the sentence not make any sense. Instead it should be be "so" or "and."

17. E. There is no error in this sentence.

18. A. This is a dangling modifier. The phrase should be placed in the sentence to modify frogs and not little girls.

19. D. This is the wrong verb tense. It should read "was given."

20. B. "careful" is an adverb so it should read "carefully."

21. E. There is no error in this sentence.

22. C. This is an error in pronoun usage. It should be "him" (objective case) and not "he." (Other objective case pronouns are me, you, him, her, it, us and them.)

23. B. This is an error in both pronoun and verb use. The sentence refers to "ears" which is plural so "it was" should read "they were."

24. A. This is a case of a dangling modifier. It is modifying the person, not the cup of coffee. Its placement in the sentence should be changed so that the person is whipping around the corner rather than the cup of coffee.

25. A. This is the wrong subordinating conjunction and so the sentence does not make sense. It needs to have a conjunction such as "although" instead.

26. C. This is an example of a double negative and should be written as "I don't believe that any such thing" or "I believe that no such thing."

27. E. There is no error in this sentence.

28. A. This is an example of a dangling modifier. It should modify the subject and instead it is modifying the glasses. The glasses aren't running to the front door.

29. B. The pronoun does not match the previous pronoun and subject in gender; they are feminine so it should be "her." The hint is in the first clause: "Erin closed HER eyes."

30. E. There is no error in this sentence.

Improving Sentences

The following sentences test correctness and effectiveness of expression. Part of each sentence or the entire sentence is underlined; then beneath each sentence are five ways of phrasing the underlined material. Choice A repeats the original phrasing; the other four choices are different. If you think the original phrasing produces a better sentence than any of the alternatives, select Choice A; if not, select one of the other choices.

In making your selection, follow the requirements of standard written English; that is, pay attention to grammar, choice of words, sentence construction and punctuation. Your selection should result in the most effective sentence—clear and precise, without awkwardness or ambiguity.

1. A recent trend in popular fiction is to write about minor characters from classic novels although they attract readers who remember reading the original stories and want to find out what else has happened to these people since then.

A. although they attract readers who remember reading the original stories and want to find out what else has happened to these people since then.

B. since they attract readers who remember reading the original stories and want to find out what else has happened to these people since then.

C. even though they attract readers who remember reading the original stories and want to find out what else has happened to these people since then.

D. or they attract readers who remember reading the original stories and want to find out what else has happened to these people since then.

E. as though they attract readers who remember reading the original stories and want to find out what else has happened to these people since then.

2. The new computer at Caroline's house is both newer and more modern than Katherine's house.

A. both newer and more modern than Katherine's house.

B. both sturdier and moderner than Katherine's house.

C. both sturdier and more complicated than the computer at Katherine's house.

D. both sturdier and more complicated than Katherine's.

E. both sturdier and more complicated than the one at Katherine's house.

3. Full of calories, sugar and carbohydrates, the models avoided eating the chocolate birthday cake as if it was laced with cyanide.

A. the models avoided eating the chocolate birthday cake as if it was laced with cyanide.

B. the chocolate birthday cake, as if laced with cyanide, was avoided by all of the models.

C. avoided as if laced with cyanide, the chocolate birthday cake the models avoided eating.

D. the chocolate birthday cake was avoided by the models as if it were laced with cyanide.

E. the models, as if laced with cyanide, avoided eating the chocolate birthday cake.

4. The question of whether or not schools should include art and physical education in their curriculum is debated by everyone from teachers and administrators to parents and students.

A. or not schools should include art and physical education in their curriculum is debated

B. or not schools should include art and physical education in their curriculum are debated

C. or not schools, art and physical education in their curriculum, are debated

D. or not curriculum, such as art and physical education, in schools is debated

E. or not schools in their curriculum, art and physical education, should be included is debated

5. The orchestra's conductor was shocked to find the perfect violin he'd been hoping to have for years preparing for the huge debut that night at the Orpheus.

A. The orchestra's conductor was shocked to find the perfect violin he'd been hoping to have for years preparing for the huge debut that night at the Orpheus.

B. Shocked, the orchestra's conduction found the perfect violin he'd been hoping to have for years preparing for the huge debut that night at the Orpheus.

C. Preparing for the huge debut that night at the Orpheus, the orchestra's conductor was shocked to find the perfect violin he'd been hoping to have for years.

D. To his shock, the orchestra's conductor found the perfect violin for the huge debut that night at the Orpheus that he'd been hoping to have for years.

E. Finding the perfect violin he'd been hoping to have for years preparing for the huge debut that night at the Orpheus, the orchestra conductor was shocked.

6. Personal computers which once belonged only to huge, wealthy corporations are now found in more homes than indoor plumbing.

A. Personal computers which once belonged only to huge, wealthy corporations are

B. Personal computers, only belonging to huge, wealthy corporations are

C. Belonging only to huge, wealthy corporations, personal computers are

D. Personal computers, which once belonged only to huge, wealthy corporations, are

E. Huge, wealthy corporations, personal computers, only belonging are

7. Plugging in his electric guitar, the lead singer prepared to walk out on the stage and thrill his audience with the newest hit single.

A. Plugging in his electric guitar, the lead singer

B. The electric guitar, plugging in, the lead singer

C. The lead singer, his electric guitar plugging in

D. Plugging in, the lead singer, his electric guitar

E. The leader singer, plugging in his electric guitar, he

8. The film finally started fifteen minutes late the audience was already getting extremely restless and noisy.

A. fifteen minutes late the audience was already

B. fifteen minutes late; the audience was already

C. fifteen minutes late, the audience was already

D. fifteen minutes late: the audience was already

E. fifteen minutes late—the audience was already

9. The park was full of people out enjoying the unexpected warmth children were playing, dogs were running and there was a feel of excitement in the air.

A. unexpected warmth children were playing

B. unexpected warmth, children were playing

C. unexpected warmth; children were playing

D. unexpected warmth although children were playing

E. unexpected warmth—children were playing

10. The personnel at the jewelry store realized that more was missing than they had thought, seven diamond rings, three bracelets, five necklaces, eight brooches and more than two dozen loose stones.

A. missing than they had thought, seven diamond rings

B. missing than they had thought—seven diamond rings

C. missing than they had thought for seven diamond rings

D. missing than they had thought: seven diamond rings

E. missing than they had thought. Seven diamond rings

11. Grabbing the last piece of pizza, the telephone rang just as she took the very first bite.

A. Grabbing the last piece of pizza, the telephone rang just as she took the very first bite.

B. Just as she took the very first bite, the telephone rang grabbing the last piece of pizza.

C. The telephone rang just as she took the very first bite, grabbing the last piece of pizza.

D. The very first bite she took as the telephone rang and she grabbed the last piece of pizza.

E. Grabbing the last piece of pizza, she took the very first bite and the telephone rang.

12. "Eliminating all credit card debt is certainly possible, said Mr. Cunningham, "and it is far easier than you ever imagined."

A. is certainly possible, said Mr. Cunningham,

B. is certainly possible," said Mr. Cunningham,

C. is certainly possible." Said Mr. Cunningham,

D. is certainly possible; said Mr. Cunningham,

E. is certainly possible" said Mr. Cunningham,

13. The information about new species of underwater creatures are totally fascinating to hear and the photographs are absolutely astonishing to see.

A. new species of underwater creatures are totally fascinating

B. new specie of underwater creature is totally fascinating

C. new species of underwater creatures is totally fascinating

D. new species of underwater creatures were totally fascinating

E. new species of underwater creatures are total fascinating

14. The suspect was taken into custody, his fingerprints were taken and finally she was read his legal rights.

A. and finally she was read his legal rights.

B. and finally he was read her legal rights.

C. and finally he was read their legal rights.

D. and finally he was read his legal rights.

E. and finally they were read his legal rights.

15. The story of Jekyll and Hyde is a classic one which appears again and again in modern movies and novels.

A. which appears again and again

B. which, appears again and again,

C. which appears again. And again

D. which appears, again and again

E. ,which appears again and again,

16. The wine cellar was locked and thus the collection of expensive, irreplaceable bottles were safe from burglars.

A. collection of expensive, irreplaceable bottles were safe

B. collection of expensive, irreplaceable bottles was safe

C. collection of expensive, irreplaceable bottle was safe

D. collections of expensive, irreplaceable bottle was safe

E. collections of expensive, irreplaceable bottles is safe

17. The police officer reassured me repeatedly that there weren't no problems with my record.

A. that there weren't no problems with my record.

B. that there were none problems with my record.

C. that there were any problems with my record.

D. that there wasn't no problems with my record.

E. that there weren't any problems with my record.

18. The history professor, who originally came from California, was teaching at a prestigious college in Chicago today.

A. who originally came from California, was teaching

B. who originally came from California; was teaching

C. who originally came from California. Was teaching

D. who, originally came from California was teaching

E. who, originally, came from California was teaching

Answer Key:

1. B. The conjunction "since" connects the two statements meaningfully. The other conjunctions change the meaning in ways that do not make sense.

2. E. This is a case of faulty comparison. A does not repair it and B includes "moderner," which is not a real word. C is too wordy and D is confusing—the new computer is more modern than Katherine's what? Only E corrects the problem.

3. D. This modifier is in the wrong place so the second half has to be rearranged so that it correctly modifies the birthday cake. Only option D does this without changing the meaning or being too wordy. Additionally, "was"

must be changed to "were" to use the subjunctive form of the verb ("subjunctive" form is used when the thought is contrary to fact. In this sentence, the cake isn't really laced with cyanide). Option D also does this.

4. A. The sentence is best as is. Option B changes the verb incorrectly, as does C. All other options change the sentence so that it does not make sense.

5. C. This is a case of a misplaced modifier. It sounds like the violin was preparing for the debut and only option C puts the modifier where it belongs.

6. D. This sentence contains a dependent nonessential clause, which needs to set off by commas and only option D does this.

7. A. The modifier describes the lead singer so this sentence is correct as is.

8. B. This is a run-on sentence and needs the right punctuation to link the two independent clauses. The only possibilities that work are a semicolon or a period. Choice B uses the semicolon.

9. C. This is a run-on sentence and needs the right punctuation to link the clauses. The only possibilities that work are a semicolon or a period. Choice C uses the semicolon.

10. D. This sentence contains a list and that can only properly be introduced with a colon.

11. E. This misplaced modifier needs to be next to "she" and not "telephone." Only option E does this without changing the meaning of the sentence.

12. B. A second quotation mark is needed after "possible" and the sentence must retain the comma.

13. C. The subject "information" is singular so it requires a singular verb, i.e. "is" and not "are."

14. D. This is a case of figuring out the right pronouns to use. The first part of the sentence determines that the suspect is male so the pronouns have to match that in gender and number.

15. A. This sentence is correct as is.

16. B. The subject is "collection," which is singular, so the verb has to match.

17. E. This is an example of a double negative and only option E corrects it without changing the meaning of the sentence.

18. A. This is correct as it is written.

Improving Paragraphs

The following passage is an early draft of an essay. Some parts of the passage need to be rewritten.

Read the passage and select the best answers for the questions that follow. Some questions are about particular sentences or parts of sentences and ask you to improve sentence structure or word choice. Other questions ask you to consider organization and development. In choosing answers, follow the requirements of standard written English.

Passage #1

(1) Scientists have known for a long time that different parts of the brain become active depending on what a person is thinking about or doing at the time. (2) To see how music affects the brain, a few researchers performed an interesting study. (3) They asked six professional jazz piano players to participate.

(4) Each one of the musicians was put inside a long tube-shaped machine called an MRI or magnetic resonance imaging. (5) This machine is able to measure blood flow in the brain. (6)

As a person thinks about something, different parts of the brain become filled with blood. (7) The MRI can track where and when it does.

(8) First, the researchers had the musicians play some notes on a little piano keyboard. (9) Next, they had him put the notes together to create a song. (10) Finally, they had each one of them each memorize a jazz song and then play it while inside the MRI tube. (11) It might have been a song written by Cole Porter. (12) As they played, they heard a recording of other instruments playing accompaniment. (13) Improvising, which means to make up the notes to play as they went.

(1) In context, which of the following represents the best way to revise and combine sentences 4 and 5 (reproduced below)?

Each one of the musicians was put inside a long tube-shaped machine called an MRI or magnetic resonance imaging. This machine is able to measure blood flow in the brain.

A. Each one of the musicians was put inside a long tube-shaped machine called an MRI or magnetic resonance imaging although this machine is able to measure blood flow in the brain.

B. Each one of the musicians was put inside a long tube-shaped machine called an MRI or magnetic resonance imaging, which is able to measure blood flow in the brain.

C. Each one of the musicians was put inside a long tube-shaped machine called an MRI or magnetic resonance imaging whereas it is able to measure blood flow in the brain.

D. Each one of the musicians was put inside a long tube-shaped machine called an MRI or magnetic resonance imaging or this machine is able to measure blood flow in the brain.

E. Each one of the musicians was put inside a long tube-shaped machine called an MRI or magnetic resonance imaging, if it is able to measure blood flow in the brain.

(2) In context, which of the following is the best revision of sentence 10 (reproduced below)?

Finally, they had each one of them each memorize a jazz song and then play it while inside the MRI tube.

A. Finally, they had each one of them memorize a jazz song and then plays it while inside the MRI tube.

B. Finally, he had every one of them each memorizes a jazz song and then play it while inside the MRI tube.

C. Finally, they had them each memorize a jazz song and then play it while inside the MRI tube.

D. Finally, we had them all each memorize a jazz song and then play it while inside the MRI tube.

E. Finally, we had him each memorize a jazz song and then plays it while inside the MRI tube.

(3) In context, which of the following is the best revision of sentence 13 (reproduced below)?

Improvising, which means to make up the notes to play as they went.

A. Improvising, which means to make up the notes to play as they went is what they did.

B. Making up the notes to play as they went or improvising.

C. Improvising, making up the notes to play, is what they did as they went.

D. The musicians improvising, making up the notes to play as they went.

E. The musicians improvised, or made up the notes to play as they went.

(4) The writer's main reason or purpose in this essay is to

A. point out the connection between playing music and brain activity.

B. analyze how the MRI uses magnets to measure blood flow.

C. describe how jazz players learn how to improvise music.

D. prove that playing music is beneficial to brain growth.

E. predict how creating music changes overall brain function.

(5) The writer could best close this passage with information about what

A. instruments each musician liked to play best.

B. kind of jazz the pianists preferred to play.

C. the majority of jazz music sounds like.

D. the MRI tests revealed about the brain flow.

E. makes MRIs able to measure brain activity.

(6) Which of the following sentences from the passage should be removed to improve the flow?

A. Seven

B. Eight

C. Ten

D. Eleven

E. Thirteen

Answer Key:

1. B. This is the only option that retains the meaning and uses a word that appropriately links the sentences together.

2. C. This sentence has a problem with singular versus plural pronouns as well as indefinite pronouns. Only option C corrects this. Some of the other choices offered have faulty subject/verb agreement and cannot be selected as a revision.

3. E. This sentence is a fragment lacking a subject. Choice E is the best correction.

4. A. None of the other actions is relevant to the passage.

5. D. This is key information that is needed in the passage's conclusion.

6. D. This gives unnecessary information and should be removed.

Passage #2

(1) The produce sections of many of the biggest grocery stores have been getting more exotic in recent years. (2) Next to the typical fruit selections of strawberries and melons, many of them offer such unusual fruits as acai, mangosteen, pomegranate, noni and goji berries. (3) These fruits add some interesting new tastes to the dinner table. (4) According to some, they can also make a person healthier.

(5) Even though it is illegal in the United States for companies that sell these fruits to claim that the food can fight cancer, cure heart disease, strengthen the immune system or help a person live longer, they still do so. (6) Earning them the nickname of "superfruits."

(7) Of course, some nutritionists strongly disagree with the opinion that these types of fruit are any better for you than the typical apple or orange. (8) They do not necessarily say the fruits are not good for you, just not specifically better than more typical fruits. (9) Since this exotic produce means high prices, it may end up hurting a person's wallet more than helping your health.

(1) In context, which of the following represents the best way to revise and combine sentences 3 and 4 (reproduced below)?

These fruits add some interesting new tastes to the dinner table. According to some, they can also make a person healthier.

A. These fruits add some interesting new tastes to the dinner table since according to some, they can also make a person healthier.

B. These fruits add some interesting new tastes to the dinner table because according to some, they can also make a person healthier.

C. These fruits add some interesting new tastes to the dinner table and according to some, they can also make a person healthier.

D. These fruits add some interesting new tastes to the dinner table so according to some, they can also make a person healthier.

E. These fruits add some interesting new tastes to the dinner table nor according to some, they can also make a person healthier.

(2) In context, which of the following is the best revision of sentence 6 (reproduced below)?

Earning them the nickname of "superfruits."

A. The nickname "superfruits" is earned them.

B. This has earned them the nickname of "superfruits."

C. Earning them "superfruits" as a nickname.

D. "Superfruits" is the nickname earned for them.

E. This the nickname "superfruits" has earned them.

(3) In context, which of the following is the best revision of sentence 9 (reproduced below)?

Since this exotic produce means high prices, it may end up hurting a person's wallet more than helping your health.

A. Since this exotic produce means high prices, they may end up hurting a person's wallet more than helping your health.

B. Since this exotic produce means high prices, it may end up hurting your wallet more than helping a person's health.

C. Since this exotic produce means high prices, you may end up hurting one's wallet more than helping a person's health.

D. Since this exotic produce means high prices, it may end up hurting a person's wallet more than helping a person's health.

E. Since this exotic produce means high prices, it may end up hurting the wallet instead of helping your health.

(4) The author's main purpose in writing this essay is to

A. prove that all types of fruit are created equal.

B. point out the importance of eating a variety of foods.

C. analyze how some companies lie to the American public.

D. convince the reader that these fruits can help them live longer.

E. highlight the fact that some new fruits on the market are being sold as extra healthy.

(5) The logical flow of the passage as a whole would be most improved by adding the following sentence after which of the essay's lines?

Supposedly these fruits contain ingredients like antioxidants that have been proven in certain studies to improve health and protect against disease.

A. After sentence 1

B. After sentence 4

C. After sentence 5

D. After sentence 7

E. After sentence 9

(6) Which of the following statements would make the best conclusion to the essay?

A. In order to support the claims of these companies, more research needs to be done on these so-called "superfruits."

B. These fruits cost so much more than typical produce that even if they are good for you, it is simply not worth it.

C. Most of these fruits come from other countries and have to be flown in at great expense to the stores and consumers.

D. "Superfruits" are said to contain antioxidants which have many supposed health benefits.

E. Companies are always looking for ways to exploit consumers' ongoing desire for healthy alternatives.

Answer Key:

1. C. This adds the correct conjunction to keep the original meaning of the sentence.

2. B. This is a fragment and is missing a subject. Only option B adds one that makes sense.

3. D. The problem in this sentence is that it switches from third person to second person so the pronoun must be changed for consistency.

4. E. The other options are not supported by the details in the essay.

5. B. This is where the statement would best fit as it fits the topic of the sentence before and after it. The other places are too early or too late.

6. A. This is a neutral position between the two opinions in the essay and it addresses both viewpoints evenly. The others are either too strong an opinion or would belong in a different part of the essay rather than appearing in the conclusion.

Essay

Think carefully about the issue presented in the following excerpt and the assignment below.

Being loyal—faithful or dedicated to someone or something—is not always easy. People often have conflicting loyalties, and there are no guidelines that help them decide to what or whom they should be loyal. Moreover, people are often loyal to something bad. Still, loyalty is one of the essential attributes a person must have and must demand of others.

Adapted from James Carville, *Stickin': The Case for Loyalty*
Note: This is an actual example of a writing prompt used in the March 2008 SAT.

Assignment: Should people always be loyal? Plan and write an essay in which you develop your point of view on this issue. Support your position with reasoning and examples taken from your reading, studies, experience or observations.

Good Sample Answer:

I believe that always being loyal is almost as impossible to achieve as always being honest or always being kind. Even though each one of these is an admirable goal, to always be anything, regardless of the circumstances or the situation, seems foolish. There are circumstances in life where being loyal, honest or kind is not the wisest choice to make.

For example, a few years ago, one of my best friends began spending time with several new kids at school. They were involved not only in using drugs but also in selling it to others. Before long, my friend was entangled too. I watched a happy person and a good student slowly sink down into becoming a frantic person and a horrible student. The rules of loyalty may have dictated that I stay his friend and keep my mouth shut, but instead I talked to his parents and they quickly got him into rehab. Perhaps that was violating my loyalty but it was still the right thing to do. I was proud of my actions and even though I risked our friendship, I would do it all over again.

Time and again, I have seen the principle of loyalty turn sour in our culture. Sometimes it is a politician staying loyal to unions or lobbies, even at the cost of the people they are supposed to serve. Other times it might be loyalty to an employer, even when the employer is involved in nefarious or illegal activities. Loyalty is just not the best choice in all situations.

Loyalty is an important value for all people, including me. It is one that I consider essential but not unalterable. While I plan to uphold the ethic as long as I can, I will also recognize that there are times, places, people and circumstances that change the meaning and significance of the word.

SCORE: 6 points

Comments: This is an excellent essay. It hits all the nails on the head, to use a don't-use-it-in-your-essay idiom. It addresses the topic directly. It states an opinion clearly in the first paragraph. It supports the opinion with a personal example in the second paragraph and with worldly examples in the third paragraph. Then, the fourth paragraph restates the opinion and brings it all to a solid conclusion. It is a good length and uses excellent vocabulary. Bravo!

Bad Sample Answer:

Here is another essay on the same subject:

Being loyal is important. Everyone should do it. That is what friendship is all about. I think that I am a loyal friend to people.

The news is always full of stories about people who are not loyal to each other. There are stories about spouses hurting their partners or their children. There are stories about politicians not being loyal to the people they work for. There are even stories about employees who just don't remain loyal to their employers even though that is where their paychecks come from.

I think that if you care about someone, then being loyal is just part of it. It is what makes you a good friend and an overall good person. You should always be loyal to the people you hang with just like you should always be nice. It's just the best way to live your life.

SCORE: 3 points

Comments: On the positive side: The student does address the topic and express her opinion on it. She also provides several examples to support her opinion. That is about it, however. On the negative side: The essay is too short. It uses slang and no examples of a strong vocabulary. It is somewhat repetitive and the sentences are choppy. This earns just a grade of average.

Practice Test #2

Identifying Sentence Errors

The following sentences test your ability to recognize grammar and usage errors. Each sentence contains either a single error or no error at all. No sentence contains more than one error. The error, if there is one, is underlined and lettered. If the sentence contains an error, select the one underlined part that must be changed to make the sentence correct. If the sentence is correct, select choice E. In choosing answers, follow the requirements of standard written English.

1. The four Irish singers came (A) out on the stage and (B) all the young women began screaming and yelling (C) out each singer's name (D). No error (E).

2. The cherry trees lining Main Street (A) were blossoming (B) already since (C) it was far too early (D) in the season. No error (E).

3. Julio and Emilio jogged along the park's track (A), chatting (B) about their homework and kidding (C) each other about the good-looking new girl that just moved to his school (D). No error (E).

4. Setting the table (A), the dishes she (B) used were elegant and fragile (C), giving the entire room (D) a sophisticated look. No error (E).

5. Even though (A) the sign said that the restaurant was open, there wasn't no cars (B) in the parking lot, the doors were (C) locked and there were no lights (D) on in the whole place. No error (E).

6. Because (A) the temperature was predicted (B) to go above 100 degrees that afternoon (C), it was (D) at that moment quite comfortable with a light breeze blowing. No error. (E)

7. Maria was so tired that she could not wait to go home, change clothes, grab her book,
A B C
reading until midnight and then go to bed. No error.
D E

8. Theodore fought against going to sleep, although his eyelids kept fluttering shut and
A B
his head kept falling forward as him lost the battle. No error.
C D E

9. The ushers finished seating people just as the house lights blinked on and off and
A B
within a few minutes, all the noise stopped as the audience waited for the overture to
C D
begin. No error.
E

10. The babysitter tiptoed across the room as quiet as she could so that the baby
A B C
would not wake up from his much needed nap. No error.
D E

11. The twin sisters fell in love with the twin brothers, which resulted in some very
A B C
unusual family reunions. No error.
D E

12. Carefully docking into the harbor, the passengers watched and cheered on the captain
A B
as he maneuvered the unwieldy ship. No error.
C D E

13. The leopards paced back and forth in our cage before finally settling down and
A B C
getting comfortable with their new surroundings. No error.
D E

14. The high school football team were ready for the evening's important game and
A B C
had been for over a week. No error.
D E

15. Jasmine moved (A) into her apartment (B) this week and spent (C) each day scrubbing the floors, washing the windows, she painted (D) the walls and unpacking all of her boxes. No error. (E)

16. The actor in all of those popular movies were so popular (A) that he could not go out in public without being mobbed (B) by either (C) a worshiping group of fans or nosey paparazzi (D) hoping for a photograph. No error. (E)

17. My older sister reminded (A) me that I should never judge a book by its cover (B) and so I am rethinking (C) my opinion of the man I (D) met last night. No error. (E)

18. The brand new manager fortunately (A) allow (B) me to take the time I needed to visit (C) my sick grandmother (D) in Texas. No error. (E)

19. The computer technician patiently (A) told me how to reconnect (B) to the Internet yet (C) reminded me to unplug my (D) router on a semi-regular basis. No error. (E)

20. My sister and me (A) headed straight for the beach because (B) it (C) was the best place to be on the very first day (D) of summer vacation. No error. (E)

21. Franklin covered his (A) ears when the ambulance went by and (B) didn't want no one (C) to talk to him (D) until it was out of range. No error. (E)

22. Changing the channels (A), the television offered no interesting shows (B) or movies whatsoever (C) and finally, I just turned (D) the whole thing off in frustration. No error. (E)

23. The telephone rang constantly that afternoon but no one was willing to leave the
A B C
pool long enough to see who was calling. No error.
D E

24. The list of chores that his mother handed to him was intimidating because it included
A B
clean the bathrooms, putting away the laundry, making all of the beds and even
C
washing all the dishes. No error.
D E

25. This morning I got out of the wrong side of the bed and so I am not feeling patient or
A B
friendly to anyone who lives in my house. No error.
C D E

26. Watching *American Idol* for most people is not about hearing new singers but about
A B
listening to the three judges' comments. No error.
C D E

27. I decided to go the extra mile and do the optional book report that my history
A B
teacher had suggested since it was worth 50 points. No error.
C D E

28. Even though the teacher had told the class to be quiet, one student was so excited
A B
about being in the contest that he could not help but whisper quite loud. No error.
C D E

29. The three tenors came out on the stage and as soon as the first note of music began,
A B
they started singing a beautiful Celtic melody that delighted the appreciative audience.
C D
No error.
E

30. Their road trip was going to be an amazing adventure or they were eager
A B C
to get started the second the sun came up over the horizon. No error.
D E

Answer Key:

1. E. There is no error in this sentence.

2. C. This transition word does not fit well with the meaning of the sentence. It should have been something like "even though."

3. D. The pronoun "his" is wrong as the sentence is about two boys. It should be "their."

4. A. This is a misplaced modifier and looks like it is describing the dishes' actions instead of the actions of the person setting the table.

5. B. This is an example of a double negative and should read "there were no cars" or "there weren't any cars."

6. A. The sentence is introduced by the wrong subordinate conjunction as it does not fit the meaning of the sentence. It should be something closer to "although" or "even though."

7. D. This is an example of faulty parallelism. The word should be "read" to match the other verbs.

8. D. This is the wrong pronoun to use. It should be "he."

9. E. There is no error in this sentence.

10. B. The word is meant to be an adverb and should be "quietly" instead of "quiet."

11. E. There is no error in this sentence.

12. A. This is a misplaced modifier making it appear as if the passengers were docking the ship.

13. B. This is the wrong pronoun as it is first person and the rest of the sentence is written in third person.

14. B. The verb is plural but the subject is a singular, collective noun. It should be "was" and not "were."

15. D. This is faulty parallelism. It should be "painting."

16. A. The subject is "actor", which is singular and therefore needs a singular verb. It should be "was."

17. B. This expression is an idiom and should be replaced.

18. B. The tense for the verb "allow" is incorrect. It should be "allowed."

19. C. The word "yet" does not correctly join these two thoughts. It would be better with "and."

20. A. The pronoun needed is "I" and not "me." If you find compound subjects confusing, try separating them into two individual sentences: "My sister headed for the beach" and "I headed for the beach." You would not say "Me headed for the beach" so you know that the only choice is "My sister and I..."

21. C. This is an example of a double negative and should read "didn't want anyone" or "wanted no one."

22. A. This is a misplaced modified making it sound like the television was changing the channels instead of the person.

23. E. There are no errors in this sentence.

24. C. This is an example of faulty parallelism. It should be "cleaning" and not "clean."

25. A. This is an idiom that needs to be replaced.

26. E. There are no errors in this sentence. You might be tempted to think that choice D is incorrect, but there are three judges (plural) so the apostrophe must come after the "s" to make it plural possessive.

27. A. This is an idiom that needs to be replaced.

28. D. The word "loud" is an adverb and should be "loudly."

29. E. There are no errors in this sentence.

30. B. This conjunction does not fit the sentence. Instead it needs "so" or "and."

Improving Sentences

The following sentences test correctness and effectiveness of expression. Part of each sentence or the entire sentence is underlined; beneath each sentence are five ways of phrasing the underlined material. Choice A repeats the original phrasing; the other four choices are different. If you think the original phrasing produces a better sentence than any of the alternatives, select Choice A; if not, select one of the other choices.

In making your selection, follow the requirements of standard written English; that is, pay attention to grammar, choice of words, sentence construction and punctuation. Your selection should result in the most effective sentence—clear and precise, without awkwardness or ambiguity.

1. The outdoor pool at the Cooper's house is both larger and deeper than the Hopman's house.

A. both larger and deeper than the Hopman's house.

B. both larger and more deep than the Hopman's house.

C. both larger and deeper than the pool at the Hopman's house.

D. both larger and deeper than the Hopman's.

E. both larger and more deep than the pool that is at the Hopman's house.

2. In recent years, popular singers from the modern music era have sold numerous CDs by singing songs that were well known in the 1940s and 1950s since they give the old numbers a new style.

A. since they give the old numbers a new style.

B. although they give the old numbers a new style.

C. or they give the old numbers a new style.

D. whereas they give the old numbers a new style.

E. as though they give the old numbers a new style.

3. Overflowing with chocolate, jelly beans and pink plastic grass, the girls eagerly opened their Easter baskets and squealed when they spotted their favorite candy.

A. the girls eagerly opened their Easter baskets and squealed when they spotted their favorite candy.

B. the girls squealed when they spotted their favorite candy as they eagerly opened their Easter baskets.

C. squealing when they spotted their favorite candy, the girls eagerly opened their Easter baskets.

D. the Easter baskets were eagerly opened by the girls, who squealed when they spotted their favorite candy.

E. spotting their favorite candy, the girls eagerly opened their Easter baskets and squealed.

4. The advantage of learning neat penmanship during the computer age when keyboarding has taken over is dubious at best.

A. is dubious at best.

B. are dubious at best.

C. were dubious at best.

D. will be dubious at best.

E. is being dubious at best.

5. The photo journalist was delighted to see the perfect shot he had been looking for all day taking candid pictures for a feature story in a national magazine.

A. The photo journalist was delighted to see the perfect shot he had been looking for all day taking candid pictures for a feature story in a national magazine.

B. Delighted, the photo journalist saw the perfect shot he had been looking for all day taking candid pictures for a feature story in a national magazine.

C. The perfect shot he had been looking for all day, the photo journalist was delighted to be taking candid pictures for a feature story in a national magazine.

D. A feature story in a national magazine, the photo journalist was delighted to see the perfect shot he had been looking for all day taking pictures.

E. Taking candid pictures for a feature story in a national magazine, the photo journalist was delighted to see the perfect shot he had been looking for all day.

6. Cell phones which a few decades ago belonged only to international spies and millionaires are not considered to be necessary equipment for people of all ages.

A. Cell phones which a few decades ago belonged only to international spies and millionaires

B. Cell phones, which a few decades ago belonged only to international spies and millionaires

C. Cell phones which a few decades ago belonged only to international spies and millionaires,

D. Cell phones, which a few decades ago belonged only to international spies and millionaires,

E. Cell phones; which a few decades ago belonged only to international spies and millionaires;

7. Taking the leash off her dog, Sheila was glad to be home after such a long walk out in the cold winter wind.

A. Taking the leash off her dog, Sheila was glad

B. Off her dog, Sheila was glad to take the leash

C. Sheila was glad to take the leash off her dog

D. Her dog, Sheila was glad to take the leash off

E. Taking the leash off her dog, glad was Sheila

8. The werewolf legend has been around for many years it is found in literature, movies and art within different cultures.

A. for many years it is found in literature

B. for many years, it is found in literature

C. for many years: it is found, in literature

D. for many years; it is found in literature

E. for many years—it is found in literature

9. The football stadium was packed with eager fans they could not wait to cheer their team on to victory in the championship.

A. packed with eager fans they could not wait

B. packed with eager fans, they could not wait

C. packed with eager fans. They could not wait

D. packed with eager fans—they could not wait

E. packed with eager fans' they could not wait

10. The first-year college student could not believe how much homework he had been given, three book reports, one lab experiment, one research paper and four workbook pages.

A. how much homework he had been given, three book reports

B. how much homework he had been given—three book reports

C. how much homework he had been given: three book reports

D. how much homework he had been given; three book reports

E. how much homework he had been given. Three book reports

11. Listening to the music, the doorbell rang just as Julia sat down to relax.

A. Listening to the music, the doorbell rang just as Julia sat down to relax

B. Listening to the music, Julia sat down to relax just as the doorbell rang.

C. Just as Julia sat down to relax, the doorbell rang listening to music.

D. The doorbell rang, listening to the music, just as Julia sat down to relax.

E. Julia sat down to relax, listening to the music, just as the doorbell rang.

12. "Your research paper is worth half of your overall grade" explained Professor Lincoln, "so be sure and do a good job on it."

A. is worth half of your overall grade;" explained Professor Lincoln,

B. is worth half of your overall grade?" explained Professor Lincoln,

C. is worth half of your overall grade explained Professor Lincoln,

D. is worth half of your overall grade." explained Professor Lincoln,

E. is worth half of your overall grade," explained Professor Lincoln,

13. The discovery of several new moons within the galaxy are extremely exciting to astronomers all over the globe.

A. several new moons within the galaxy are

B. several new moons within the galaxy is

C. several new moon within the galaxy is

D. several new moons within the galaxy were

E. several new moons within the galaxy will be

14. The new attorney grabbed her briefcase, walking into the courtroom and prepared to give her opening statement.

A. walking into the courtroom and prepared to give her opening statement.

B. walking into the courtroom and preparing to give her opening statement.

C. walks into the courtroom and prepares to give her opening statement.

D. walked into the courtroom and preparing to give her opening statement.

E. walked into the courtroom and prepared to give her opening statement.

15. Kristin loved to go horseback riding, which was convenient since her parents owned a horse ranch.

A. which was convenient since her parents owned a horse ranch.

B. which was convenient, since her parents owned a horse ranch.

C. which was convenient; since her parents owned a horse ranch.

D. which was convenient. Since her parents owned a horse ranch.

E. which was convenient—since her parents owned a horse ranch.

16. The bookstore was nearby so her purchase of several mysteries and a romance novel were easily returned.

A. her purchase of several mysteries and a romance novel were

B. her purchase of several mysteries and a romance novel are

C. her purchase of several mysteries and a romance novel was

D. her purchases of several mysteries and a romance novel is

E. her purchase of several mystery and a romance novel are

17. The physician kept reassuring me that there weren't no abnormalities on any of my medical tests.

A. that there weren't no abnormalities

B. that there wasn't no abnormalities

C. that there aren't no abnormalities

D. that there were no abnormalities

E. that there is not no abnormalities

18. The new kid in school, who had moved here from Pasadena, California, was placed in Mrs. Harshberger's class.

A. who had moved here from Pasadena, California, was placed

B. who had moved here, from Pasadena, California, was placed

C. who had moved here from Pasadena, California was placed

D. who had moved, here from Pasadena, California, was placed

E. who had moved here from Pasadena, California; was placed

Answer Key:

1. C. This is a case of faulty comparison. Option B changes deeper to more deep which is incorrect. Option D does not explain what it being compared. Option E is too wordy and awkward.

2. B. The conjunction "since" does not work because a contrast is needed. Option B provides that. Option C, D and E do not make sense.

3. D. As written it appears that the girls are overflowing with all of these things. The modifier has to be moved so it is next to Easter baskets. Only option D does this.

4. A. This sentence is correct as written. The other options change the verb incorrectly. Since the subject is singular, the verb must be singular too. It must also stay in the present tense. Both options D and E use the wrong verb tense.

5. E. This is a misplaced modifier that makes it appear as if the shot is taking pictures. Only E places the modifier where it belongs.

6. D. This sentence includes a nonessential dependent clause which needs to be set off by commas before and after it.

7. A. The sentence is correct as is. The modifier is next to Sheila where it is supposed to be. The other options only make it awkward or grammatically incorrect.

8. D. This is an example of a run-on sentence and the only punctuation that repairs it is a semicolon or a period. The other punctuation marks are not correct.

9. C. This is another run-on sentence. The only punctuation that repairs it is a semicolon or a period as in option C.

10. C. This sentence includes a list that needs to be introduced by a colon.

11. B. This is a misplaced modifier and it has to be moved so that it is next to Sheila. Only option B does this correctly.

12. E. There is a missing comma that needs to be inserted as in option E. The other options use incorrect punctuation marks.

13. B. The verb needs to be present tense and singular since the subject is singular. Only option B has these requirements.

14. E. This sentence has faulty parallelism. All verb tenses have to match and this occurs only in option E.

15. A. This sentence is correct as it is written. You might be tempted to think that a comma before "since" is correct. However, when a dependent clause appears at the end of a sentence, the subordinate conjunction is not preceded by a comma.

16. C. The subject of this sentence is "purchase." It is singular so it needs a singular verb. The verb must also remain in past tense.

17. D. This is a case of a double negative and only option D repairs the sentence correctly.

18. A. This sentence is correct as written. The dependent clause is nonessential and therefore should be set off commas.

Improving Paragraphs

The following passage is an early draft of an essay. Some parts of the passage need to be rewritten.

Read the passage and select the best answers for the questions that follow. Some questions are about particular sentences or parts of sentences and ask you to improve sentence structure or word choice. Other questions ask you to consider organization and development. In choosing answers, follow the requirements of standard written English.

Passage #1

(1) For decades, people have believed that hobbits only existed in J.R.R. Tolkien's fantasy world. (2) A report of finding hobbit-like bones from the island of Flores in Indonesia changed all that.(3) The skeletons found there has been dated to between 1400 and 3000 years ago.

(4) The bones have told researchers many secrets. (5) They have facial features have a great deal in common with *Homo sapiens*. (6) They are quite human-like from head to toe except for their overall height. (7) Some scientists theorize that these people had diminished height due to a phenomenon known as island dwarfism. (8) This is not the same thing as being a midget, however. (9) Creatures, human and animal, often have an overall smaller stature if they live on a remote island instead of on the mainland. (10) Why this happens has yet to be determined.

1. In context, which of the following represents the best way to revise and combine sentences 1 and 2 (reproduced below)?

For decades, people have believed that hobbits only existed in J.R.R. Tolkien's fantasy world. A report of finding hobbit-like bones from the island of Flores in Indonesia changed all that.

A. For decades, people have believed that hobbits only existed in J.R.R. Tolkien's fantasy world while a report of finding hobbit-like bones from the island of Flores in Indonesia changed all that.

B. For decades, people have believed that hobbits only existed in J.R.R. Tolkien's fantasy world; however, a report of finding hobbit-like bones from the island of Flores in Indonesia changed all that.

C. For decades, people have believed that hobbits only existed in J.R.R. Tolkien's fantasy world, even though a report of finding hobbit-like bones from the island of Flores in Indonesia changed all that.

D. For decades, people have believed that hobbits only existed in J.R.R. Tolkien's fantasy world, whereas a report of finding hobbit-like bones from the island of Flores in Indonesia changed all that.

E. For decades, people have believed that hobbits only existed in J.R.R. Tolkien's fantasy world; meanwhile, a report of finding hobbit-like bones from the island of Flores in Indonesia changed all that.

2. In context, which of the following is the best revision of sentence 3 (reproduced below)?

The skeletons found there has been dated to between 1400 and 3000 years ago.

A. The skeletons found there had been dated to between 1400 and 3000 years ago.

B. The skeletons found there will have been dated to between 1400 and 3000 years ago.

C. The skeletons found there have been dated to between 1400 and 3000 years ago.

D. The skeletons found there is dated to between 1400 and 3000 years ago.

E. The skeletons found there dated to between 1400 and 3000 years ago.

3. In context, which of the following is the best revision of sentence 5 (reproduced below)?

They have facial features that have a great deal in common with Homo sapiens.

A. The characters have facial features that have a great deal in common with *Homo sapiens.*

B. The researchers have facial features that have a great deal in common with *Homo sapiens.*

C. The hobbits have facial features that have a great deal in common with *Homo sapiens.*

D. The skeletons have facial features that have a great deal in common with *Homo sapiens.*

E. The scientists have facial features that have a great deal in common with *Homo sapiens.*

4. The writer's main reason or purpose in this essay is to

A. discuss the possibility of island dwarfism.

B. explain where hobbits came from originally.

C. point out where Tolkien got his inspiration.

D. convince the reader about the age of the skeletons.

E. entertain readers with an amusing bit of history.

5. The writer could best close this passage with information about what

A. causes island dwarfism.

B. the population of Indonesia is like.

C. teams the scientists will form.

D. the small humans used to eat and drink.

E. the hobbit creatures can teach researchers.

6. Which of the following sentences from the passage should be removed to improve the flow?

A. Five

B. Six

C. Seven

D. Eight

E. Ten

Answer Key:

1. B. This is the only option that preserves the meaning and uses a word that appropriately links the sentences together.

2. C. The verb has to be plural and past tense to match the rest of the sentence and only option C does this.

3. D. The problem with this sentence is that the pronoun is vague. "They" could be referring to the researchers or the skeletons. It has to be clarified and only option D does this correctly.

4. A. Tolkien's inspiration is never discussed, there is no persuasion involved and there is nothing funny in the essay.

5. E. Option A is wrong because it states that the cause is unknown. Option B is incorrect because it would be irrelevant information. Option C is wrong because it would be irrelevant and Option D is wrong because this would be a minor detail that would not lend much to the essay. Option E is the only logical choice.

6. D. This sentence is irrelevant to the rest of the passage and should ideally be removed.

Passage #2

(1) Cheese lovers have a new reason to cheer. (2) There is a new cheese on the market that has high levels of heart healthy fats. (3) These are the type that may be able to help fight heart disease, cancer and even diabetes. (4) While some will be lining up to get a taste of this new cheese, other people might not be in such a hurry when they find out where the cheese comes from.(5) It is made from the milk of yaks.

(6) Yaks are long haired, humped animals that is a common sight in countries like Tibet, Asia and Mongolia. (7) When the cheese made from the yak's milk was compared to the cheese made from dairy cows, they found that yak cheese had four times higher amounts of the helpful fatty acids. (8) For people concerned about their health, getting a helping of yak cheese might be just what they want to add to their dinner table.

1. In context, which of the following represents the best way to revise and combine sentences 3 and 4 (reproduced below)?

Cheese lovers have a new reason to cheer. There is a new cheese on the market that has high levels of heart healthy fats.

A. Cheese lovers have a new reason to cheer although there is a new cheese on the market that has high levels of heart healthy fats.

B. Cheese lovers have a new reason to cheer yet there is a new cheese on the market that has high levels of heart healthy fats.

C. Cheese lovers have a new reason to cheer there is a new cheese on the market that has high levels of heart healthy fats.

D. Cheese lovers have a new reason to cheer or there is a new cheese on the market that has high levels of heart healthy fats.

E. Cheese lovers have a new reason to cheer because there is a new cheese on the market that has high levels of heart healthy fats.

2. In context, which of the following is the best revision of sentence 6 (reproduced below)?

Yaks are long haired, humped animals that is a common sight in countries like Tibet, Asia and Mongolia.

A. Yaks are long haired, humped animals that are a common sight in countries like Tibet, Asia and Mongolia.

B. Yaks are long haired, humped animals that has been a common sight in countries like Tibet, Asia and Mongolia.

C. Yaks are long haired, humped animals that will be a common sight in countries like Tibet, Asia and Mongolia.

D. Yaks are long haired, humped animals, which is a common sight in countries like Tibet, Asia and Mongolia.

E. Yaks are long haired, humped animals being a common sight in countries like Tibet, Asia and Mongolia.

3. In context, which of the following is the best revision of sentence 7 (reproduced below)?

When the cheese made from the yak's milk was compared to the cheese made from dairy cows, they found that yak cheese had amounts of helpful fatty acids in quantities four times higher than the cow cheese.

A. When the cheese made from the yak's milk was compared to the cheese made from dairy cows, the cows found that yak cheese had amounts of helpful fatty acids in quantities four times higher than the cow cheese.

B. When the cheese made from the yak's milk was compared to the cheese made from dairy cows, the yaks found that yak cheese had amounts of helpful fatty acids in quantities four times higher than the cow cheese.

C. When the cheese made from the yak's milk was compared to the cheese made from dairy cows, the chefs found that yak cheese had amounts of helpful fatty acids in quantities four times higher than the cow cheese.

D. When the cheese made from the yak's milk was compared to the cheese made from dairy cows, the researchers found that yak cheese had amounts of helpful fatty acids in quantities four times higher than dairy cheese.

E. When the cheese made from the yak's milk was compared to the cheese made from dairy cows, the people found that yak cheese had amounts of helpful fatty acids in quantities four times higher than the cow cheese.

4. The author's main purpose in writing this essay is to

A. describe cheese in these countries

B. point out a new healthy food product

C. explain what a yak's life is like

D. convince readers to try a new cheese

E. discuss what makes something heart healthy

5. The logical flow of the passage as a whole would be most improved by adding the following sentence after which of the essay's lines?

These beneficial acids are officially known as conjugated linoleic acid.

A. After sentence 2

B. After sentence 4

C. After sentence 6

D. After sentence 7

E. After sentence 8

6. Which of the following statements would make the best conclusion to the essay?

A. The researchers in this study are stationed in Nepal and Canada.

B. Yaks are common animals in some countries, much like pets in the U.S.

C. Sometimes eating heart healthy means being willing to experiment a bit.

D. Cheese is one of the most popular types of dairy food on the market today.

E. This study was published in the Journal of Agricultural and Food Chemistry.

Answer Key:

1. E. This option has the only connecting word that makes sense with the rest of the sentence. Option C takes out the connecting word and this just creates a run-on sentence.

2. A. The subject is plural so the verb has to be plural too. Only option A does this without changing the verb tense.

3. D. The pronoun "they" is completely unidentified in this sentence, so a noun is needed to replace it. None of the other options make any sense.

4. B. None of the other options are mentioned or supported within the essay.

5. A. This adds information to what is stated in the previous sentence. The other options are not good choices because the added sentence would be out of place.

6. C. The other options are extra information that could potentially be added but would not work as a conclusion. Only option C fits the requirement.

ESSAY

Think carefully about the issue presented in the following excerpt and the assignment below.

Winning feels forever fabulous. But you can learn more from losing than from winning. Losing prepares you for setback and tragedy more than winning ever can. Moreover, loss invites reflection and a change of strategies. In the process of recovering from your losses, you learn how to avoid them the next time.

Adapted from Pat Conroy, *My Losing Season*
Note: This is an actual example of a writing prompt used in the March 2008 SAT.

Assignment: Do people learn more from losing than from winning? Plan and write an essay in which you develop your point of view on this issue. Support your position with reasoning and examples taken from your reading, studies, experience or observations.

Good Sample Answer:

If we don't have rain, we can't appreciate sunshine. If we don't have sorrow, we can't appreciate happiness. And, if we don't lose, we can never truly appreciate the rush of winning. Losing teaches us the most powerful lessons, but that doesn't mean we have to enjoy ourselves in the process.

Last year, I joined the track team and in the beginning, I lost every single competition. It began to get rather discouraging, but I tried to look at each race and figure out what I needed to learn from it so that I could carry that experience to my next competition. I began to improve and soon I was winning more than losing.

My mother is a fantastic example of someone who grew and developed through the process of losing. She had seven jobs over the course of one year. Each one she took taught her more about what she did not want to do with her life. Finally, using those lessons, she ended up getting a job that not only matched her abilities but also her passion.

History has proven this principle again and again. Those leaders who have failed end up going on to become the best at their jobs. Losing one battle gives us the edge to win the next one. The examples are endless.

Perhaps the key to learning more from losing is having the right point of view. If you see each failure as a weakness that cannot be improved or rectified, then its lessons are wasted on you. If, however, you see each one as a golden opportunity to find out more about your abilities and your goals, then even in losing, you are winning.

SCORE: 6 points

Comments: This essay hits the mark on all counts. The author states a direct answer to the question in the first paragraph. The opinion is then supported by examples from personal experience, the work record of his/her mother and a reference to leaders in history. Finally, in the last paragraph, he/she brings it to a strong conclusion and refers back to the prompt to give it closure.

Bad Sample Answer:

Let's look at a second essay on this topic:

Losing is a part of life. It's a part that most of us don't like though. I do agree that a person can learn more from losing than winning, but that doesn't make it any easier to deal with, does it?

I have lost plenty of times in my life. Most of the time, I try to figure out what I did wrong so then next time around I can make sure not to do it again. I admit that now and then I forget to do that though. Then I just walk around and complain a lot.

Everyone loses. Famous people throughout history have failed at something. Just look at Colonel Sanders from Kentucky Fried Chicken. He tried a whole lot of jobs before he finally founded his multi-million dollar franchise. His determination to succeed won out.

Losing just isn't any fun. But if we find the lesson in it, then it had a purpose anyway. If you don't lose, you won't appreciate what it is like to win.

SCORE: 3

Comments: This essay attempts to express an opinion and then to support it, but the paragraphs tend to ramble. The author uses a lot of words to say little. It does not have any solid examples other than the vague one about the founding of KFC. This just passes.

Practice Test #3

Identifying Sentence Errors

The following sentences test your ability to recognize grammar and usage errors. Each sentence contains either a single error or no error at all. No sentence contains more than one error. The error, if there is one, is underlined and lettered. If the sentence contains an error, select the one underlined part that must be changed to make the sentence correct. If the sentence is correct, select choice E. In choosing answers, follow the requirements of standard written English.

1. Whenever Dad comes home, the dog begins jumping, to bark and wagging its tail
A B
frantically to let us all know that he has finally arrived. No error.
C D E

2. The history professor continued to remind everyone in the classroom that if a society
A B
did not learn from its mistakes, it would be doomed to repeat them. No error.
C D E

3. The "Spring Fling Choir Concert" was ready to begin or the choir director
A B C
had still not arrived at the school. No error.
D E

4. Dr. Connors and Dr. Julian walked to the teacher's lounge together, comparing notes
A B
on how her first period classes had done on the final exams. No error.
C D E

5. Reading the newspaper, the dog would not leave me alone until I stopped reading and
A B C
let her out to chase the squirrel in the backyard. No error.
D E

6. Although she promised to meet me at the coffee shop at noon, she was not nowhere in
A B
sight when I arrived, so I gave up and went home. No error.
C D E

7. Although the weather report had predicted thunderstorms all afternoon, the barbeque
A B
at our house was postponed until the following weekend. No error.
C D E

8. Kevin looked at his list of homework and knew he would be spending the evening
A
reading his history book, figuring out his math problems, finish his book report and
B C
working on his speech. No error.
D E

9. When I answered the question about Shakespeare's play in my English class, my
A B
teacher told me that I had hit the nail on the head. No error.
C D E

10. Mitch called to tell us that the keys us found in between the cushions of our couch
A B C
belonged to him after all. No error.
D E

11. The Search and Rescue workers were called in immediately so that the search for the
A B
missing hikers could start as soon as possible. No error.
C D E

12. Her part-time job was far more demanding than she had thought it would be, although
A B C
she learned as quick as she possibly could. No error.
D E

13. Cooper watched the tall, historical ships gracefully sailing across the river,
A B C
while eating a quick lunch. No error.
D E

14. The purse belongs to me, the umbrella is hers, the baseball cap is hims and the
A B C
set of car keys have not yet been claimed. No error.
D E

15. Stomping loudly, the stairs shuddered as the excited teenager ran to show off
A B
his brand new driver's license to the rest of his family. No error.
C D E

16. The coach kept asking if everyone were ready to go because the game
A
is going to start in less than 30 minutes and we still had to go over the night's plays. No error.
B C D E

17. The song “Summer Wine” was made famous in the 1960s by Nancy Sinatra, but
A B
recently a duet by the Corrs and Bono produced an excellent version. No error.
C D E

18. When I ran out of allowance money this week, my Uncle Phil kindly reminded me
B B C
that money was the root of all evil in the world. No error.
D E

19. The book told readers all about the best 100 places to be kissed in the city of Portland,
A B
Oregon nor I was eager to give every single one of them a try with my new boyfriend.
C D
No error.
E

20. The author of all those bestselling books are planning to give a presentation at noon,
A B
followed by a book signing and then a brief question and answer session. No error.
C D E

21. “Don’t no one move!” shouted the villain. “If you do, I will cut off your rations,
A B
take away your Internet services and turn off your cell phones!” No error.
C D E

22. The cafeteria is planning to serve pizza every Friday from now on; and
A
every other Monday, the cooks will make peach or apple cobbler. No error.
B C D E

23. “It is clear that you are walking around with a huge chip on your shoulder, son,” Mr.
A B
Howards said as he and Kevin took the garbage out together. No error.
C D E

24. My English teacher absentmindedly grant permission for me to leave class early in
A B C
order to get to my dentist appointment on time. No error.
D E

25. The spring garden was in full bloom already unless my favorite plant had
A B C
yet to produce any blossoms, which was disappointing. No error.
D E

26. My two brothers, my mother and me were all more than ready to go on vacation but
A B
we had to wait patiently until our car's air conditioning and radiator were repaired.
C D
No error.
E

27. They finally installed the projection monitor in their living room but by that time,
A B C
everyone was too tired to care about watching a movie. No error.
D E

28. Pounding on the front door, the cat jumped out the back window, frightened by the
A B
unexpected sound that the Federal Express man was making. No error.
C D E

29. I really wanted to go to the movies and out to dinner with all of my friends, but
A B
ever since that morning I had felt under the weather. No error.
C D E

30. My twin brother and I told the teacher that there wasn't no way we were going to sign
A B
up for the debate team even though we were experts at arguing with each other. No error.
C D E

Answer Key:

1. B. This is faulty parallelism. The verb should be "barking" to match the others in tense.

2. E. There are no errors in this sentence.

3. B. This is the wrong coordinating conjunction so it does not make sense. The conjunction should show contrast of the two clauses. A good choice would be "but."

4. C. Since the subject is plural, the pronoun must be also. It should be "their." Another hint is the word "classes," which tells you that the two professors are comparing notes on both of their classes.

5. A. This is a misplaced modifier as it sounds like the dog is the one reading the newspaper.

6. B. This is a double negative. It should read "was nowhere" or "was not anywhere" to be correct.

7. A. The subordinate conjunction is wrong as it does not fit the meaning of the sentence. It should be something like "Because" or "Since."

8. C. This is an example of faulty parallelism. The verb should be "finishing" so that it matches the others in the sentence.

9. D. This is an idiom and should be replaced with a phrase that is not a cliché and better explains the meaning.

10. B. This is an error in pronoun usage. It should be "we."

11. E. There is no error in this sentence.

12. D. Since "quick" is an adverb, it should be written as "quickly."

13. D. This is a misplaced modifier that makes it appear as if the ships rather than Cooper are eating a quick lunch.

14. C. This is an error in pronoun choice. It should be "his" and not "hims."

15. A. This is a misplaced modifier that makes it appear as if the stairs are stomping instead of the teenager.

16. B. You might think that A is the part of the sentence that is incorrect. But that isn't the case. Even though the subject "everyone" is singular, it is subjunctive, which means that it suggests something that is not a known fact. (A verb that is subjunctive often appears in a clause begun by the subordinate conjunction "if"; for example, "if I were the king of the world.") The real problem with the sentence is B. The verb should be "was going" rather than "is going."

17. E. There is no error in this sentence.

18. D. This is an idiom and should be replaced.

19. C. This coordination conjunction does not make any sense with the rest of the sentence and should be "and" or "so."

20. B. The subject (author) is singular so the verb must match. It should be "is" instead of "are." Don't let prepositional phrases get you off track. You must still look for the subject in order to match it with the correct verb.

21. A. This is a case of a double negative and should be "No one move" or "Don't anyone move."

22. E. There is no error in this sentence.

23. B. This is an idiom that needs to be replaced.

24. B. The tense for the verb "grant" should be in the past to match the rest of the sentence so it should be "granted."

25. C. This is not the correct subordinate conjunction as it does not make sense in the statement. "Unless" implies a cause and effect relationship which doesn't exist. This needs a contrasting conjunction such as "although" or "even though."

26. B. This should be "I" and not "me." If you are not sure on questions like these, try thinking of each subject separately in its own sentence. You could say, "My two brothers were ready" and "My mother was ready." You would not say, "Me was ready"; so you know that when you put the three shorter sentences together, you'd make this sentence: "My two brothers, my mother and I …"

27. E. There is no error in this sentence.

28. A. This is a misplaced modifier because it appears as if the cat is pounding on the door.

29. D. "Under the weather" is an idiom that needs to be replaced.

30. B. This is a case of a double negative. It should be "there wasn't any way" or "there was no way."

Improving Sentences

The following sentences test correctness and effectiveness of expression. Part of each sentence or the entire sentence is underlined; beneath each sentence are five ways of phrasing the underlined material. Choice A repeats the original phrasing; the other four choices are different. If you think the original phrasing produces a better sentence than any of the alternatives, select Choice A; if not, select one of the other choices.

In making your selection, follow the requirements of standard written English; that is, pay attention to grammar, choice of words, sentence construction and punctuation. Your selection should result in the most effective sentence—clear and precise, without awkwardness or ambiguity.

1. Spring break has to be <u>one of my favorite times of year everyone gets to stay home</u> from school and a lot of people go on vacation.

A. one of my favorite times of year everyone gets to stay home

B. one of my favorite times of year, everyone gets to stay home

C. one of my favorite times of year although everyone gets to stay home

D. one of my favorite times of year. Everyone gets to stay home

E. one of my favorite times of year, everyone, gets to stay home

2. The spring break party at Leah's house is <u>both bigger and more fun than Carmen's house.</u>

A. both bigger and more fun than Carmen's house.

B. both bigger and funner than Carmen's house.

C. both bigger and more fun than the spring break party at Carmen's house.

D. both bigger and funner than Carmen's.

E. both bigger and more fun than the party at Carmen's.

3. Walking in the forest, <u>the wind blew through the trees and Daniel was sure he could hear every single leaf whispering to him to hurry home.</u>

A. the wind blew through the trees and Daniel was sure he could hear every single leaf whispering to him to hurry home.

B. the wind blew through the trees and Daniel was sure he could hear whispering to him to hurry home every single leaf.

C. Daniel was sure he could hear every single leaf whispering to him to hurry home as the wind blew through the trees.

D. wind blowing through the trees, Daniel was sure he could hear every single leaf whispering to him to hurry home.

E. through the trees the wind blew and Daniel was sure he could hear every single leaf whispering to him to hurry home.

4. There is so many creatures living under the surface of the world's oceans that it will take decades to discover, study and name even a small portion of them.

A. There is so many creatures living under the surface of the world's oceans

B. There is so many creature's living under the surface of the worlds oceans

C. There was so many creatures living under the surface of the world's oceans

D. There were so many creatures living under the surface of the world's oceans

E. There are so many creatures living under the surface of the world's oceans

5. The fisherman was thrilled to catch the biggest fish of his life spending the summer afternoon on his best friend's yacht.

A. The fisherman was thrilled to catch the biggest fish of his life spending the summer afternoon on his best friend's yacht.

B. The fisherman spending the summer afternoon on his best friend's yacht was thrilled to catch the biggest fish of his life.

C. Thrilled, the fisherman caught the biggest fish of his life spending the summer afternoon on his best friend's yacht.

D. Spending the summer afternoon on his best friend's yacht, the biggest fish of his life the fisherman was thrilled to catch.

E. The biggest fish of his life, the fisherman was thrilled to catch spending the summer afternoon on his best friend's yacht.

6. College scholarships which are somewhat easier to obtain than most students believe are quite helpful when parents get ready to send their children for further education.

A. College scholarships which are somewhat easier to obtain than most students believe

B. College scholarships, which are somewhat easier to obtain than most students believe

C. College scholarships, which are somewhat easier to obtain than most students believe,

D. College scholarships; which are somewhat easier to obtain, than most students believe

E. College scholarships: which are somewhat easier to obtain than most students believe,

7. Eavesdropping on the conversation, I tried to be as quiet as I could so they would not know I was on the telephone.

A. Eavesdropping on the conversation, I tried to be

B. I tried, eavesdropping on the conversation, to be

C. Eavesdropping, I tried to be, on the conversation

D. On the conversation, I tried to be eavesdropping

E. I tried, eavesdropping, to be on the conversation

8. Vampire stories have never been as popular as they are right now everyone seems to be telling a tale of those garlic-hating, blood-loving monsters.

A. as they are right now everyone seems to be telling

B. as they are right now; everyone seems to be telling

C. as they are right now, everyone seems to be telling

D. as they are right now: everyone seems to be telling

E. as they are right now (everyone seems to be telling)

9. The new student in charge of the sports equipment tried to carry far too much six baseballs, three catcher's mitts, eight bats and 20 hats.

A. to carry far too much six baseballs, three catcher's mitts, eight bats and 20 hats.

B. to carry far too much, six baseballs, three catcher's mitts, eight bats and 20 hats.

C. to carry far too much. Six baseballs, three catcher's mitts, eight bats and 20 hats.

D. to carry far too much; six baseballs, three catcher's mitts, eight bats and 20 hats.

E. to carry far too much: six baseballs, three catcher's mitts, eight bats and 20 hats.

10. Caroline reluctantly reached for the ringing telephone, attempting to take a much needed nap.

A. Caroline reluctantly reached for the ringing telephone, attempting to take a much needed nap.

B. Caroline, attempting to take a much needed nap, reluctantly reached for the ringing telephone.

C. Reluctantly reaching for the ringing telephone, Caroline attempting to take a much needed nap.

D. Attempting to take a much needed nap, the ringing telephone was reluctantly reached for by Caroline.

E. The ringing telephone, attempting to take a much needed nap, Caroline reluctantly reached for.

11. "Buffy the Vampire Slayer is an example of pop culture television," explained Profession Hendricks, "so get ready to watch four episodes and then write a book report over it."

A. example of pop culture television," explained Profession Hendricks,

B. example of pop culture television" explained Profession Hendricks,

C. example of pop culture television, explained Profession Hendricks,

D. example of pop culture television explained Profession Hendricks,

E. example of pop culture television." explained Profession Hendricks,

12. The new Indiana Jones movie about grand new adventures in archeology are sure to please old and new fans alike.

A. grand new adventures in archeology are sure to please

B. grand new adventure in archeology are sure to please

C. grand new adventures in archeology is sure to please

D. grand new adventures in archeology was sure to please

E. grand new adventures in archeology were sure to please

13. The busy mother of four young children picked up the dry cleaning, bought some groceries, washes the car and paid all of the month's bills.

A. bought some groceries, washes the car and paid all of the month's bills.

B. buys some groceries, washes the car and paid all of the month's bills.

C. buys some groceries, washed the car and pays all of the month's bills.

D. bought some groceries, washed the car and paid all of the month's bills.

E. bought some groceries, washed the car and pays all of the month's bills.

14. The family decided to move into the new apartment that was located right above a locally owned bakery.

A. that was located right above a locally owned bakery.

B. that was located, right above a locally owned bakery.

C. that was located: right above a locally owned bakery.

D. that, was located right above a locally owned bakery,

E. that was located; right above a locally owned bakery.

15. The mechanic eventually convinced me that there wasn't nothing wrong with my truck's engine after all.

A. that there wasn't nothing wrong

B. that there weren't nothing wrong

C. that there were nothing wrong

D. that there wasn't anything wrong

E. that there were anything wrong

16. My favorite band, which was on tour throughout the country for 18 months, was finally coming to my town and I could not wait.

A. which was on tour throughout the country for 18 months,

B. which was on tour, throughout the country for 18 months

C. which was on tour throughout the country for 18 months

D. which was on tour (throughout the country for 18 months)

E. which was on tour; throughout the country for 18 months

17. The many fans of *Lost* are always wondering what will happen next according to the media, so are most of the television show's actors.

A. wondering what will happen next according to the media,

B. wondering what will happen next; according to the media,

C. wondering what will happen next, according to the media,

D. wondering what will happen next, according to the media;

E. wondering what will happen next—according to the media,

18. "Taking good photographs is less about having an expensive camera," explained Mr. Thompson, and more about knowing what light and angles to use."

A. explained Mr. Thompson, and more about knowing what light and angles to use."

B. explained Mr. Thompson and more about knowing what light and angles to use."

C. explained Mr. Thompson. And more about knowing what light and angles to use."

D. explained Mr. Thompson, "and more about knowing what light and angles to use."

E. explained Mr. Thompson, "and more about knowing what light and angles to use.

Answer Key:

1. D. This is a run-on sentence which needs either a period or semicolon to repair. Only option D does this.
2. E. This is a case of faulty comparison. Option B and D use "funner" which is not a real word. C is too wordy.
3. C. This is a misplaced modifier that has to be moved next to Daniel and not the wind.
4. E. The verb needs to be plural and present tense in order to match the rest of the sentence and option E does both of these things.
5. B. As it is written the big fish spent the day on the yacht. The modifier has to be moved next to the fisherman.
6. C. This sentence includes a nonessential dependent clause which needs to be set off by commas. The other options are either missing a necessary comma or use the wrong punctuation.
7. A. There is no error in the way this sentence is written. The rest of the options do not make sense.
8. B. This is a run-on sentence and it needs to be repaired with a period or a semicolon. Only option B does this.
9. E. This sentence needs to have a colon introduce the list.
10. B. This is a misplaced modifier and has to be moved so it is next to Caroline and not telephone.
11. A. There is no error in the way this sentence is written. All of the punctuation is correct.
12. C. The verb "movie" has to be singular and present tense to fit the sentence. Only option C does both of these things. Notice that "adventures" is the object of the preposition "about." This means that "adventures" is NOT the subject. Don't let prepositional phrases confuse you.
13. D. This is an example of faulty parallelism. All verbs must be in the same tense.

14. A. There is no error in the way this sentence is written. There is no other punctuation needed.

15. D. This is a double negative and only option D fixes it and uses the right verb.

16. A. There is no error in the way this sentence is written. As a nonessential dependent clause, it has to be set off by commas.

17. B. This is a run-on sentence and needs a semicolon to join the two together.

18. D. This sentence is missing a quotation mark. Only option D adds it without inserting unnecessary additional punctuation.

Improving Paragraphs

The following passage is an early draft of an essay. Some parts of the passage need to be rewritten.

Read the passage and select the best answers for the questions that follow. Some questions are about particular sentences or parts of sentences and ask you to improve sentence structure or word choice. Other questions ask you to consider organization and development. In choosing answers, follow the requirements of standard written English.

Passage #1

(1) A new, but limited study has revealed some relatively unexpected information about how marriage affects a person's health. (2) Over 200 married people and almost 100 singles were involved in the study. (3) They all wore devices that randomly recorded their blood pressure over 24 hours. (4) Married participants also filled out questionnaires about their marriages.

(5) The first result from their study was that people who reported the most satisfaction with their spouses had the lowest average blood pressure. (6) However, spouses that scored low in satisfaction with their relationships had higher average blood pressure than the single people.

(7) Correlating blood pressure measurements and marital contentment is a somewhat new idea in medical research. (8) Although the study was too small to be conclusive. (9) It does intrigue researchers enough to initiate further study on the concept. (10) So they will do it in the future.

1. In context, which of the following represents the best way to revise and combine sentences 3 and 4 (reproduced below)?

They all wore devices that randomly recorded their blood pressure over 24 hours. Married participants also filled out questionnaires about their marriages.

A. They all wore devices that randomly recorded their blood pressure over 24 hours since married participants also filled out questionnaires about their marriages.

B. They all wore devices that randomly recorded their blood pressure over 24 hours, after married participants also filled out questionnaires about their marriages.

C. They all wore devices that randomly recorded their blood pressure over 24 hours, provided that married participants also filled out questionnaires about their marriages.

D. They all wore devices that randomly recorded their blood pressure over 24 hours and married participants also filled out questionnaires about their marriages.

E. They all wore devices that randomly recorded their blood pressure over 24 hours. or married participants also filled out questionnaires about their marriages.

2. In context, which of the following is the best revision of sentence 8 (reproduced below)?

Although the study was too small to be conclusive.

A. The study was too small, although, to be conclusive.

B. The study was too small to be conclusive.

C. Although the study was too small.

D. To be conclusive, although the study was too small.

E. Too small, although the study was conclusive.

3. In context, which of the following sentences would be best if removed from the passage altogether?

A. Two

B. Four

C. Seven

D. Nine

E. Ten

4. The writer's main reason or purpose in this essay is to

A. prove that marriage is the best choice for everyone to make in life.

B. convince readers to keep a close eye on blood pressure readings.

C. point out an interesting study correlating health and relationships.

D. warn people to get out of unhappy marriages to preserve their health.

E. explain why physicians will be changing their advice about blood pressure.

5. The writer could best close this passage with information about what

A. other studies might be initiated based on this new information.

B. what steps couples need to make to improve their marriages.

C. the types of lifestyle changes that can effectively lower blood pressure.

D. the questionnaires the couples filled out revealed about their relationships.

E. kinds of health issues singles tend to have that married couples do not experience.

6. Which of the following sentences from the passage should be revised to make it easier for the reader to understand?

A. One

B. Four

C. Six

D. Seven

E. Nine

Answer Key:

1. D. Only the addition of "and" joins these sentences in a way that makes sense and doesn't change the meaning.

2. B. The statement, as it reads, is a dependent clause and cannot stand on its own as a complete sentence. The conjunction "although" must be removed. The other options do not make sense grammatically.

3. E. This statement adds nothing to the passage and is too vague to be helpful.

4. C. This is the only relevant and accurate purpose and the only one supported by passage details.

5. A. None of the other additional information would be relevant to the main topic other than option A.

6. C. This is the only statement that states a technical idea that could use some additional explanation.

Passage #2

(1) The idea that better to give than receive may just have some medical backup, according to some new research. (2) A study showed that people who use their money to help others experience a boost in their overall happiness levels.

(3) To test the theory that sharing your wealth with others makes you happier, the researchers surveyed more than 600 male and female Americans. (4) In this survey, people reported their general happiness along with their annual income broken down into spending and donations to charity. (5) There was a distinct correlation between the money shared and higher levels of joy in life.

(6) A second small study also got the same results. (7) Students were divided up into two different groups. (8) All were given a small amount of money. (9) It was $20 or less. (10) Half were instructed to spend the money on themselves. (11) The other half were told to spend it on others, friends or strangers. (12) Those who shared the money reported feeling happier at the end of the day than those who did not.

1. In context, which of the following is the best revision of sentence 1 (reproduced below)?

The idea that better to give than receive may just have some medical backup, according to some new research.

A. Better to give than receive, the idea may just have some medical backup, according to some new research.

B. The idea that it is better to give than receive may just have some medical backup, according to some new research.

C. According to some new research, the idea that better to given than receive may just have some medical backup.

D. The idea better to give than receive, according to some new research, may just have some medical backup.

E. Some medical backup, according to some new research, is the idea that it's better to give than receive.

2. In context, which of the following is the best revision of sentence 3 (reproduced below)?

To test the theory that sharing your wealth with others makes you happier, the researchers surveyed more than 600 male and female Americans.

A. To test the theory that sharing one's wealth with others makes them happier, the researchers surveyed more than 600 male and female Americans.

B. To test the theory that sharing our wealth with others makes us happier, the researchers surveyed more than 600 male and female Americans.

C. To test the theory that sharing wealth with others makes people happier, the researchers surveyed more than 600 male and female Americans.

D. To test the theory that sharing my wealth with others makes me happier, the researchers surveyed more than 600 male and female Americans.

E. To test the theory that sharing their wealth with others makes him happier, the researchers surveyed more than 600 male and female Americans.

3. In context, which of the following represents the best way to revise and combine sentences 8 and 9 (reproduced below)?

All were given a small amount of money. It was $20 or less.

A. All were given a small amount of money, it was $20 or less.

B. $20 or less was given to all, a small amount of money.

C. All were given $20 or less, it was a small amount of money.

D. All were given a small amount of money of $20 or less.

E. A small amount of money, all were given $20 or less.

4. The author's main purpose in writing this essay is to

A. point out how sharing seems to affect some.

B. convince readers to start donating to charity.

C. show people the key to constant happiness.

D. demonstrate how some people use their money.

E. explain why some people are more generous than others.

5. Which of the following ideas would make the best conclusion paragraph?

A. A closer look at which charities people choose the most often

B. Additional studies on how charity seems to affect people's emotions

C. The top ten best ways to help others with $20 or less

D. The percentage of a person's income that is spent on personal expenses

E. How many different things can be purchased for $20 or less

6. A quote from which of the following people would add the most credit to the main idea of the passage?

A. A person who was given money by another

B. The head of a non-profit organization

C. An organizer for a major charity group

D. A student who did not share any of his/her money

E. A researcher who conducted one of the studies

Answer Key:

1. B. The sentence is missing the clause "it is." Only option B provides this and preserves the meaning.

2. C. The problem with this sentence is that it uses "you" when the rest of the passage does not. The passage is written in 3rd person, so all the pronouns must be in 3rd person. Additionally, the pronouns must match in number. None of the options fit both criteria except C.

3. D. This the only option that merges the two sentences smoothly without losing meaning or sounding awkward.

4. A. This is the only option that fits the main idea of the passage.

5. B. The main point of this passage is to explore how people's spending habits affect their emotions, so the best material to add should be related directly to that. Only option B does that.

6. E. Options A through D would not be significantly relevant. A quote from one of the researchers, however, would lend credence to the idea.

ESSAY

Think carefully about the issue presented in the following excerpt and the assignment below.

Many persons believe that to move up the ladder of success and achievement, they must forget the past, repress it, and relinquish it. But others have just the opposite view. They see old memories as a chance to reckon with the past and integrate past and present.

Adapted from Sara Lawrence-Lightfoot
Note: This is an actual example of a writing prompt used in the June 2005 SAT.

Assignment: Do memories hinder or help people in their effort to learn from the past and succeed in the present?

Good Sample Answer:

Whether or not memories help people or hinder them depends not on the memories but on the people themselves. It is like many other things in life, from money to power. Alone they are neutral, neither good nor bad. It is how a person uses them that makes the difference.

I have done my best to use my memories as lessons on what to do and not to do in my life. I look back at the times I spent with my grandparents and it teaches me to be respectful of my elders. The memories remind me to be patient with people who might be slower than I am and to realize the incredible experiences elderly people carry around in their heads and in their hearts. We just have to take the time to listen to them.

There are many other memories that I call on at different times of my life to help me. I think of the times I have been extremely successful and that helps me to have the initiative and encouragement to keep succeeding. I also think of the times I have failed in my life—since everyone does now and then. Those memories are important because they remind me of what not to repeat.

There have been times that I know both of my parents have also relied on memories of their own parents and their childhoods to guide their own lives. Perhaps their examples are why I follow the tradition. As they repeat the lessons they have learned, I have internalized those lessons too.

Recently a friend of mine surprised me when he refused to dwell on some mistakes he had made earlier. He told me that he preferred to just block it out of his mind and never think about it again. I struggle with this idea because even if we, as humans, do something incredibly irresponsible or even dangerous, ignoring it isn't the answer. Instead, we need to think about those memories and use them as springboards for making good decisions today and in the future.

SCORE: 6

Comments: This is truly an excellent essay. It states the student's opinion in the opening paragraph and then supports that opinion with strong personal examples. It uses good grammar, spelling and usage. It demonstrates a good vocabulary. The conclusion refers back to the original opinion and brings everything to a close.

Bad Sample Answers:

Let's look at another essay that is a response to the same prompt:

Memories can be pretty rotten. I have a lot of them in my head I would prefer not to have. I try to forget them but it's hard. Why is it that we forget the things we want to remember? And then vice versa?

I think memories can help you. They can also hinder me. It just depends on the memory. I mean, if I think about how crappy I did on a test, it can either make me study harder for the next one or I can get so bummed out that I don't even care about trying. It just depends on my mood, I guess.

So memories can help. They can hinder. They are just part of life. You have to deal with it, you know? You have to hang tough.

SCORE: 3

Comments: This essay tries to answer the question but fails pretty solidly. It doesn't state a clear opinion, wobbling back and forth between them. It gives vague examples but nothing clear. There are grammatical errors. It is full of slang and idioms.

The End: Final Thoughts

SECTION 9

The End: Final Thoughts

Unless you are cheating and reading this part of the book first (and if so, shame on you!), you should now have a much better handle on what to expect with the new writing portion of the SAT. Before you take the actual test review your notes (you did take some, right?) and run through a few of the practice questions to limber up your brain.

Before I bid you a fond farewell, I have four final thoughts:

(1) **Writing is a learned process just like anything else.** Learning to write well is a lot like learning to drive a car. The first time you sat in a car during Driver's Education, you may have been completely overwhelmed at all you were expected to do. How in the world could any one normal person watch the side mirrors, rearview mirrors, speedometer and traffic on all four sides, plus do simple things like turn on the radio, drink a cup of coffee or remember how to get someplace? It just seemed impossible (especially if you had to shift a manual transmission!) to keep all of that in mind at the same time. However, by doing these same things over and over every time you got behind the wheel, it soon became habit. Soon you did not even have to consciously remind yourself to check the mirrors; you just did it. Writing is the same way. By learning how to do it and doing it often, the skills become second nature. You don't have to keep an eye on verb tense, spelling or punctuation because somewhere along the line, you learned it well enough to do it subconsciously.

Just like there was a time you could not drive and now you can, there is a time you may not have been able to write but with enough attention, determination and practice, now you can.

(2) **The key to doing anything well is practice.** This is true for riding a bike, making touchdowns, doing cartwheels or writing well. If you do not practice the skills, they will not sink into your brain while you are sleeping so that you awaken ready to go. Writing well means practicing the elements that go into writing well, from spelling the words correctly to using the right verb tense. There is no way around it: you can't bribe anyone to do it for you, you can't pretend it isn't there; you can't expect your parents to take care of it for you. Good writing takes practice. If you want to do well on the SAT, you have to practice. The format and the requirements must be familiar and comfortable. Ok? Enough said. Now go practice!

(3) **Thinking positively.** When it comes to taking the SAT, who is the one person who can absolutely guarantee you bomb it? Your parents? Nope. Your teachers? Hardly. The people who wrote the test? Not even close. The number one culprit is you.

Perhaps one of the most effective ways to make sure you do a lousy job on the SAT is to tell yourself you will. "What?" you exclaim. "Why would I do that?" Well, think about it for a moment. Imagine it is the day of the test and you are walking in to take the first part. Listen to your inner thoughts for a moment. What are you telling yourself? What thoughts are running through your head? Tell me if any of these sound somewhat familiar:

> *I hate this test. I know I'm gonna flunk the writing portion.*
>
> *I am going to screw this up and never get into college.*
>
> *I didn't study hard enough for this test and now I'll pay the price.*
>
> *Everyone in this room will do better on this test than I will.*
>
> *This is a stupid, worthless test, and I am ticked off I even have to take it.*

Your subconscious mind is listening to every single thought you have. When you have negative thoughts like these running through your head, it hears them. "Oh, ok," it says. "You're going to do badly on this test? Sure, I can help with that. C'mon buddy, let's go mess this up together." On the other hand, what is a subconscious mind going to do if it hears statements like:

> *I am going to do my best on this test today.*
>
> *Things are going to go better and easier than I ever expected.*
>
> *This is going to be an interesting and enjoyable challenge.*
>
> *I am completely prepared to take the SAT now.*
>
> *I am ready to do a terrific job on this test.*

"Oh!" says the subconscious mind. "You are going to ace this test. Well ok, let's go do it!"

It is vital to think positively as you walk into that classroom. Give your brain the encouragement and optimism it needs to help you perform wonderfully.

You may remember a great show that used to be on PBS called "Reading Rainbow." Host LeVar Burton would recommend a book but then he would say, "But don't take my word for it" and let kids do their own reviews. So, I'm going to do the same thing here. I may believe that positive thinking is one of the most important parts of taking the SAT, but hey, don't just take my word for it. Here are what some others have to say:

> "Positive thinking will let you do everything better than negative thinking will." ~ Zig Ziglar
>
> "Learn to think like a winner. Think positive and visualize your strengths." ~ Vic Braden
>
> "If constructive thoughts are planted positive outcomes will be the result. Plant the seeds of failure and failure will follow." ~ Sidney Madwed

"It takes but one positive thought when given a chance to survive and thrive to overpower an entire army of negative thoughts."
~ Robert Schuller

(4) **As important as SAT scores are, they are NOT the end of the world.** Please do not put so much pressure on yourself to do well on these tests that you do yourself harm. SAT scores are an important part of getting into college, yes, but they are not a life or death situation either. Do the best job you can and then move on. Remember that colleges will also be looking at your grades, admission essays, teacher recommendations and activities before deciding whether or not to let you in. (Keep in mind that more than 700 colleges in this country do not base acceptance on SAT scores at all. To find a list of them, visit www.fairtest.org/optinit.htm.) The SAT is just one piece of the admission puzzle, and you can still get accepted even if this piece is not your strongest asset.

By investing the time to read this book, you have the skills to do well on the SAT essay. Now, it's just a matter of learning, practicing, accepting and doing. You have the power, the ability, the determination and the drive–use it and see where it takes you.

Happy writing!

Useful Websites

Ah, the wonders (not wanders!) of the Internet. It is full of some great preparation tips, strategies, ideas and practice questions, so spend some time exploring these web sites and see what you can learn.

- SuperCollege
  www.supercollege.com
- The College Board (they are the SAT experts!)
  www.collegeboard.com and
  www.collegeboard.com/student/testing/sat/prep_one/prep_one.html
- Test Prep Review
  www.testprepreview.com
- Free SAT Prep 1
  www.freesat1prep.com
- Kaplan
  www.kaptest.com
- Princeton Review
  www.review.com

For information on a variety of tests, try…

- College Power Prep
  www.powerprep.com
- SAT Prep
  www.takesat.com

If you want more choices, just go to your favorite search engine and put in the terms "SAT," "prep," "essay," "writing," "test" or "practice" in any of thousands of possible combinations. Bring a lunch. You will have a lot to look over!

Special Thanks

Ned Johnson

Ned Johnson is the founder and president of PrepMatters, Inc., a company of test-prep geeks who serve clients in the Washington, DC metropolitan area. The PrepMatters approach includes expert knowledge, test-specific strategies and insights on maximizing performance gleaned from working tens of thousands of hours with thousands of successful students for over a decade. Find out more about PrepMatters at www.prepmatters.com.

Dr. Samuel Barnett

Samuel Barnett has a Ph.D. from Purdue University. He has taught at multiple universities for the last 20 years, as well as worked in admissions, counseling and financial aid. In 2003, he focused on developing his solo practice, SchoolFutures. This consulting business continues to grow today. Currently, in addition to running SchoolFutures, Mr. Barnett serves as Adjunct Assistant Professor at University of Maryland University College.

Kaaren Dolinsky

Kaaren Dolinsky has taught at Bauder College and Perimeter College. She has been a grader for the SAT II essays and GMAT, TOEFL and AP Literature exams.

More Great Books & Resources by SuperCollege

Don't let your grades stop you from getting a great education

- Complete profiles of 100 great colleges that don't emphasize grades and test scores in their admission decisions
- Admission tips for overcoming less than perfect grades or test scores
- Information on academics, majors and what the colleges seek
- Inside advice from students, counselors and admission officers
- Win free money for college with scholarships based on more than grades and test scores
- Thrive in college by successfully managing your time and balancing academic and social priorities

Get your copy at bookstores or visit www.supercollege.com

America's Best Colleges for B Students

By: Tamra B. Orr

ISBN: 9781932662221

Price: $19.95

Access Billions of Dollars of Free Cash for College!

- More than 1.5 million awards
- Scholarships you can use at any college
- Detailed information on eligibility requirements and how to apply
- Insider advice on how to create winning applications
- Key indexes to pinpoint the best scholarships for you
- The most up-to-date information available
- Complete scholarship directory and comprehensive strategy guide

Get your copy at bookstores or visit www.supercollege.com

The Ultimate Scholarship Book 2009

By: Gen and Kelly Tanabe

ISBN: 9781932662276

Price: $26.95

Learn every conceivable way to pay for college

- Find the best scholarships
- Pay in-state tuition even if you're an out-of-state student
- Jump-start your college savings with 529 Savings Plans and Coverdell ESAs
- Claim your $1,650 Hope Tax Credit and $2,000 Lifetime Learning Credit
- Avoid taxes on your tuition
- Get your share of the $97 billion in financial aid awarded each year
- Get the state to pay for your college education
- Have your student loans forgiven
- And much more

Get your copy at bookstores or visit www.supercollege.com

1001 Ways to Pay for College: Practical Strategies to Make College Affordable

By: Gen and Kelly Tanabe

ISBN: 9781932662207

Price: $19.95

"I read this book from cover to back and got ACCEPTED to Cornell."
—JASON CLEMMEY
Accepted!
SECOND EDITION
50 Successful College Admission Essays
Step-by-step guide to writing a powerful essay
Writing strategies from top students and admission officers
25 essay mistakes to avoid
Gen and Kelly Tanabe Harvard graduates and of Get Into Any College

About the Author

I am absolutely positive that this will be your favorite part of the book, since it is all about me! I respect your valuable time enough, however, not to start with, "I was born in a small town…" I promise just to hit the highlights.

For me, writing is as much a part of life as breathing. From a pretty early age, I loved to read and write. I have journals dating all the way back to when I was ten years old (and are they a hoot for me to read now!) until the present. I wrote short stories in elementary school, and in junior high and high school, I began writing even more. I was one of those students that many of you really don't like because when the teacher assigned a book report, essay or term paper, I was happy about it. (I learned not to make my delight obvious, however, at the risk of life and limb.) I probably would have cheered at the concept of an essay on the SAT, especially if I could have found a way to skip all of the math.

When I graduated from high school, I went on to college where I majored in (you'd never have guessed, I am sure!) Secondary Education and English. I thought I would be a high school teacher eventually, but life held other plans for me. Instead of entrenching myself into a specific school, I had the audacity to meet my future husband, have a whirlwind romance and get married. This brought a move to another part of the state and an all new school system for me to learn about. I did some subbing (yes, I was one of those poor substitute victims) and then life made different plans for me again and I got pregnant with my first child. Over the course of the next 13 years, I did that a total of four times (yup, four kids and still sane, can you believe it?) and I chose to stay at home with them.

Afraid that my writing skills would wither away and die if not maintained by something more than the occasional journal entry and baby book notation, I decided to turn my skills to becoming a freelance writer instead of a teacher. For years, it was a fun little hobby that paid me enough to put gas in the car and food on the table but not much more. As my children grew up, however, I had more time to devote to it and by 1999, it was my full-time job.

Fast forward to 2008, and I am a full-time freelance writer and author. We no longer live in Indiana but have moved to the beautiful state of Oregon. My kids are now 24, 18, 15 and 12. I have written more than 100 books (on a gloomy day, I go to Amazon and look up my titles to cheer me up). The books I have written so far cover such diversified subjects as fire ants, terrorism, Ronald Reagan, test tube babies, school violence, Slovenia, astronauts and home education. I also write for more than two dozen magazines and a dozen educational testing companies. (Yes, some of you can blame me for the state tests you have taken in school. The good questions were mine, of course.)

Although there are days where writing is more of a chore than a creative passion, I still love my job and think I have to be one the luckiest people on earth. I would write for free if I had to (hopefully, none of my editors are reading this) and feel rather blessed that I actually get paid to do what brings me such pleasure.

Winston Churchill once said, "Writing a book is a horrible, exhausting struggle, like a long bout of some painful illness. One would never undertake such a thing if one were not driven by some demon whom one can neither resist nor understand." Sorry Winston, I have to disagree with you. I had a wonderful time writing this book. I feel like for most of it, I was sitting in the living room with all of you readers, sucking down root beer, pigging out on double pineapple pizza and listening to some great music while we figured out how to best conquer this mandatory essay. I hope that you had a little fun with it now and then as well, that you will think kindly of me on SAT test day and perhaps even send me a virtual hug when you get your SAT scores back. I wish you the best of luck on the entire test and on all of the life and writing that goes on long after the SAT is just a vague memory.

The End

(OH! So NOW you cheer!)